THE

CONSTITUTION

OF

GOOD

SOCIETIES

EDITED BY

KAROL EDWARD SOŁTAN AND STEPHEN L. ELKIN

THE

CONSTITUTION

OF

GOOD

SOCIETIES

THE PENNSYLVANIA STATE UNIVERSITY PRESS
UNIVERSITY PARK, PENNSYLVANIA

Library of Congress Cataloging-in-Publication Data

The constitution of good societies / edited by Karol Edward Sołtan and
    Stephen L. Elkin.

    p.   cm.
    Includes bibliographical references and index.
    ISBN 0-271-01564-0 (cloth : alk. paper)
    ISBN 0-271-01565-9 (pbk. : alk. paper)
    1. Public interest. 2. Common good. 3. State, The. 4. Public
institutions. 5. Social institutions. I. Sołtan, Karol Edward,
1950– . II. Elkin, Stephen L.
JC330.15.C68   1996
303—dc20   95-48949
                                                 CIP

Published by The Pennsylvania State University Press,
University Park, PA 16802-1003

It is the policy of The Pennsylvania State University Press to use acid-free
paper for the first printing of all clothbound books. Publications on uncoated
stock satisfy the minimum requirements of American National Standard for
Information Sciences—Permanence of Paper for Printed Library Materials,
ANSI Z39.48-1992.

CONTENTS

PREFACE

The purpose of this book is to help develop, through a variety of exploratory essays, the art and science of institutional design. But this is puzzling. If in fact this is our purpose, why did we entitle the book *The Constitution of Good Societies?* Any why is the book organized in the way it is? The answers to these two questions can be traced to our conception of institutional design, and of what is required to perform it well.

Let us begin with the title. The phrase "constitution of good societies" could be understood in a number of narrow legal and political ways. Indeed, the word "constitution" often brings to mind legal documents and political systems. Yet this is not how we use the word. Rather, it should be read as equivalent to the *making*, or *crafting*, of good societies. One could even call it the *design* of good societies. The aim is to look at good societies as artifacts, as products—at least partly—of design, and to consider how societies can be crafted well.

But why "good societies"? The main reason is to be as inclusive as possible. The knowledge relevant to the art and science of institutional design helps us answer a multitude of sometimes crosscutting practical questions, of various degrees of generality and concerning a broad range of entities. We believe it is important to push forward simultaneously on all fronts—hence the diversity of practical questions in this book.

Philip Green considers how to diminish the influence of some specific impediments to equality (viz., gender and class hierarchies). Gar Alperovitz asks what sorts of institutions can best serve the values of equality, liberty, and democracy. Stephen Elkin asks how we can promote deliberative virtues. Charles Anderson considers what distinguishes his three good societies (Costa Rica, Denmark, Wisconsin) from all the others. In all these chapters the social scale is large, and we consider whole complexes of institutions.

We also need to ask practical questions about situations defined on a smaller scale, albeit ones that may be encountered more often. Thus Elinor Ostrom writes about solutions to the common-pool resource problem. Viktor Vanberg and James Buchanan worry about the problem of constitutional knowledge. Karol Sołtan considers human error-proneness and interdependence. All these questions involve specific impediments and strategies for overcoming them. In the chapters by John Dryzek and Karol Sołtan, moreover, we also have some effort to move beyond the elaboration of what can be called "instrumental" or "technical" rationality, through a discussion of various *forms* of competence.

If we define as our task the making of good societies, we can incorporate *all* of these efforts. We can divide our labor in multiple ways, which are sometimes mutually inconsistent, and we can follow multiple strategies. This, we think, is the best way to proceed. Looking at whole societies, and at complexes of institutions, complements and informs our approach to the institutional microscale. Understanding the microscale, on the other hand, often makes the difference between empty slogans and realistic political proposals. "The Constitution of Good Societies," then, is simply an appropriately inclusive name for all the work necessary if we are to make some progress in the art and science of institutional design.

This book is a product of the Committee on the Political Economy of the Good Society (PEGS), and it is part of the Committee's larger effort to promote the art and science of institutional design. It is the second volume emerging from the Committee's work, following *A New Constitutionalism* (1993). A third volume, *Citizen Competence and Democracy*, is in preparation. The present volume began as a set of papers prepared for a conference cosponsored by PEGS and the Committee on Social Thought and Ethics at Yale. That conference, which took place at Yale University in January 1991, was made possible thanks to a generous grant from the John Castle Fund. Much time and effort separates us from that conference, offering many opportunities to incur various kinds of debts. We give special thanks to Bruce Ackerman, Benjamin Barber, Joshua Cohen, Kathryn Doherty, Diana Elkin, John Ferejohn, Herbert Gintis, Russell Hardin, Jeffrey Isaac, Jyl Josephson, Duncan Kennedy, Jack Knight, Charles Lindblom, Jane Mansbridge, Michael McPherson, Emily Millians, Jennifer Nedelsky, Douglas Rae, Alan Ryan, Thomas Schelling, Ian Shapiro, Jeremy Shearmur, Rogers Smith, Anna Sołtan, and Margaret Sołtan.

Karol Edward Sołtan
Stephen L. Elkin

Introduction: Imagination, Political Competence, and Institutions

KAROL EDWARD SOŁTAN

IMAGINATION RULES the world. Surely this must be the statement of a naive dreamer, or of some utopian, perhaps even (God forbid) a poet. Not exactly: Napoleon is said to have made the claim, and it is difficult to doubt his political realism. He certainly did not merely dream of different worlds: he changed the one he was in. Let us consider, then, the form of realism Napoleon's statement represents. To rule is to change the world, but to do that you need a good idea of the changes you want to introduce. You must imagine a different world from the one you live in. And it is not enough to be able to imagine: what you imagine must plausibly be better, must be workable, acceptable to relevant parties, and so on. Not just any kind of vivid imagination can be said to rule the world—certainly not the imagination of utopian dreamers. Only a properly educated, skilled imagination can effectively rule the world.

New Constitutionalism and Political Competence

Let us call "political competence" the set of skills involved in such imaginative and effective rule. There is a long history of attempts to describe the necessary skills: books containing advice to rulers and princes (Machiavelli [1514] 1988) or advice to statesmen, lawmakers, and constitutionmakers (from Plato and Aristotle to the *Federalist* papers and the constitutionalist tradition). There are also increasing numbers of contemporary practitioners. Some are policy centered (cost–benefit analysis; welfare economics; Dror 1993; Reich 1990), whereas others are more law centered (Posner 1972–92; Ackerman 1984). Still others focus on principles of organizational design and good management (from Williamson 1975 and 1985 to Peters and Waterman 1982). In each sphere (policy, law, organization and management) we have a similar intellectual situation: a rather precisely articulated perspective deriving from economics (welfare economics, cost–benefit analysis, and some version of public-choice theory or game theory) is challenged by various critiques, none quite so well developed as the economic perspective.

The essays in this volume are varied, both intellectually and politically. But they are all contributions to the development of a more elaborate alternative to a too simple combination of welfare economics (with cost–benefit analysis) and game theory. These essays derive from the work of the Committee on the Political Economy of the Good Society (PEGS), which is based on the premise that we need a better understanding of political competence—both with respect to specific institutional contexts, such as law and private organization, and with respect to the state as well as the more complex systems of institutions or regimes (e.g., the evolving global system of markets interacting with putatively sovereign states). The most important questions concern not case-by-case policymaking but the creation and reform of institutions. We assume that tinkering with the world here and there (through new policies and incremental legislative reforms) may not be enough in the end. We must be prepared to reconsider seriously the most general problems of institutional design and large-scale change. Thus we use the term "political economy" in the name of our organization (and not, for example, "policy") and "new constitutionalism" in the title of our previous book. We aim to give the study of political competence an *institutionalist* turn.

The present book, our previous one (*A New Constitutionalism* [Elkin and Sołtan 1993]), and the organization whose work these volumes represent (PEGS) all focus on institutions as the most promising instruments for building a better world. Our best hope, we believe, lies not in influencing the character of people and decisions directly, but in doing so through institutions.

This itself is an important strategic and intellectual decision, based on unfortunate experiences with the available alternatives: social change through revolution turns out to be predictably disastrous, social change through individual repentence or therapeutic transformation turns out to be not much of a social change. Again, institutions are the most promising avenue for changing the world. This is not to say that it is *only* institutions which matter, but it does mean that even if we want to transform human character, to develop and strengthen civic virtue and competence (for example), we do so best through institutions, not through "direct action."

The most *important* decisions, and the social changes they introduce, are those whose consequences are pervasive across society and long term in their effects. They require either revolution or extensive institutional reform. This large scale of social action, which requires us to achieve things through institutions or organizations, rather than through spontaneous action, is also the most *difficult*. The "new constitutionalism," then, is concerned to develop knowledge and skills useful for those with a practical interest in improving our most *important* and *difficult* decisions.

Self-styled realists have repeated many times the admonition that politics is the art of the possible. Yet the politics and policy that result from too much, and too serious, attention to this admonition simply end up small-minded, cynical, and narrow. Such a politics is deficient in *imagination*, so it cannot take advantage of existing opportunities for dramatic change and reform. Indeed, it was so busy adjusting realistically to the power of communist systems that it did not foresee their collapse. A more admirable realistic politics can be described as the art of the difficult and the important. A decision or action is important when it is connected to a serious end (i.e., when it is a necessary means to that end, or when it is itself that end, or even when it provides an opportunity for averting errors that could jeopardize the achievement of that end). A decision or action is difficult when skill and sacrifice are needed to overcome impediments.

The social sciences can contribute to the improvement of such an art—that is, to the improvement of political competence—and this is the aim of the new constitutionalism. Institution building and institutional reform are central to political competence. Trying to improve individual decisions (with the help, say, of policy analysis) is likely to lead only to frustration unless we operate within institutions that are conducive to such improvement (Buchanan 1990). And this seems, if anything, even more true for attempts to transform human mentalities and human character. Institutions are instrumental both for better decisions and for better people. Focus on institutions is the main distinctive characteristic of the new constitutionalism among the various practical social sciences.

The new constitutionalism is a family of theoretical perspectives, all of which share an effort to understand institutions from the designer's (or creator's, or founder's, or framer's, or reformer's) perspective. This is not simply the point of view of social engineers, of experts constructing institutions from the foundation up. It seems more appropriate to see it as the point of view of *citizens,* of persons with an active interest in the improvement or reform of the institutional framework within which they live.

Practical social sciences in general, and new forms of constitutionalism in particular, come in a variety of styles: pragmatic (Anderson 1990 and Selznick 1992); Marxist and neo-Marxist (e.g., Habermas 1973 or Bowles and Gintis 1986); Aristotelian and Straussian (Strauss 1959, 1989); contractarian (Buchanan and the Virginia School [Brennan and Buchanan 1985]); and utilitarian or wealth maximizing (as in the economic analysis of law [Posner 1972–92]). New constitutionalism, then, is not necessarily a contractarian perspective, imagining what sort of institutions would be chosen in a suitably arranged contract. The contractarian work of James Buchanan and the Virginia school of political economy is only one possible path in the new constitutionalist repertoire. It is represented in this volume by Chapter 2. New constitutionalism is also not necessarily pragmatic (though Anderson is, see Chapter 5), nor is it Aristotelian (though one can detect the influence of Aristotle among many of us). It is a broader and more inclusive tradition—without clear boundaries but with enough shared methodology, added to a few shared substantive conclusions, to constitute a distinctive perspective within the social and political sciences.

Moral Competence

What are the elements of political competence?[1] A good place to start is with the distinction between moral and instrumental competence. Moral competence consists of skills needed in the choice of ends. Instrumental competence, on the other hand, consists of skills used in choosing the best means to those ends. This distinction seems straightforward, and it is found in most systematic discussions of the subject in contemporary political theory (see, e.g., Thompson's account [1976] of J. S. Mill's theory of representative democracy or Dahl's discussion [1989] of guardianship as an alternative to democracy). We can try to build some detail into this basic distinction.

Moral competence involves the choice of ends. If we know our ends clearly, the practical problem reduces to the choice of best means, which is a problem for *instrumental* reason. The methods we adopt to solve the instrumental problem will not help us, however, if our goals and ideals either have not been chosen or are not clear; that is to say, if we do not know what we want. We need, then, methods for the choice of ends or for clarification of ends.

We need ways to choose, discover, elaborate, or clarify our ultimate goals, ends, values, rules, and quality standards. We can simply

---

1. Or the "competence of an ideal citizen," as I call it in "What is the New Constitutionalism?" (Sołtan 1996) and in Chapter 4 of this volume.

assume a goal, such as wealth maximization. Or we can use various techniques of standard empirical science, hermeneutics, or rational reconstruction to make the process less arbitrary.

When we do not know what we want, we must discover our own goals, values, ideals, and preferences; we must determine what is for us better or worse (what counts for us as an indicator of success). One important family of strategies for doing so involves a process now commonly called "rational reconstruction." It typically proceeds as follows: we identify clear successes and clear failures in some sphere, and we then reconstruct the standards that we must have used in making those identifications. We begin by not knowing much about what we want (or what counts as a success); though we do know *something*, which allows this process to get off the ground. We end by knowing much more about what we want: we do so by increasing our capacity to distinguish success from failure, and greater success from lesser success (or right from wrong, better from worse).

One good example is generative grammar, as pioneered by Noam Chomsky (1965). This is an empirical science whose subject consists of the judgments made by the speakers of a language with respect to the grammaticalness (or linguistic acceptability) of sentences rendered in that language. These are the "successes" and "failures" (grammatical and ungrammatical sentences) that generative grammar considers. The task for linguistic theory is the rational reconstruction of the rules of grammar that could have produced the judgments we find—a set of rules that will allow sentences that the population finds acceptable (successes) and forbid sentences that the population does not find acceptable (failures).

A very different form of rational reconstruction can be found in common law. Here the precedents chosen by a judge in the process of justifying a decision in law are the "successes." The task of rational reconstruction is to propose a set of principles or rules that will both justify these precedent decisions and decide the case at hand. Reflective equilibrium, of the kind proposed by John Rawls as a method for ethics, is similar, with considered moral judgments playing the role of precedents. Finally, the policy-capturing method of developing new policy works basically the same way.

The best example I know of "policy capturing" is found in the procedures for creation of the typical job-evaluation scheme, a management tool to systematize and justify wage differentials in large organizations. We begin by picking a set of uncontroversial wages in the existing system to serve as precedents for the new system (this is typically a small subset of the existing system). We then pick a set of properties of jobs in the organization, properties that can be used to justify one job being paid more than another (usually these are a job's diffi-culty, importance, and unpleasantness). A simple regression equa-tion—where the job properties are independent variables, and where the wages chosen to be precedents are the dependent variables—gives us the weight each job property must have in the system. We now have a new system which essentially articulates and systematizes the success-ful (uncontroversial) aspects of the old system (Sołtan 1987).

There are many different styles of rational reconstruction. It can be quite rigorous and empirical-minded, closer to the style of hard science than to that of philosophy, but it can also be more literary or hermeneutic. It is easy to lose track of this diversity if one relies exclu-sively on the Habermas account of rational reconstruction. The value of Chomsky and generative grammar, for example, as models of a cer-tain kind of empirical investigation, committed to the highest stan-dards of rigor, is more than a bit diluted when we read about it only in neo-Marxist German social philosophy, whose aims, interests, and standards are quite different.

Rational reconstruction is not the only way to add content and precision to our conceptions of moral competence. Many kinds of em-pirical research can be helpful. One possible strategy begins with the economic conception. For the economic account of moral competence restricts us to the goal of wealth maximization, or its various close cous-ins (welfare maximization, utility maximization, Pareto optimality), and we have much evidence that this goal is widely accepted and acted on. One way to broaden our conception of moral competence beyond wealth maximization is to search for *other* such broadly acceptable ends. Empirical evidence, including experiments, provide a very use-ful tool here.

Thus, for example, experimental evidence (Frohlich and Oppen-heimer 1992) shows that people are inclined to prefer something other than simple wealth maximization or the Rawlsian maximin. They pick instead a rule that maximizes average wealth with a "floor constraint" (i.e., with a guaranteed social minimum). If this is the goal we incorpo-rate into the moral component of political competence, we will be bet-ter able to give support to one of the main aspirations of the modern welfare state: to establish and maintain such a minimum.

We can use experimental evidence to expand our conception fur-ther. Those accounts of moral competence which are limited to wealth maximization (or wealth maximization with a floor constraint) fail per-haps most spectacularly when we consider the constitutional law of liberal democracies (e.g., the United States). There is no plausible way to present as wealth maximizing the American Bill of Rights (or the

French Declaration of Rights), the principle of "one person, one vote," or the prohibition of slavery and involuntary servitude.[2]

Fortunately we have another set of experimental results that can serve us here. These results provide empirical justification for adding a purely procedural ideal to the list of ends we recognize in our account of moral competence. The empirical evidence comes from a large number of psychological experiments that model various judicial and quasi-judicial settings and that elicit subject evaluation of those settings. When subjects are asked which procedures they prefer (independent of result) and which they find more fair, two strong patterns emerge. Subjects both prefer and find more fair procedures that treat all parties equally, and subjects both prefer and find more fair procedures that give all parties a greater opportunity to influence outcomes (Tyler 1990).

We can formalize these two "preferences" in order to make them axioms of what I would call a liberal-democratic procedural ideal. If we then add other axioms which simply define a procedural ideal as procedural, we can derive (I believe)[3] at least the following two conclusions:

1. A "principle of subsidiarity," according to which a smaller scale of collective decisions is preferred to a larger scale. This is a form of argument for individual liberty (an individual's decisions being the smallest scale), and it also supports smaller communities against incursions by larger ones.
2. A preference for majority rule in choices between two alternatives.

The moral foundation of this liberal-democratic procedural ideal lies in equal respect for all. This is a much rehearsed idea in the liberal tradition of political theory, but it has suffered from vagueness surrounding the notion of "respect." In the axiomatized procedural ideal I am referring to here, the notion of respect can be formulated in a precise behavioral way. The procedural ideal demands that we give each person maximum respect compatible with equal respect for all, and *giving respect* is identified with *giving an opportunity to influence* deci-

---

2. Mueller (1996) comes closest to succeeding (it seems to me) in his new book on constitutional design, but he articulates a contractarian, not a wealth-maximizing position.

3. There are some formal difficulties in doing so, which I have been unable to solve. I suspect these are simply technicalities that do not affect the result, but I may be wrong. See Sołtan 1994.

sions. In this way, we turn everyone into as much of an authority as is compatible with all being equal as authorities.

If we add this procedural ideal to our picture of moral competence, we will see institutions as morally more complex. We will see them as efforts to balance equal *concern* for everyone (articulated in the principle of wealth maximization with a floor constraint) against the procedural ideal reflecting a principle of maximum *respect* for all (compatible with equality of respect). At the heart of moral competence, which we will have constructed entirely in an empirically driven way, will be something like equality of concern and respect, a principle that for Dworkin (1977) lies at the heart of the American legal system, but whose applicability is obviously not limited to that restricted legal sphere.[4]

Instrumental Competence

Instrumental competence involves the choice of means. Our goal is a more perfect world. But this is difficult because we face many impediments. One of them lies in the fact that we usually do not know what we want with any precision; we do not know what would make for a more perfect world. *This* problem falls under the heading of moral competence, but there are many other problems. In the standard rational-choice treatment of the subject, we focus on the power of self-interest (or narrow interest, what has been known in constitutional thought as the "problem of faction"), the problem of uncertainty and risk, and the problem of scarcity. A fuller treatment would include also the problem of human error-proneness and mutual dependence, as well as the problems of conflicts and contradictions between our goals and our available means (leading to various paradoxes and tragedies of human decisionmaking [see, e.g., Calabresi and Bobbitt 1978]).

These are only the most general and widespread impediments to successful human action. There are many more, which affect us in more specific circumstances: these include the challenges of environmental destruction, of national and ethnic conflict, of action and reform in postcommunist societies.

Many of the key issues for institutional design concern the boundaries of what is humanly possible: what is easy, what is difficult, and what is entirely impossible. We can respond to such boundaries, limits, or impediments in two very different ways: we can adapt to them or we can attempt to modify them, to expand the boundaries of the possible.

4. In *Causal Theory of Justice* (Sołtan 1987) I consider a different set of ideals which could also be added to our account of moral competence while still keeping its empirical grounding.

Consider the example of a budget constraint for a firm. In the usual market situation the budget constraint is hard-and-fast, and the firm's only option is to adapt. It picks the best alternative allowed by the budget. In other settings, notoriously those of enterprises in a "late communist" economy, an organization's budget constraint may be modifiable by bargaining (with, for example, the central planning office). The budget constraint is then soft, and the rational strategy is to expand it as much as possible.

Self-limitation is one well-known and well-tried method of adapting to our limits. We accept the fact that people are neither angels nor geniuses, and that they face a situation of scarcity. We respond by self-limitation in order to prevent ourselves from doing what we do not really want to do, or what we ought not attempt, given the limits of our capacities. We impose on ourselves general and rigid rules, or we accept long-term commitments. Examples range from Ulysses facing the sirens, through the institution of marriage, to the more properly constitutionalist devices of the rule of law and a rigid, judicially enforceable constitution (see Elster 1979; Elster and Slagstad 1988).

We can also attempt to expand the boundaries of the possible. On this front, one crucial instrument—considered at length in this volume—is deliberation. What is deliberation? It is a form of interpersonal or intrapersonal interaction, a debate, an exchange, and a test of reasons. It is not exactly a "marketplace of ideas," but it *is* a testing ground for the persuasive force of rational arguments. Deliberation is a method whereby we can weigh alternative means to serve our purposes (as in cost–benefit analysis, for example). And deliberation in the form of rational debate is an instrument of morally informed action. The subject of deliberation is a pervasive theme in the essays that follow (see especially Chapters 2, 3, 5, 6).

How can we strike a balance between adapting to limits and trying to expand those limits? Abstract, scientifically developed knowledge will have little to say on the subject. This is a matter of judgment. How we exercise it will determine, among other things, where we are on the political spectrum. This judgment can also be educated, but the education will necessarily take a very different form from that of scientific education.

Institutional design and institutional reform should strike a balance between these various considerations, including efforts to deal with (diminish the force of, make the most of, rationally adapt to) the many impediments to successful human action. Each element of this complex set of considerations gives us one aspect of instrumental competence. From each element, we can derive partial strategies of institutional reform. For each impediment, then, we have a different view of what it is that institutions require, each view allowing us to see aspects of what makes a good institution (aspects that are not clearly visible elsewhere). Let me go down the list of the most important and universal of the impediments that instrumental competence must recognize.

If we consider the impediment of narrowly interested or self-interested human motivation, we will see institutions as, for example, solutions to the problem of faction, to the Prisoners' Dilemma game (Elster 1976), or to the problem of collective action (Taylor 1987). The work of Elinor Ostrom (see Chapter 1) is an important contribution to our understanding of this aspect of institutions.

Second, we can also look at institutions as ways to handle human error-proneness. Institutions provide us with mechanisms for error correction, including low-cost "exit" in a market, periodic elections in a democracy, and fallibilist procedures in science—all the elements, in short, of a flexible Popperian open society (Popper 1945). Institutional arrangements can also help us *prevent* errors. Rigid commitments and rigid rules are useful in this regard (Elster 1979; Heiner 1983), as are various forms of learning and education, the division of labor, and social differentiation. We make fewer errors after we have been educated, and we make fewer errors if we can concentrate on smaller tasks (i.e., if we specialize). These are all features, it should be noted, that reliably appear on most lists of what distinguishes modern from traditional societies (Parsons 1971; Janos 1986). The task of institutional reform on this front can be described, then, as *modernization*.

Institutions can also be seen as efforts to handle our mutual dependence and mutual influence. In this case, institutions are instruments or products of the art of separation (see Walzer 1984). The capacity to separate various types of action, kinds of decisionmakers, and institutional spheres is important to economic performance (this is a truism of economic thought, the reason why stable and secure property rights are so valuable). Economic systems can operate well only when they are reasonably independent from the political system, and stable and secure property rights are one good way of achieving such separation.

Finally, institutions can be seen as instruments for the handling (avoidance, management, or resolution) of conflicts and contradictions. Here we might consider how contradictions and conflicts among various goals, ideals, and institutional arrangements can be avoided, overcome, or resolved. This requires an understanding of the workings of complex institutional wholes, complex mutual interdependencies, and the many ways of handling large-scale contradictions. The relevant literature ranges from various forms of "institutionalist" Marxism (Carnoy 1984; Skocpol 1979), through much of Critical

Legal Studies (Kennedy 1976; Kelman 1987), to the historical institutionalism of Orren and Skowronek (1994) and systems theory or cybernetics.

The Whole and the Parts in Institutional Design

The new constitutionalism aims to develop and promote the knowledge necessary for institutional reform and institutional creation. It is cognizant of the fact that, unlike architects, institutional reformers (including engaged citizens) do not build from the ground a brand-new construction. They are more like shipbuilders trying to rebuild a ship while at sea, but with limited knowledge. They know something about planks, wind, waves, and promising directions for sailing, but they have no sound notion of the Ideal Ship and no knowledge of the precise location of the ports.

On some views of institutional design, no judgment is necessary to perform well. When we assume one basic goal, say wealth maximization, and a simple model of human motivation, then institutional design is algorithmic. Proper institutions can be logically deduced from the axioms of the theory, as in the simpler versions of Posnerian Economic Analysis of Law. We can then safely leave institutional design to the experts, and leave the citizens out.

But institutional design is more complex than that. There are multiple ends, and institutions can serve to redefine those ends. Moreover, the constraints institutions face are also ones that can be either adapted to or changed. It is a matter of judgment how to balance the considerations imposed by these facts of the human situation. Hence the design of institutions is not a simple algorithmic application of axioms: it is a more creative process, more loosely connected to the relevant microprocesses. It is an exercise in practical reason.

We can learn to exercise practical reason, and the political judgment that expresses it, by studying appropriately chosen *cases.* Among possible cases will be whole designs, whether successful or notable for their failure, and thus we study in detail examples of good or bad regimes. Alternatively we study cases of good (or bad) solutions to a particular design problem, or we study the design of "institutional components." We look, for example, at the sources of success and failure of markets (there is, of course, a large literature here) or of self-limiting social movements of the kind made famous by Mohandas Gandhi and Martin Luther King, Jr.

To perform this sort of complex task competently we need skills falling into two *methodologically* distinct groupings, not unlike those we would also encounter when analyzing the professional knowledge of architects or medical doctors. The first aspect of competence involves understanding the general features of the human situation and human nature relevant to institutional creation and reform. Most of the skills that fall into the traditionally recognized categories of moral and instrumental competence, as presented above, can be developed in this way. That is to say, they can be expressed in abstract, conventionally scientific form. But not all of political competence can be so expressed.

The second aspect of competence involves development of the particular judgment, based on practical reason, that is required to deal with specific cases of design and reform of large, complex combinations of institutions in a context of conflicting considerations. This judgment is best developed not simply through a mastery of scientific knowledge, but through detailed attention both to various large-scale case studies and to the ways in which large-scale complexity and internal contradictions can be handled.

We face, therefore, two conflicting intellectual pressures. On the one hand, we have pressure toward the micro level, toward analytical precision and systematic reliance on empirical evidence. This is essential in order to avoid vague truisms and empty slogans. Most of instrumental and moral competence can be subdivided into small and analytically tractable elements, some of them very general in their range of applicability.

On the other hand, though, we have pressure toward the macro level, needed to avoid a certain form of utopianism which ignores the way things are related to each other. Thus we are concerned not simply with politics or with economics, but with the politico-economic system. And the ultimate goal is not a better local neighborhood, municipality, or even a better "society" (if we identify "societies" with nations or territorial states, thus inviting abstraction from international interdependencies). The ultimate goal is rather a better *world*, a better global society.

The difficulties in reconciling contradictory principles and institutions when building large-scale systems can easily disappear from view if we split our problem into parts, for that problem concerns the relationship *among* the parts. Basic conflicts we may need to handle will include those between market and democracy, between procedural and substantive aspects of democracy, between participation and competence, between the rational and the sacred (or charismatic) dimensions of institutional legitimacy, and between those arrangements necessary to obtain things worth paying for and those arrangements necessary to obtain things worth dying for. A good society will need to reconcile at least some of these conflicting considerations.

So political competence (both in its moral and its instrumental components) is composed, first, out of various analytically tractable elements. Were it not, we would have little to add to common sense. But it cannot end with those elements, or be reduced to them: we do not learn how to handle conflicts among various aspects of complex arrangements by looking at each of their parts separately. The new worlds we imagine must be internally coherent ones, composed of parts that work together well. Thus, political competence includes skill in imagining large-scale and complex institutional wholes—combinations, say, of democratic states and competitive markets based on private property and freedom of contract.

I can think of two strategies for maintaining political realism while developing the skill to imagine very different (but workable) worlds. In both we begin where we are, with the best of the institutions we have inherited; we begin (in short) with capitalist democracy. The first strategy pushes one institutional aspect of where we are much further. Either it pushes capitalist markets into spheres where they are now absent, or it extends democracy much further than it is now extended. One approach calls for more extensive development of the institutions of capitalism, especially the market. In practice, its proponents are often hostile to the democratic state. Various anarcho-capitalists and libertarians are examples. The other approach calls for the extension of democracy into all spheres and is often hostile to capitalist markets. We have here various democratic socialists and radical democrats (Green [Chapter 8], Alperovitz [Chapter 7], Dahl [1985], Bowles and Gintis [1986], and others).

The alternative strategy also begins where we are. It identifies that place, however, not with any particular set of institutions, but—roughly—with the method that has produced those institutions: a set of principles for institution construction (a conception, in short, of political competence). A method does not change the world by itself, though. Only people can change the world. If we do not identify a good society with any particular set of institutions, then, we must at least require that the relevant method have a chance to be effective, that the institutionmakers in that society must adopt it. And for any conception of political competence that could plausibly generate a capitalist *democracy*, the institutionmakers cannot simply be some strategically located individuals. They cannot be the Great Lawmaker (a Solon, say), nor an elite group of Guardians (as Plato would like). The relevant competence must be spread out as widely as possible within the body of citizens.

At the end of the road of the first strategy is capitalism without democracy, or democracy without capitalism. The tensions, conflicts, and contradictions of capitalist democracy are resolved by one sphere triumphing over the other. At the end of the road of the second strategy we might be able to find completely new forms of capitalist democracy.[5] Its characteristic conflicts are not abandoned or overcome: neither side (market or democracy) "wins," and a balance is still required.

On this second view, the most important characteristic feature of a good society is *not* institutional; it is neither "more democracy" nor "more markets." What matters most is in people's minds. The pervasiveness of a certain attitude, a combination of skills and motives, separates the good societies from the rest. What is that attitude? The narrowest conception sees it as limited to "civic virtue," relying on one possible literal meaning of that term. Here citizenship is a form of membership in the state, and civic virtue is exclusively concerned with the design and reform of the state. We arrive at a broader conception by thinking of citizenship more generally as a type of membership in *any* institution. Then civic virtue and civic competence are skills in the making of institutions more generally.

But we can push further, as Charles Anderson does in this volume. In order to describe the distinctive feature of good societies, as he sees it, Anderson invokes Veblen's concept of "the instinct of workmanship." When applied to public institutions, this instinct amounts to a form of civic virtue, but it is more pervasive: it shows itself in carefulness and in attention to quality, in economic as well as in political activity. It is good craftsmanship across the political economy.

With the help of a more detailed look at the very book of Veblen's on which Anderson relies, we can push further still. Veblen writes:

> Chief among the instinctive dispositions that conduce directly to the material well-being of the race, and therefore to its biological success, is perhaps the instinctive bias here spoken of as the sense of workmanship. The only other instinctive factor of human nature that could with any likelihood dispute this primacy would be the parental bent. Indeed the two have much in common. They spend themselves on much the same concrete objective ends, and the mutual furtherance of each by the other is indeed so broad and intimate as often to leave it a matter of extreme difficulty to draw a line between them. (Veblen [1914] 1964, 25)

In Veblen's difficulty with distinguishing the "sense of workmanship" from the "parental bent," we can see the outlines of an even broader characterization of the mentality that distinguishes the good society: a

---

5. I take it that Stephen Elkin, in Chapter 6 and elsewhere, uses the expression "commercial republic" to emphasize the possibility, and the desirability, of such completely new forms.

form of love, the creator's love for what she creates. This distinctive kind of creator's love is known in the Christian tradition as *agape* (God's love for humanity); in the writings of Gandhi, it is *ahimsa,* a conception broader and more affirmative than its usual literal translation as "nonviolence" (Dhawan 1946). It is, I take it, a highly generalized form of the morality of *care,* whose content and development have been much studied recently in moral psychology and feminist theory (Gilligan 1982).

This creator's love is a form of love that celebrates what its object has already become and that strives to make it the best it can be. So, for example, when we direct this love toward law, we approach law from the "internal point of view" (Hart 1961; Finnis 1980; Dworkin 1985, 1986), trying to make law "the best it can be."[6] We bring together expertise, understanding, and a special kind of respect, one that values law in a way essential to improving it.

This kind of loving point of view can be our perspective on institutions, and on the material objects we create, not just on people. The pervasiveness of this love in a population can then be used as part of our definition of a good society. This form of love cannot be identified with any *emotions* or feelings, for it is a set of attitudes, skills, and motives that must be quite hard-nosed and *realistic.* But we are not speaking here about the cynical realism of Realpolitik and of politics as the art of the possible. We have here, rather, a skilled and motivated *imagination* which can create new institutions, new forms of material objects, and which can build character.

The Organization of the Book

The organization of this volume reflects the basic methodological division I discussed above: a division between two fundamentally different intellectual tasks in thinking about institutional design and institutional reform. Part 1, "Human Capabilities and Institutional Design," will consider how human capabilities affect institutional design. It will take into account some of the boundaries of what is humanly possible in politico-economic designs and will address the role of deliberation and the process of adapting to limits. Part 2, "Conceptions of the Good Society," will consider different notions of good society, including examples of both the search for a Third Way and the search for a better form of capitalist democracy.

6. This approach to law is most fully elaborated in the legal theory of Ronald Dworkin, based on hermeneutic principles combining the dimensions of "charity" and "fit" (see also Arthur 1989).

REFERENCES

Ackerman, Bruce. 1984. *Reconstructing American Law*. Cambridge: Harvard University Press.

Anderson, Charles. 1990. *Pragmatic Liberalism*. Chicago: University of Chicago Press.

Arthur, John. 1989. *The Unfinished Constitution*. Belmont, Calif.: Wadsworth.

Bowles, Samuel, and Herbert Gintis. 1986. *Democracy and Capitalism*. New York: Basic Books.

Brennan, Geoffrey, and James Buchanan. 1985. *The Reason of Rules*. Cambridge: Cambridge University Press.

Buchanan, James. 1990. "The Domain of Constitutional Economics." *Constitutional Political Economy* 1:1–18.

Calabresi, Guido, and Philip Bobbitt. 1978. *Tragic Choices*. New York: W. W. Norton.

Carnoy, Martin. 1984. *The State and Political Theory*. Princeton, N.J.: Princeton University Press.

Chomsky, Noam. 1965. *Aspects of the Theory of Syntax*. Cambridge: MIT Press.

Dahl, Robert. 1985. *A Preface to Economic Democracy*. Berkeley and Los Angeles: University of California Press.

———. 1989. *Democracy and Its Critics*. New Haven, Conn.: Yale University Press.

Dhawan, Gopi Nath. 1946. *The Political Philosophy of Mahatma Gandhi*. Bombay: The Popular Book Depot.

Dror, Yehezkel. 1993. "Public Policy Analysis and Development." New York: United Nations Development Program.

Dworkin, Ronald. 1977. *Taking Rights Seriously*. Cambridge: Harvard University Press.

———. 1985. *A Matter of Principle*. Cambridge: Harvard University Press.

———. 1986. *Law's Empire*. Cambridge: Harvard University Press.

Elkin, Stephen, and Karol Sołtan, eds. 1993. *A New Constitutionalism*. Chicago: University of Chicago Press.

Elster, Jon. 1976. "Some Conceptual Problems in Political Theory." In Brian Barry, ed., *Power and Political Theory*. London: Wiley.

———. 1979. *Ulysses and the Sirens: Studies in Rationality and Irrationality*. Cambridge: Cambridge University Press.

Elster, Jon, and Rune Slagstad, eds. 1988. *Constitutionalism and Democracy*. Cambridge: Cambridge University Press.

Finnis, John. 1980. *Natural Law and Natural Rights*. Oxford: Clarendon Press.

Frohlich, Norman, and Joe Oppenheimer. 1992. *Choosing Justice: An Experimental Approach to Ethical Theory*. Berkeley and Los Angeles: University of California Press.

Gilligan, Carol. 1982. *In a Different Voice*. Cambridge: Harvard University Press.

Habermas, Jürgen. 1973. *Theory and Practice*. Boston: Beacon Press.

Hart, H.L.A. 1961. *The Concept of Law*. Oxford: Clarendon Press.

Heiner, Ronald. 1983. "The Origins of Predictable Behavior." *American Economic Review* 73:560–95.

Janos, Andrew. 1986. *Politics and Paradigms*. Stanford, Calif.: Stanford University Press.

Kelman, Mark. 1987. *A Guide to Critical Legal Studies*. Cambridge: Harvard University Press.

Kennedy, Duncan. 1976. "Form and Substance in Private Law Adjudication." *Harvard Law Review* 89:1685–1778.

Machiavelli, Niccolò. (1514) 1988. *The Prince*. Cambridge: Cambridge University Press.

Mueller, Dennis. 1996. *Constitutional Democracy*. New York: Oxford University Press.

Orren, Karen, and Stephen Skowronek. 1994. "Beyond the Iconography of Order: Notes for a New Institutionalism." In Lawrence Dodd and Calvin Jillson, eds., *The Dynamics of American Politics*. Boulder, Colo.: Westview.

Parsons, Talcott. 1971. *The System of Modern Societies*. Englewood Cliffs, N.J.: Prentice-Hall.

Peters, Thomas, and Robert Waterman. 1982. *In Search of Excellence*. New York: Harper & Row.

Popper, Karl. 1945. *The Open Society and Its Enemies*. London: Routledge & Sons.

Posner, Richard. 1972–92. *Economic Analysis of Law*. 1st to 4th eds. Boston: Little, Brown.

Reich, Robert, ed. 1990. *The Power of Public Ideas*. Cambridge: Harvard University Press.

Selznick, Philip. 1992. *The Moral Commonwealth*. Berkeley and Los Angeles: University of California Press.

Skocpol, Theda. 1979. *States and Social Revolutions*. Cambridge: Cambridge University Press.

Sołtan, Karol Edward. 1987. *Causal Theory of Justice*. Berkeley and Los Angeles: University of California Press.

———. 1993. "What Is the New Constitutionalism?" In Stephen Elkin and Karol Edward Sołtan, eds., *A New Constitutionalism*. Chicago: University of Chicago Press.

———. 1994. "A Liberal and Democratic Procedural Ideal." Paper presented at the meetings of the American Political Science Association.

Strauss, Leo. 1959. *What Is Political Philosophy?* Glencoe, Ill.: Free Press.

———. 1989. *The Rebirth of Classical Political Rationalism*. Edited by Thomas Pangle. Chicago: University of Chicago Press.

Taylor, Michael. 1987. *The Possibility of Cooperation*. Cambridge: Cambridge University Press.

Thompson, Dennis. 1976. *John Stuart Mill and Representative Government*. Princeton, N.J.: Princeton University Press.

Tyler, Tom. 1990. "Justice, Self-Interest, and the Legitimacy of Legal and Political Authority." In Jane Mansbridge, ed., *Beyond Self-Interest*. Chicago: University of Chicago Press.

Veblen, Thorstein. (1914) 1964. *The Instinct of Workmanship and the State of the Industrial Arts.* New York: W. W. Norton.

Walzer, Michael. 1984. "Liberalism and the Art of Separation." *Political Theory* 12:315–30.

Williamson, Oliver. 1975. *Markets and Hierarchies: Analysis and Anti-Trust Implications.* New York: Free Press.

———. 1985. *The Economic Institutions of Capitalism.* New York: Free Press.

PART ONE

Human Capabilities and Institutional Design

The chapters in this section concern the microfoundations of the problem of institutional design. One good place to begin this discussion is with the standard formulation of the problem in economics. The basic elements are as follows:

1. Wealth maximization or Pareto optimality is the social goal. The goal is taken as a given, so that the problem of the choice of goals is not considered.
2. The main choice for policymakers and institutional designers is the choice between provision of goods and services through a government agency or through the market.
3. There are three main impediments facing the institutional designer.
   a. Scarcity—to get something, we have to give up something else.
   b. Limited information, requiring decisions in situations of uncertainty or risk.
   c. Narrowly interested motivation.

The entire toolbox of rational-choice theories elaborates on these constraints and on ways of dealing with them. Thus we have, among others, maximization of expected utility, maximin, budget constraints, and game theory.

In her essay (Chapter 1), Elinor Ostrom describes the results of the research she and others have been conducting about practical solutions to the problem of "common-pool resources." Her conclusions are complex and detailed, but the main emphasis is on two ways in which this standard economic picture is inadequate. First, the best solutions to the common-pool resources problem are neither those imposed by a central government nor those relying on a market mechanism. The set of alternatives we must consider must be broader and must include spontaneously evolving local institutions. Second, she stresses the importance of social capital, a form of "capital" absent from the standard economic models and consisting of "shared knowledge, understandings, and patterns of interaction," usable resources in the creation and the improvement of institutions.

If we adopt Ostrom's categories, we can see the subject of the chapter by Vanberg and Buchanan as one particularly important form of social capital: "constitutional knowledge." Vanberg and Buchanan distinguish two components of our constitutional preferences: the interest and the theory components. The kind of constitution I want (or, more generally, the kind of institution I want) depends on my interests, but it also depends on my "constitutional theories," my understanding of how various constitutions will in fact operate and what consequences they will have. Most contractarianism (including previous work by these authors) focuses on the interest problem, but in Chapter 2 the focus is on the knowledge problem.

Vanberg and Buchanan introduce the notion of constitutional discourse as the set of factors that alleviate this knowledge problem (by helping eliminate disagreement and by improving the quality of constitutional understandings). They then consider two kinds of limitation on this discourse: motivational limits, producing the problem of rational ignorance, and cognitive limits. Among the possible solutions of the problem of rational ignorance are mandatory constitutional training, the use of specialized experts, and constitutional competition. For solutions to the problem of limited reason, the authors draw on the work of Popper and Hayek; they stress the value of incremental evolution of practices and understandings, based on a process of trial and error, and they discuss the possibility of constitutional learning.

The contributions by Dryzek and Sołtan (Chapters 3 and 4) take one additional step beyond the standard economic treatment of the institutional design problem. Both try to add to instrumental rationality in the accounts they present. The Sołtan chapter first suggests a more complicated conception of instrumental rationality, adding human error-proneness and human interdependence to the standard considerations from economics. Thus, the craft of institutional design is seen to include the art of preventing and correcting errors (a subject considered also by Vanberg and Buchanan for the special case of constitutional knowledge) and the art of separation, a fundamental skill for the design of liberal institutions. Sołtan continues with an account of one possible methodology for the description of moral competence. It is a methodology guided by the ideal of objectivity, a commitment to which Sołtan derives both from the traditional constitutionalist concern with natural law and natural rights and from the more contemporary rhetoric of truth in Gandhi's *satyagraha,* or Havel's "living in truth."

Dryzek's path beyond instrumental rationality is different. Where Sołtan adds moral competence to instrumental competence, Dryzek multiplies competences. He asks us to consider communicative, self-referential, dramaturgical, and ecological competence. Given these multiple competences, we are faced with a problem of choice not just among alternative courses of action, but also among the alternative competences that we can use in deciding among actions. The significance of autonomy for Dryzek arises from this predicament which we all face, because autonomy is (for Dryzek) the capacity to decide reflectively which competence to invoke.

CHAPTER ONE

Covenants, Collective Action, and Common-Pool Resources

ELINOR OSTROM

UNTIL RECENTLY, students of constitutional choice focused almost entirely on formal documents written for national governments during an overt constitutional process. During the past three decades, however, considerable analytical and empirical work has centered on how individuals covenant together to create local enterprises in order to provide public goods or common-pool resources. Buchanan and Tullock's foundational *Calculus of Consent* (1962) concentrated on the logic used by a group of farmers who were creating a public enterprise to provide a local road. Mancur Olson's *The Logic of Collective Action* (1965) started with a problem facing a group that wanted to lower local tax rates. Todd Sandler's recent *Collective Action: Theory and Applications* (1992) ranges in its focus from problems of global warming and destruction of the ozone layer to how individuals can create and sustain local neighborhood clubs.

Besides examining phenomena that are both smaller and larger than national governments, scholars have also begun to recognize the importance of covenants made among individuals to create nongovernmental organizations for solving collective-action problems. The presence of written, legal documents and external enforcers is no longer seen as the necessary foundation for a successful effort at constitutional change. All too many formal constitutional documents have been little more than words on paper, without any impact on the political and social order that follows their pronouncement. In response to many collective-action problems, actors covenanting together to follow a set of rules and to monitor and enforce rule conformance themselves has been a more effective remedy than policy prescriptions formally made in a nation's capital.

The establishment of the Panel on Common Property Resources

at the National Academy of Sciences (NAS) during the mid-1980s has stimulated even further the theoretical and empirical research on collective-action problems specifically related to common-pool resources. Common-pool resources (CPRs) are natural or man-made resources where exclusion is nontrivial (but not necessarily impossible) and where the yield is subtractable (E. Ostrom, Gardner, and Walker 1994). CPRs include inshore and ocean fisheries, irrigation systems, grazing areas, and forests as well as bridges and other man-made resources. When the NAS panel was first created, many social scientists interested in natural resource policy problems presumed that the "appropriators" (a general term used to describe all persons who harvest or withdraw benefits, and who thus "appropriate," from a CPR) were unlikely to develop their own norms and institutions to reduce the costs of externalities associated with the use of CPRs.

On the assumption that no evolution of local norms, rules, or rights would occur, recommendations were made that external agents should impose solutions to CPR problems. The imposed solutions were frequently presented as "the *only* way" to reduce these externalities and increase efficiency. One proposed solution was control of natural resources by a central government agency; another was the imposition of private property. Something had to be wrong with the theories, their interpretation, or the policy prescriptions based on the theories, however, if solutions as different as state control and market control were both proposed as the *only* way to manage natural resources efficiently.

Research in this area has come a long way over the past decade.[1] The initial publication of the summary volume of the NAS panel (National Research Council 1986), the many important books recently published (McCay and Acheson 1987; Fortmann and Bruce 1988; Wade 1988; Berkes 1989; Pinkerton 1989; Sengupta 1991; Dasgupta and Mäler 1992; V. Ostrom, Feeny, and Picht 1993; Netting 1993), the revision of the NAS volume (Bromley et al 1992), the influential article by Feeny et al. (1990), and recent important work on property rights (Libecap 1989; Eggertsson 1990; Bromley 1991) have all contributed to this progress. Books by those associated with the Workshop in Political Theory and Policy Analysis at Indiana University (E. Ostrom 1990 and 1992; E. Ostrom, Gardner, and Walker 1994; Blomquist 1992;

---

1. Of course, that progress drew on an immense body of scholarly work that already existed in scattered sources. The theoretical breakthroughs probably would not have occurred if many scholars in different disciplines had not already undertaken in-depth and detailed studies of particular natural resource systems. See F. Martin (1989 and 1992) for a bibliographic overview of this literature.

Tang 1992; F. Martin 1989 and 1992; Sproule-Jones 1993; Thomson 1992) have contributed as well.

Emergence and Consequences of Self-Organized CPR Institutions

While many of those affected by the threat of overuse and potential destruction of CPRs find ways of constituting their own institutions, others do not. Empirical research both in the field and the laboratory has now yielded a series of important findings regarding the emergence and consequences of institutions. These findings can be summarized as follows:

1. Overuse, conflict, and potential destruction of CPRs producing highly valued products is likely to occur where those involved act independently owing to a lack of communication or an incapacity to make credible commitments.
2. If those who directly benefit can communicate, agree on norms, monitor each other, and sanction noncompliance to their own covenants, then overuse, conflict, and the destruction of CPRs can be reduced substantially.
3. Locally developed systems of norms, rules, and property rights that are not recognized by external authorities may collapse if the legitimacy of these covenants is challenged or if large, exogenous economic or physical shocks occur.
4. Control of local or regional CPRs by state authorities is effective in some settings but is frequently less effective and efficient than control by those directly affected, especially in settings related to smaller-scale natural resource systems.
5. Efforts to establish marketable property rights to natural resource systems have substantially increased efficiency in some cases and encountered difficulties of implementation in others.

At a general level, these findings can be summarized with three statements. Open-access resources—those characterized by *no* property rights—will be overused, generate conflict, and may even be destroyed. All types of institutions—including private property, common property, and state property—may be used to reduce the costs of open-access regimes. Performance of diverse institutions depends on how well the attributes of the resource, the social and economic attributes of those using the resource, and the specific rules used work together. Thus, evolved or self-consciously designed institutions are needed to regulate the use of natural resource systems, but all such regimes have limits. If those who know the most about local time-and-place information and incentives are given sufficient autonomy to reach and enforce local covenants, they frequently are able to devise rules well tailored to the problems they face.

The dominant theories of a decade ago have not been proved wrong. Rather, their claim to universal applicability has been challenged both theoretically (Sandler 1992) and empirically (E. Ostrom, Gardner, and Walker 1994). Empirical research readily confirms that when those using open-access regimes are limited by physical and institutional constraints to act independently and not to take each other's interests into account, then the predictions derived from the "tragedy of the commons" (G. Hardin 1968), the finitely repeated prisoner's dilemma game (R. Hardin 1982), and the logic of collective *in*action (Olson 1965) are empirically supported. In the simpler environment of an experimental laboratory, findings from repeated experiments that do not allow subjects to communicate about their contributions to public goods (Isaac, Walker, and Williams 1994) or their investments in common-pool resources (Walker, Gardner, and Ostrom 1990) are quite consistent with predictions of low levels of "cooperative" behavior. On the other hand, when symmetric subjects are given opportunities in a laboratory to communicate and devise their own agreements and sanctioning arrangements, then the outcomes approximate optimality (E. Ostrom, Walker, and Gardner 1992; see also E. Ostrom and Walker 1991 and Isaac and Walker 1991). These findings are surprising for many theorists, because the capacity to communicate without an external enforcer for monitoring and sanctioning behavior inconsistent with covenantal agreements is considered to be mere "cheap talk" having no impact on the strategic structure of the game (but see Banks and Calvert 1992a, 1992b). Hackett, Schlager, and Walker (1994) find that, even in experimental environments where the players are not symmetric but have different endowments, face-to-face communication is a very effective institution for greatly increasing efficiency. Charles Plott (1983) has shown that in the experimental lab it is possible to impose markets or regulatory institutions that enable subjects to achieve close-to-optimal results.

Because we can create conditions in a laboratory that enable subjects to come close to optimality, however, should not encourage us to think that there are optimal solutions that can be imposed on all natural resource problems within large and diversified countries. The complexity of natural settings is immense. The particular features of a natural setting that might effectively be used by local users in selecting rules cannot be included in general models. The likelihood is small that any set of uniform rules for all natural resource systems within a large territory will produce optimal results. This is unfortunately the case whether or not the particular rules can be shown to generate optimal rules in a sparse theoretical or experimental setting. Rather, theoretical and empirical research can be used to help inform those who are close to particular natural resource systems (as well as those in larger, overarching agencies) about principles they can use to improve performance.

Design Principles and Robust Institutions

In addition to knowing that various types of institutions can be used to reduce the externalities usually involved in the management and use of natural resource systems, we also are beginning to understand the design principles used by robust institutions. Robust institutions are those in which the systems have survived for very long periods of time and where operational rules have been devised and modified over time according to a set of collective-choice and constitutional-choice rules (Shepsle 1989). Robust institutions tend to be characterized by most of the design principles listed in Table 1. Fragile institutions tend to be characterized by only some of these design principles. Failed institutions are characterized by only a few of these principles. Initial analysis also finds that farmer-governed irrigation systems, which are characterized by most of these principles, are associated with higher agricultural yields and crop intensities, controlling for the physical characteristics of the systems (Lam, Lee, and Ostrom, forthcoming). The theoretical reasons why these design principles work in practice have been presented elsewhere and will not be repeated here (see E. Ostrom 1990; Weissing and Ostrom 1991, 1993; E. Ostrom and Gardner 1993; E. Ostrom, Gardner, and Walker 1994).

The design principles are stated generally. The specific ways that individuals have crafted rules to meet these principles vary in their particulars. Successful, long-enduring irrigation institutions, for example, have developed different ways of meeting the second design principle of achieving congruence or proportionality between the costs of building and maintaining irrigation systems and the distribution of benefits. Some examples will illustrate the diversity of specific rules that meet the second design principle.[2]

The Zanjeras *of the Northern Philippines*

Zanjeras are self-organized systems that obtain use rights to previously unirrigated land from a large landowner by building a canal

2. The following section draws from my previous work (E. Ostrom 1992, 76–78).

Table 1. Design Principles Illustrated by Long-Enduring CPR Institutions

---

1. Clearly Defined Boundaries
   Individuals or households with rights to withdraw resource units from the CPR and the boundaries of the CPR itself are clearly defined.

2. Congruence between Appropriation and Provision Rules and Local Conditions
   Appropriation rules restricting time, place, technology, and/or quantity of resource units are related to local conditions and to provision rules requiring labor, materials, and/or money.

3. Collective-Choice Arrangements
   Most individuals affected by operational rules can participate in modifying operational rules.

4. Monitoring
   Monitors, who actively audit CPR conditions and appropriator behavior, are accountable to the appropriators and/or are the appropriators themselves.

5. Graduated Sanctions
   Appropriators who violate operational rules are likely to receive graduated sanctions (depending on the seriousness and context of the offense) from other appropriators, from officials accountable to other appropriators, or from both.

6. Conflict Resolution Mechanisms
   Appropriators and their officials have rapid access to low-cost, local arenas in order to resolve conflict among appropriators or between appropriators and officials.

7. Minimal Recognition of Rights to Organize
   The rights of appropriators to devise their own institutions are not challenged by external governmental authorities.

For CPRs that are part of larger systems:

8. Nested Enterprises
   Appropriation, provision, monitoring, enforcement, conflict resolution, and governance activities are organized in multiple layers of nested enterprises.

SOURCE: E. Ostrom 1990, 90.

that irrigates both the landowner's land and that of the *zanjera*. At the time that the land is allocated, each farmer willing to abide by the rules of the system receives a bundle of rights and duties in the form of *atars*. Each *atar* defines three parcels of land located in the head, middle, and tail sections of the service area where the holder grows his or her crops. Responsibilities for construction and maintenance are allocated by *atars*, as are voting rights. In the rainy seasons, water is allocated freely. In a dry year, water may be allocated only to parcels located in the head and middle portions. Thus, everyone receives water in plentiful and scarce times in rough proportion to the amount of *atars* they possess. *Atars* may be sold to others with the permission of the irrigation association and are inheritable (see Siy 1982; Coward 1979).

Thulo Kulo, Nepal

When the Thulo Kulo system was first constructed in 1928, twenty-seven households contributed to a fund to construct the canal and received shares of the resulting system proportionate to the amount they invested. Since then, the system has been expanded several times by selling additional shares. Measurement and diversion weirs or gates are installed at key locations so that water is automatically allocated to each farmer according to the proportion of shares owned. Routine monitoring and maintenance is allocated to work teams so that everyone participates proportionally, but emergency repairs require labor input from all shareholders regardless of the size of their share (see E. Martin and Yoder 1983; E. Martin 1986).

The Huerta of Valencia, Spain

In 1435, eighty-four irrigators, served by two interrelated canals in Valencia, gathered at the monastery of St. Francis to draw up and approve formal regulations to specify who had rights to water from these canals, how the water would be shared in good and bad years, and how responsibilities for maintenance would be shared. The modern *Huerta* of Valencia, composed of these plus six additional canals, now serves about sixteen thousand hectares and fifteen thousand farmers. The right to water inheres in the land itself and cannot be bought and sold independently of the land. Rights to water are approximately proportionate to the amount of land owned, as are obligations to contribute to the cost of monitoring and maintenance activities (see Maass and Anderson 1986).

These three systems differ substantially from one another. The *zanjeras* are institutional devices for landless laborers to acquire use rights to land and water, and this system could be called a communal system. The Thulo Kulo system comes as close to allocating private and separable property rights to water as is feasible in an irrigation system. The *Huerta* of Valencia has maintained centuries-old land and water rights that forbid the separation of water rights from the land being served. The Valencian system differs both from "communal" and from "private property" systems because water rights are firmly attached to private ownership of land. Underlying these differences, however, is the basic design principle that the costs of constructing, operating, and maintaining the system are roughly proportional to the benefits that irrigators obtain.

It is important to keep these differences in mind when making policy prescriptions. Slogans such as "privatization" may mask important underlying principles rather than provide useful guides for reform. Strict privatization of water rights is not a feasible option within the broad institutional framework of many countries. On the other hand, authorizing the suppliers and users of irrigation water to participate in the design of their own systems—design principles 3 and 7 combined—is a feasible reform within the broad institutional framework of many countries.

Not only is a substantial variety of rules used to reduce the cost of externalities from unregulated use of natural resources, but neighboring systems that appear to face similar situations frequently adopt different solutions. Within a few miles of Valencia is Alicante, where irrigators long ago adopted rules separating water from the land and still participate in an active weekly market for water. Adjacent to Thulo Kulo is Raj Kulo, where the allocation of water (and labor responsibilities) is in accord with the amount of land owned. Near the *zanjeras* of the northern Philippines are many irrigation systems with quite different rules for distributing water and input responsibilities.

The Importance of Social Capital

Searching for outside solutions to problems of collective action, instead of elucidating the design principles that underlie robust institutions in use around the world, has led to an emphasis on physical capital without much attention to the social capital that may already exist in a location. All forms of capital are created by spending time and effort in transformation and transaction activities (E. Ostrom, Schroeder, and Wynne 1993). In other words, all forms of capital are created as the result of an investment process whereby resources that could be used for current consumption are invested instead in activities that have long-term consequences.

Physical capital is the stock of material resources that can be used to produce a flow of future income (Lachmann 1978). The origin of physical capital is the process of spending time and other resources to construct tools, plants, facilities, and other material resources that can, in turn, be used to produce other products. The construction of physical capital establishes physical restraints that (1) create the possibilities for some events to occur that would not otherwise occur (e.g., channeling water from a distant source to a farmer's field) and (2) constrain physical events to a more restricted domain (e.g., water is held within a channel rather than being allowed to spread out). Physical capital thus opens up some opportunities while restricting others.

Human capital is the acquired knowledge and skills that any individual brings to productive activity. Human capital is formed consciously through education and training and unconsciously through experience. Human capital also opens up some opportunities while restricting others. The acquisition of new skills enables an artisan to create artifacts that he or she could not have created prior to the acquisition of the new skill. The pursuit of any skill, however, precludes certain activities from occurring. One has to learn what *not* to do as much as what to do.

Social capital is the shared knowledge, understandings, and patterns of interaction that a group of individuals brings to any productive activity (Coleman 1988; Putnam 1993). Social capital is created when individuals learn to trust each other so that they are able to make credible commitments and rely on generalized forms of reciprocity rather than on narrow sequences of specific quid pro quo relationships. "Smith and Jones" can accomplish far more per unit of time if they do not have to negotiate each and every task in an arm's-length relationship. They can be far more productive with whatever physical and human capital they bring to the joint activity if they can covenant with one another and credibly commit themselves to a sequence of future actions. This covenant may be negotiated overtly. Or it may be based on mutual learning that both understand implicitly but have never tried to put into explicit language. It can be based on an agreement that Smith will follow Jones's commands (or vice versa) pertaining to the activity. Or it can be based on the evolution or construction of a set of norms or rules for how the activity will be carried out over time and how commitments will be monitored and sanctions imposed if nonperformance should occur.

Social capital also opens up some opportunities while restricting others. A decision to establish majority rule as the decision rule for making particular collective choices about a joint facility, for example, opens up opportunities that did not previously exist. Majority-rule decisionmaking does not exist in nature. The opportunity to use majority-rule voting is created by rules. A rule that forbids a driver from exceeding seventy miles an hour, or a participant in a discussion from speaking until recognized by the chair, limits alternative actions to a smaller set than was available before the creation of the rule.

The shared cognitive aspects of social capital help to account for two of its unusual characteristics that differ from those of physical capital. First, social capital does not wear out upon being used more and more. It may, in fact, improve with use so long as participants continue to keep prior commitments. Using social capital for an initial purpose creates mutual understandings and ways of relating that frequently can be used to accomplish entirely different joint activities at much lower start-up costs. It is not that learning curves for new activities disappear entirely. Rather, one of the steepest sections of a learning curve—learning to make commitments and to trust one another in a joint undertaking—has already been surmounted. A group that has learned to work together effectively in one task can take on other similar tasks at a cost in time and effort that is far less than that of bringing together an entirely new group of people who must learn everything from scratch. The fungibility of social capital, of course, is limited to broadly similar activities. No tool is useful for all tasks. Social capital that is well adapted to one broad set of joint activities may not be easily molded to other activities that require vastly different patterns of expectation, authority, and distribution of rewards and costs.

Second, social capital, if unused, deteriorates at a rapid rate. Individuals who do not exercise their own skills can lose human capital rapidly. When several individuals must all remember the same routine in the same manner, however, the probability that at least one of them will forget some aspect increases rapidly over time. Further, as time goes on, some individuals leave and others enter any social aggregation. If newcomers are not introduced to an established pattern of interaction as they enter (through job training, initiation, or any of the myriad of other ways that social capital is passed from one generation to the next), social capital can dissipate through nonuse. No one is quite sure how they used to get a particular joint activity done. Either the group has to pay some of the start-up costs all over again, or it must forgo the joint advantages that had once been achieved.

Factors Affecting the Creation of New Social Capital

Recent empirical research provides evidence that individuals frequently do design new institutional arrangements—and thus create social capital themselves through covenantal processes. Strong evidence also exists that effective formation of social capital does not always occur when it is needed. A major factor affecting whether individuals are able to develop new institutions for coping with CPR problems is the set of metarules at a collective-choice or constitutional level that is used for changing old rules or creating new ones (Knight 1992; E. Ostrom 1990). The metarules may assign differential advantages to participants in the rule-changing process. Those with the most voice in a covenantal process may not benefit from rule changes even though the aggregate benefits are greater. To explain a change in rules one needs to analyze not only the status quo distribution of costs and benefits, but also the distributional effects of the proposed rules (Libecap 1989) and how these relate to the metarules used for making and changing rules.

Thus, to explain investments in social capital—or institutional change—one needs to analyze the relationships between variables characterizing the resource, the community of individuals involved, and the metarules for making and changing rules. Sufficient theoretical and empirical research has been conducted on this and the closely related theory of collective action to enable us to specify important variables and the direction of their impact (E. Ostrom 1990). The following variables appear to be conducive to the selection of institutions and norms that reduce the externalities:

1. Accurate information about the condition of the resource and about the expected flow of benefits and costs are available at low cost.
2. Participants are relatively homogeneous in regard to asset structure, information, and preferences.
3. Participants share an understanding about the potential benefits and risks associated with the continuance of the status quo as contrasted with feasible changes in norms and rules.
4. Participants share generalized norms of reciprocity and trust that can be used as initial social capital.
5. The group using the resource is small and stable.
6. Participants' discounting of the future is sufficiently low.
7. Participants have the autonomy to make many of their own operational rules, and if made legitimately those rules will be supported and potentially enforced by external authorities.
8. Participants use collective-choice rules that fall between the extremes of unanimity or control by a few (or even by a bare majority) and thus avoid high transaction or high deprivation costs.
9. Participants can develop accurate and low-cost monitoring and sanctioning arrangements.

Many of these variables are in turn affected by the type of larger regime in which users are embedded. If the larger regime is facilitative of local self-organization by providing accurate information about natural resource systems, providing arenas in which participants can engage in discovery and conflict-resolution processes, and providing mechanisms to back up local monitoring and sanctioning efforts, then the probability of participants adapting more-effective norms and rules over time is higher than in regimes that ignore resource problems or presume that all decisions about governance and management need to be made by central authorities.

Future Research on Institutions

We now have a reasonably good understanding of the emergence of norms and institutions in simple, small, and isolated natural resource systems characterized by (1) a small and stable set of users able to communicate on a face-to-face basis, (2) predictable and easy-to-measure flows of benefits and costs, and (3) symmetry of information, asset structures, capabilities, and preferences. In field settings approximating the above conditions, those involved are highly likely to invest in social capital and arrive at covenantal agreements leading to the assignment of rights and duties that enhance efficiency.

Many natural resource problems, however, occur in settings that are not so conducive to self-organization. Large natural resource systems, particularly those that cross national borders (Young 1982; Keohane 1989; Dasgupta and Mäler 1992; McGinnis and Ostrom 1992; Haas, Keohane, and Levy 1993), involve substantial difficulties. These are associated with large, heterogeneous numbers of individual and corporate actors and the problem of making credible commitments. Further, many natural resources, particularly multispecies fisheries and forests, manifest complex transformation functions whose structure is hard to determine. No one—neither those directly involved nor external officials—has good enough models or sufficient accurate data to estimate future flows of benefits and costs accurately. Moreover, resources such as forests and the atmosphere have such long time-horizons that the value of future benefits and costs is difficult to assess.

In future work, consequently, it will be important to pursue theoretical and empirical studies that specifically address how heterogeneity of participants, multispecies or multiproduct resource systems, and long time-horizons affect the selection and performance of institutions. One theoretical and empirical program of research that will tackle these questions is the International Forestry Resources and Institutions (IFRI) database developed by a team at Indiana University with extensive input from colleagues at other institutions. We are conducting original field research on the types and performance of local forestry institutions in India, Nepal, Bolivia, and Uganda (as well as other countries if funding permits). These data will be archived and analyzed using a relational database structure (see E. Ostrom, Huckfeldt, Schweik, and Wertime 1993).

Understanding the emergence and performance of forestry institutions does not automatically answer questions about very large natural resource systems. The complexity, long time-horizons, and involvement of heterogeneous actors in the use of forests, however, should enable us to move from analysis of the simpler environments studied previously to the analysis of ever more difficult and complex environments. Further, forests are linked to the global atmospheric commons through their impact on greenhouse gases. If the rate of deforestation is to be reduced in many parts of the world, more must be learned about how individuals do covenant with each other to take collective action concerning local common-pool resources that are linked with global resources. We have come a great distance in understanding covenantal processes among small and homogeneous groups. The next challenge in gaining an effective understanding of such processes is to analyze larger, interlinked, and heterogeneous groups. The survival of the global commons is dependent upon further work on these important questions.

REFERENCES

Banks, Jeffrey S., and Randall L. Calvert. 1992a. "A Battle-of-the-Sexes Game with Incomplete Information." *Games and Economic Behavior* 4:1–26.
———. 1992b. "Communication and Efficiency in Coordination Games." Working paper. Rochester, N.Y.: University of Rochester, Department of Economics and Department of Political Science.
Berkes, Fikret, ed. 1989. *Common Property Resources. Ecology and Community-Based Sustainable Development*. London: Belhaven Press.
Blomquist, William. 1992. *Dividing the Waters: Governing Groundwater in Southern California*. San Francisco: Institute for Contemporary Studies Press.
Bromley, Daniel W. 1991. *Environment and Economy: Property Rights and Public Policy*. Oxford: Basil Blackwell.
Bromley, Daniel W., et al., eds. 1992. *Making the Commons Work: Theory, Practice, and Policy*. San Francisco: Institute for Contemporary Studies Press.
Buchanan, James M., and Gordon Tullock. 1962. *The Calculus of Consent*. Ann Arbor: University of Michigan Press.
Coleman, James. 1988. "Social Capital in the Creation of Human Capital." *American Journal of Sociology* 94(supp.):S95–120.
Coward, E. Walter, Jr. 1979. "Principles of Social Organization in an Indigenous Irrigation System." *Human Organization* 38(1):28–36.
Dasgupta, Partha, and Karl Göran Mäler. 1992. *The Economics of Transnational Commons*. Oxford: Clarendon Press.

Eggertsson, Thráinn. 1990. *Economic Behavior and Institutions.* Cambridge: Cambridge University Press.

Feeny, David, Fikret Berkes, Bonnie J. McCay, and James M. Acheson. 1990. "The Tragedy of the Commons: Twenty-two Years Later." *Human Ecology* 18(1):1–19.

Fortmann, Louise, and John W. Bruce, eds. 1988. *Whose Trees? Proprietary Dimensions of Forestry.* Boulder, Colo.: Westview.

Haas, Peter, Robert O. Keohane, and Marc A. Levy. 1993. *Institutions for the Earth: Sources of Effective International Environmental Protection.* Cambridge: MIT Press.

Hackett, Steven, Edella Schlager, and James M. Walker. 1994. "The Role of Communication in Resolving Commons Dilemmas: Experimental Evidence with Heterogeneous Appropriators." *Journal of Environmental Economics and Management* 27:99–126.

Hardin, Garrett. 1968. "The Tragedy of the Commons." *Science* 162:1243–48.

Hardin, Russell. 1982. *Collective Action.* Baltimore: Johns Hopkins University Press.

Isaac, R. Mark, and James M. Walker. 1991. "Costly Communication: An Experiment in a Nested Public Goods Problem." In Thomas R. Palfrey, ed., *Laboratory Research in Political Economy.* Ann Arbor: University of Michigan Press.

Isaac, R. Mark, James M. Walker, and Arlington Williams. 1993. "Group Size and the Voluntary Provision of Public Goods: Experimental Evidence Utilizing Large Groups." *Journal of Public Economics* 54(1):1–36.

Keohane, Robert O. 1989. *International Institutions and State Power: Essays in International Relations Theory.* Boulder, Colo.: Westview.

Knight, Jack. 1992. *Institutions and Social Conflict.* Cambridge: Cambridge University Press.

Lachmann, Ludwig M. 1978. *Capital and Its Structure.* Kansas City: Sheed, Andrews & McMeel.

Lam, Wai Fung, Myungsuk Lee, and Elinor Ostrom. Forthcoming. "The Institutional Analysis and Development Framework: Application to Irrigation Policy in Nepal." In Derek Brinkerhoff, ed., *Policy Analysis Concepts and Methods: An Institutional and Implementation Focus.* JAI Policy Studies and Developing Nations Series, vol. 15. Greenwich, Conn.: JAI Press.

Libecap, Gary D. 1989. *Contracting for Property Rights.* Cambridge: Cambridge University Press.

Maass, Arthur, and Raymond L. Anderson. 1986. *. . . and the Desert Shall Rejoice: Conflict, Growth and Justice in Arid Environments.* Malabar, Fla.: R. E. Krieger.

McCay, Bonnie J., and James M. Acheson. 1987. *The Question of the Commons: The Culture and Ecology of Communal Resources.* Tucson: University of Arizona Press.

McGinnis, Michael, and Elinor Ostrom. 1992. "Design Principles for Local and Global Commons." In *Proceedings of a Conference on Linking Local and Global Commons.* Edited by Robert Keohane, Michael McGinnis, and Elinor

Ostrom. Bloomington: Indiana University, Workshop in Political Theory and Policy Analysis.

Martin, Edward G. 1986. "Resource Mobilization, Water Allocation, and Farmer Organization in Hill Irrigation Systems in Nepal." Ph.D. diss., Cornell University.

Martin, Edward G., and Robert Yoder. 1983. "The Chherlung Thulo Kulo: A Case Study of a Farmer-Managed Irrigation System." In *Water Management in Nepal: Proceedings of the Seminar on Water Management Issues, July 31–August 2*. Kathmandu, Nepal: Ministry of Agriculture, Agricultural Projects Services Centre, and the Agricultural Development Council.

Martin, Fenton. 1989. *Common-Pool Resources and Collective Action: A Bibliography*. Vol. 1. Bloomington: Indiana University, Workshop in Political Theory and Policy Analysis.

———. 1992. *Common-Pool Resources and Collective Action: A Bibliography*. Vol. 2. Bloomington: Indiana University, Workshop in Political Theory and Policy Analysis.

National Research Council. 1986. *Proceedings of the Conference on Common Property Resource Management*. Washington, D.C.: National Academy Press.

Netting, Robert McC. 1993. *Smallholders, Householders: Farm Families and the Ecology of Intensive, Sustainable Agriculture*. Stanford, Calif.: Stanford University Press.

Olson, Mancur. 1965. *The Logic of Collective Action: Public Goods and the Theory of Groups*. Cambridge: Harvard University Press.

Ostrom, Elinor. 1990. *Governing the Commons: The Evolution of Institutions for Collective Action*. New York: Cambridge University Press.

———. 1992. *Strategies of Political Inquiry*. Beverly Hills, Calif.: Sage.

Ostrom, Elinor, and Roy Gardner. 1993. "Coping with Asymmetries in the Commons: Self-Governing Irrigation Systems Can Work." *Journal of Economic Perspectives* 7(4):93–112.

Ostrom, Elinor, Roy Gardner, and James Walker. 1994. *Rules, Games, and Common-Pool Resources*. Ann Arbor: University of Michigan Press.

Ostrom, Elinor, Sharon Huckfeldt, Charlie Schweik, and Mary Beth Wertime. 1993. "A Relational Archive for Natural Resources Governance and Management." Paper prepared for presentation at the Conference on Applications of Advanced Information Technologies for the Management of Natural Resources, Spokane, Wash., June 17–19.

Ostrom, Elinor, Larry Schroeder, and Susan Wynne. 1993. *Institutional Incentives and Sustainable Development: Infrastructure Policies in Perspective*. Boulder, Colo.: Westview.

Ostrom, Elinor, and James M. Walker. 1991. "Communication in a Commons: Cooperation without External Enforcement." In Thomas R. Palfrey, ed., *Laboratory Research in Political Economy*. Ann Arbor: University of Michigan Press.

Ostrom, Elinor, James Walker, and Roy Gardner. 1992. "Covenants with and without a Sword: Self-Governance Is Possible." *American Political Science Review* 86(2):404–17.

Ostrom, Vincent, David Feeny, and Hartmut Picht, eds. 1993. *Rethinking Institutional Analysis and Development: Issues, Alternatives, and Choices.* 2d ed. San Francisco: Institute for Contemporary Studies Press.

Pinkerton, Evelyn, ed. 1989. *Co-operative Management of Local Fisheries: New Directions for Improved Management and Community Development.* Vancouver: University of British Columbia Press.

Plott, Charles R. 1983. "Externalities and Corrective Policies in Experimental Markets." *Economic Journal* 92 (March): 106–27.

Putnam, Robert D. 1993. "The Prosperous Community: Social Capital and Public Life." *American Prospect* 13 (Spring): 35–42.

Sandler, Todd. 1992. *Collective Action: Theory and Applications.* Ann Arbor: University of Michigan Press.

Sengupta, Nirmal. 1991. *Managing Common Property: Irrigation in India and the Philippines.* London: Sage.

Shepsle, Kenneth A. 1989. "Studying Institutions: Some Lessons from the Rational Choice Approach." *Journal of Theoretical Politics* 1:131–49.

Siy, Robert Y., Jr. 1982. *Community Resource Management: Lessons from the Zanjera.* Quezon City: University of the Philippines Press.

Sproule-Jones, Mark. 1993. *Governments at Work: Canadian Parliamentary Federalism and Its Public Policy Effects.* Toronto: University of Toronto Press.

Sugden, Robert. 1986. *The Economics of Rights, Cooperation and Welfare.* London: Basil Blackwell.

Tang, Shui Yan. 1992. *Institutions and Collective Action: Self-Governance in Irrigation.* San Francisco: Institute for Contemporary Studies Press.

Thomson, James T. 1992. *A Framework for Analyzing Institutional Incentives in Community Forestry.* Rome: Food and Agriculture Organization of the United Nations.

Wade, Robert. 1988. *Village Republics: Economic Conditions for Collective Action in South India.* New York: Cambridge University Press.

Walker, James, Roy Gardner, and Elinor Ostrom. 1990. "Rent Dissipation in a Limited-Access Common-Pool Resource: Experimental Evidence." *Journal of Environmental Economics and Management* 19:203–11.

Weissing, Franz, and Elinor Ostrom. 1991. "Irrigation Institutions and the Games Irrigators Play: Rule Enforcement without Guards." In Reinhard Selten, ed., *Game Equilibrium Models II: Methods, Morals, and Markets.* Berlin: Springer-Verlag.

———. 1993. "Irrigation Institutions and the Games Irrigators Play: Rule Enforcement on Government- and Farmer-Managed Systems." In Fritz W. Scharpf, ed., *Games in Hierarchies and Networks: Analytical and Empirical Approaches to the Study of Governance Institutions.* Frankfurt: Campus-Verlag; Boulder, Colo.: Westview.

Young, Oran. 1982. *Resource Regimes: Natural Resources and Social Institutions.* Berkeley and Los Angeles: University of California Press.

CHAPTER TWO

Constitutional Choice, Rational Ignorance, and the Limits of Reason

VIKTOR J. VANBERG AND

JAMES M. BUCHANAN

ELEMENTARY TO ANY study of constitutional choice is the distinction between constitutional and subconstitutional *choices* and the corresponding distinction between constitutional and subconstitutional *preferences*. Constitutional choices are choices among alternative rules (constraints); subconstitutional choices are among alternative strategies available within rules (constraints). A chooser's constitutional preferences reflect trade-offs among alternative rules that might be chosen. Subconstitutional preferences reflect trade-offs among alternative courses of action or end objects which are available for choice within a defined set of rules.

For subconstitutional choices, the prevailing rules or constraints are "relatively absolute absolutes" (Buchanan 1988) in the sense that for these choices the rules are taken as parameters that define or limit the set of options. The rules are only "relative absolutes," however, since they can themselves be changed at the categorically separate constitutional level of decision. Constitutional choices, of course, may themselves be constrained by "higher" rules, relative to which they must be considered "subconstitutional." Wherever one deals with a multilayered system of rules (i.e., a system that includes rules for choosing rules) the distinction between constitutional and subconstitutional choices may be applied to any two adjoining levels of choice within a hierarchy.

In a previous paper (Vanberg and Buchanan 1989) we have discussed some of the implications that result from the fact that constitutional preferences, like any other preferences, can be assumed to embody two conceptually separable components: an *interest component* and a *theory component*. This distinction suggests that a person's preferences with respect to alternative rules, among which he can exercise choice, reflect a combination both of his *theories* about the working properties of these rules (i.e., his expectations concerning the overall pattern of outcomes that alternative rules will produce) and his *interests* in the expected outcome patterns.[1] For example, two persons may disagree on whether a law prohibiting smoking in public buildings should be adopted, either because they differ in their predictions of the law's overall effects (a theory component) or because they differ in their interests, as smoker and nonsmoker, in the same predicted effects—or, of course, because they differ in both. Because these two components underlie preferences over alternative rules, disagreement in constitutional choice may result from differences in theories as well as from differences in interests.

Neocontractarian approaches to the issue of constitutional choice (Rawls 1971; Buchanan and Tullock 1962) concentrate largely on interest divergences as a source of disagreement. Such approaches look toward a modification of the constitutional-choice setting as a way of reconciling these divergences. A principal remedy for interest-based obstacles to constitutional agreement involves the introduction of some means of ensuring that persons cannot reliably foresee how their future *particularized* interests may be affected by different rules, thereby inducing those persons to make constitutional choices on some assessment of the *general* working properties of alternative rules. The Buchanan-Tullock *veil of uncertainty* and the Rawlsian *veil of ignorance* are, in this sense, assumed to render persons uncertain or ignorant about their particularized interests, while not inhibiting their capability to anticipate accurately the general effects of potential alternative rules. Indeed, in Rawls's construction the participants in constitutional choice are assumed to be fully informed about the general working properties of potential alternative constitutions.[2]

Here our focus is quite different. Instead of considering the interest component as the principal source of problems in constitutional

1. Vanberg and Buchanan 1989, 52: "A person's constitutional theories are about matters of fact. They are his predictions (embodying assumptions and beliefs) about what the factual outcomes of alternative rules will be. These predictions may, of course, be arranged in a true or false, correct or incorrect scalar. His constitutional interests, on the other hand, are his own, subjective *evaluations* of expected outcomes, evaluations to which attributes like true or false, correct or incorrect cannot be applied."

2. Rawls 1971, 136–37. "I assume that the parties are situated behind a veil of ignorance. They do not know how the various alternatives will affect their own particular case. . . . It is taken for granted, however, that they know the general facts about human society. They understand political affairs and the principles of economic theory; they know the basis of social organization and the laws of human psychology. Indeed, the parties are presumed to know whatever general facts affect the choice of the principles of justice."

choice while taking the theory component as unproblematic, we shall explore the reverse assumption. We shall consider the interest component as unproblematic and concentrate on issues that arise when the participants in constitutional choice are assumed to be less than fully informed about the general effects of rules and to hold potentially conflicting constitutional *theories*. We shall, in other words, concentrate exclusively on the *knowledge problem* rather than the interest problem in constitutional choice. For the purposes of this paper, we shall assume that there is no conflict in constitutional interests among persons for whom, and/or by whom, a constitutional choice is to be made, so that the only issue is to find or select those rules that best serve the shared constitutional interests. Again, for example, all citizens may agree on the objective of reducing environmental pollution, and there may be no differences in their interests across the various potential regulatory measures. Disagreement my arise, however, because of differences in their predictions of the results of alternative measures: their effectiveness, their costs, their side effects, and so on. The assumption of shared interests and divergent theories, of course, is just as artificial as its obverse. In reality, both the interest problem and the knowledge problem coexist in an intertwined fashion. It is nevertheless useful for analytical purposes to separate the two conceptually and to consider their respective effects in isolation.

This paper is organized as follows. First we discuss some general characteristics of the knowledge problem in constitutional choice and draw attention to the differences between two distinct aspects: *rational ignorance* and the *limits of reason*. Then we elaborate on the first of these two aspects and consider the role of experts as a potential remedy. Next comes a discussion of the "limits of reason" problem and the role that constitutional competition can play in this context. Moving along, we argue that persons who are aware of and anticipate the knowledge problem in constitutional choice should have a predictable interest in adopting a metaconstitution that allows for and encourages explorative constitutional competition. Finally, in a concluding section, we offer some reflections on constitutional choice as a creative process.

The Knowledge Problem in Constitutional Choice

While potential interest-based conflict in constitutional choice is alleviated as the choosers' uncertainty/ignorance of their prospective particularized interests increases, potential knowledge-based disagreement obviously requires the opposite cure. So far as the interest dimension is concerned, the prospects for reaching constitutional agreement are enhanced by whatever tends to increase uncertainty—that is, by whatever tends to thicken the veil. In contrast, potential knowledge-grounded disagreement is alleviated as the participants are made more aware of the general working properties of prospective rules. Or, in terms of the veil metaphor, the knowledge problem is alleviated by whatever tends to make the veil more transparent.

There are two elements of constitutional epistemology to be distinguished here. One concerns the prospects for securing agreement in constitutional theories among persons who are empowered to choose. When we assume that the participants in a constitutional-choice setting share the same constitutional interests, the source of disagreement in expressed constitutional preferences can only be a matter of conflicting theories. If, in addition, we also assume that all participants are perfectly informed about the general working properties of the rules under consideration, then agreement would necessarily emerge on what—relative to the participants' common interests—the best rules are. Shared "perfect knowledge" is, in this sense, obviously a sufficient condition for resolving epistemological sources of constitutional conflict. Agreement, however, may emerge without "perfect knowledge." Less than perfectly knowledgeable choosers may agree on mistaken theories. This presents the second element to be considered. Rational participants who are aware of their imperfect constitutional knowledge will not only be concerned about constitutional agreement per se; they will also wish to ensure that agreement emerges on those rules that will, in fact, best serve their shared interests. And the prospects for identifying and adopting good or efficient rules (i.e., rules that serve participants' interests best) are enhanced by whatever improves mutually shared information and knowledge about the general working properties of rules.

For the knowledge problem in constitutional choice, the notion of *constitutional discourse* is, in some sense, the analogue to the notion of the veil as it is used in the Rawls-Buchanan-Tullock contractarian perspectives. The veil notion can be seen as a summary label for factors that, by increasing uncertainty, tend to alleviate potential conflicts in constitutional interests. In contrast, the notion of discourse can be interpreted as a summary label for factors that tend to alleviate the knowledge problem by eliminating disagreement in constitutional theories and, at the same time, by improving the quality of those theories.[3] On this interpretation, "discourse" includes everything that advances the acquisition, communication, and processing of general constitutional information and knowledge.

---

3. The relation between a *discourse* and a *contractarian perspective* on constitutional agreement is discussed in more detail in Vanberg and Buchanan 1989.

As we shall discuss more carefully in the following pages, the role of discourse in constitutional choice is subject to two kinds of limitations. It is subject to what may be called *motivational limitations*—i.e., limitations in the willingness of the constitutional constituency to incur the costs that participating in constitutional discourse involves—and it is subject to *cognitive limitations*—i.e., limitations in the constitutional constituency's cognitive capacity to discern and anticipate reliably the general operating properties of alternative rules. In what follows, the issue of motivational limitations will be discussed under the rubric of *rational ignorance,* the issue of cognitive limitations under the rubric of the *limits of reasons.* As will become apparent, the remedies for the problems that are associated with these two limitations are in part the same.

Constitutional Choice and Rational Ignorance

One of the most familiar principles in public choice is the rational-ignorance hypothesis (Aranson 1989–90), which states that in large electoral constituencies it is privately rational for a single voter to remain ignorant about the alternatives of collective choice because of the negligible influence of his or her own vote on the outcome. Obviously, the argument applies a fortiori where, as we assume here, there are no conflicts of interest. If the participants in a constitutional-choice setting have the same constitutional interests, an improvement in the quality of the rules that are adopted is a pure public good. Consequently, so far as any such improvement is concerned, any individual expenditure on constitutional information/knowledge is a contribution to a pure public good which rational actors cannot be expected to make. Under the assumptions made here, therefore, we should expect the members of the constitutional constituency to remain rationally ignorant and potentially to adopt inferior rules.

It is useful to recall the original, precise meaning of the rational-ignorance hypothesis. The specific, and limited, claim is that in a large constituency (with a secret ballot) the impact of a single vote on the outcome is insignificant;[4] therefore, the prospects of an individual's improving the outcome by casting a single better-informed vote do not provide significant incentive for a voter to incur the costs of becoming

---

4. Though usually not mentioned explicitly, a secret ballot has to be presumed because with public vote-casting—apart from such issues as "preference falsification" (Kuran 1989)—the actual impact of a vote on the outcome would be dependent on such contingent facts as, for example, the public standing of the voter. The crucial characteristic of a secret ballot (namely, that the impact on the outcome of any and every vote is $1/n$,) does not hold per se for an open ballot.

better informed, even when those costs are quite small. Note that the "rationality of ignorance" is claimed only with reference to the ultimate impact of a vote on the outcome of the collective choice. Wherever informational investments are potentially relevant for other activities with other prospective payoffs, it is the size of those payoffs that determines whether—and to what extent—it is rational to remain ignorant.

For the issue of constitutional choice, the rational-ignorance hypothesis does not support the unqualified conclusion that rational actors in a large constituency will remain constitutionally ignorant. Instead, whether or not it is rational to invest in constitutional information/knowledge will depend on one's involvement in other activities— other than casting votes—through which such investments may promise to pay off. It would seem obvious, moreover, that the broader category of activities that fall under the rubric of "constitutional discourse" includes some that are likely to provide incentives for some such investment. The examples that we shall consider are (1) private or public engagement in discourse on constitutional issues and (2) prospects of securing and retaining public office or acting as a political entrepreneur.

The same argument that explains why a rational actor—in the absence of selective incentives—cannot be expected to contribute to a public good can also explain why those who are part of the group of potential beneficiaries can be expected to have an interest in *others* contributing. The external benefits that contributing behavior produces, while not providing incentives for one's own contribution, create an interest in the behavior of others. And such interest, again, is likely to generate a normative expectation that others *should* contribute, an expectation that may find expression in behavior that provides selective incentives for others actually to contribute. Public-goods situations, then, are prone to generate mutually reinforced normative expectations that originate from an interest in the behavior of *others*, but that are mirrored in expectations such that everybody in the respective constitutency confronts a normatively impregnated environment.

Let us apply this argument to the problem under consideration. Rational individuals, in a constitutional constituency with the characteristics assumed above, can be expected to have an interest in others making investments in constitutional knowledge, and such interest is likely to generate a mutually reinforced and expressed normative expectation that, as a good citizen, one *should* make an effort to be informed. To the extent that, because of such shared expectations, being perceived as a "good citizen" is instrumental in getting access to valued goods, a rational actor will find it in his or her interest to make some investment in constitutional information/knowledge.[5] In this sense, an "ethic of constitutional citizenship" (Buchanan 1991, 156) may find its roots in rational self-interest.

Intertwined with, but distinguishable from, the "public goods, normative expectations" nexus is a person's interest in being respected as an informed and sought-after participant in conversations, an interest that to some extent provides incentives for investments in constitutional knowledge. A similar argument can also be made for persons who seek or hold offices for which constitutional expertise is a qualifying attribute, as well as for persons who seek the potential rewards that political entrepreneurship promises. The general conclusion from the preceeding arguments is that the rational-ignorance hypothesis has to be qualified as one goes beyond its original, limited claim concerning voting behavior in large constituencies. There are numerous other activities for which investment in constitutional knowledge promises payoffs and that, therefore, make constitutional ignorance less "rational" than an exclusive focus on voting behavior suggests.

Although, as we have argued above, various incentives may make at least some investment in constitutional information/knowledge "rational," such incentives are unlikely to sustain an overall level of expertise that would fully meet the ultimate *constitutional preferences* of individuals. That is to say: if persons could choose among constituencies with varying levels of constitutional expertise, other things equal, they can be expected to prefer one with a higher level of constitutional knowledge or wisdom than will be sustained by the incentives noted. There would, in other words, be a constellation where persons' separate, individualized choices to invest in constitutional knowledge would not generate the state of affairs that ultimately would be preferred—a constellation which is characteristic of any example of the generalized *social dilemma*. The question then arises concerning which, if any, reforms might be suggested.

Individuals in a constitutional constituency who anticipate the presence of rational ignorance, even if qualified in the above sense, can

---

5. A more complete version of this argument could be construed along the lines of David Gauthier's argument on the rationality of adopting a *moral disposition*. To be perceived as a moral person makes a person a desirable partner for cooperative activities and, thus, provides access to cooperative gains that otherwise could not be obtained. To the extent that the prospects for effective cost-saving mimicry are limited, the actual possession of a moral disposition can be a necessary prerequisite for access to such cooperative gains: hence the rationality of morality (Gauthier 1986; Vanberg and Buchanan 1990). For the present case, the logic would be that where effective mimicry is not feasible, actually doing the things that define a "good citizen" may be the precondition for obtaining access to the rewards that result from being perceived as such.

be assumed to share an interest in incorporating provisions in their constitution that promise to cure or alleviate this problem. Such provisions may be designed either to provide additional incentives for investment in constitutional knowledge or to decrease the costs of providing such knowledge. Or they may be designed simply to circumvent the problem. The first of the three options would include, for instance, adopting constitutional measures that make some kind of constitutional training mandatory—such as a requirement that everyone participate in certain programs for constitutional education. Such schemes, however, even if they would be effective in their intended purpose, are likely to be perceived as undesirable in other respects. Provisions for lowering the costs of providing constitutional knowledge would include the use of specialized experts, a device that will be discussed next. Finally, provisions for circumventing the rational-ignorance problem might include the use of what we will call *constitutional competition* (to be discussed farther on).

Rational Ignorance and Constitutional Experts

Any socioeconomic arrangement of even moderate complexity has to provide for the possibility that individuals can benefit from knowledge that they do not themselves possess privately. This point is central to Hayek's (1948) argument concerning the "use of knowledge in society" and his inference concerning the superior characteristics of markets as "utilizers of dispersed knowledge." The division of labor across markets allows participants in the exchange nexus to benefit from contributions of highly specialized experts without any necessity to acquire for themselves even a small fraction of the total expert knowledge utilized. Most of us drive cars, use computers, or telefax without knowing much about the basic technology. Possession of such knowledge is not prerequisite to the enjoyment of the benefits of these technological achievements. Could any comparable role for experts be feasible in the realm of constitutional construction?

The notion that "experts" should be entrusted with governmental-constitutional authority has, of course, a long tradition, ranging at least from Plato's "philosopher king" to the communist fiction of the "enlightened avant-garde." The objections to such notions are also well known. They mainly have to do with the implied tendency to legitimize the role of a self-appointed elite which remains beyond the control of those who are subject to government. It is obvious that the authoritarian-totalitarian version of the "constitutional expert" model does not qualify in any meaningful sense as an analogue to the abovementioned role of experts in markets. Relevant analogues can be identified, however, by considering what role rational actors, anticipating the problem of rational ignorance, would be willing to assign to *constitutional experts*.

One scheme might be an analogue to the model of political competition that is embodied in the ordinary constitutional structure of representative democracy. In terms of this model, individuals in a constitutional constituency would select from a set of competing experts those whom they consider most competent. If, as we assume here, there exist no conflicts of constitutional interest in the constituency, the selection problem reduces to that of assessing the relative competence of those who would claim to be experts. And to the extent that a comparably reliable choice among competent experts is less costly (i.e., requires less investment in constitutional knowledge) than the raw choice among constitutional alternatives themselves, rational individuals will have a reason to choose the lower-cost procedure.[6] The putative experts' motivation for acquiring constitutional competence derives from the prospects of securing the advantages attached to the office, given the constraints that the competitive setting imposes.

Closer comparison suggests that there are significant differences between the two above-mentioned roles for experts in markets and in representative democracy. For the latter, the rational-ignorance problem reasserts itself again because, in a large constituency, one person's vote is unlikely to decide which among a competing set of experts will be chosen. Hence, the effect on the electoral outcome itself cannot be considered an important source of incentives for acquiring knowledge that would make for a better-informed vote. To be sure, in the sense discussed above, there may be other reasons (besides the electoral outcome) for investing in constitutional information/knowledge. And to the extent that a reliable choice among experts involves lower information costs, the discrepancy between actually acquired and ideally required knowledge may be less for the choice among experts than for the raw choice among constitutional alternatives. The essential difference from the "market expert" model remains, however, a difference, the significance of which becomes apparent when one imagines, for instance, how a system might work if a choice among motor cars were delegated to an automotive "expert" to be chosen in some electoral process.

There are two respects here in which the procedures of choosing would be different. There is, on the one side, the difference between

6. In an article on the role of experts in constitutional choice (Buchanan and Vanberg 1989), we have discussed this aspect as well as related issues, albeit with a focus that is somewhat different from our present inquiry.

individual and collective choice and, on the other side, the difference between a choice among the experts themselves and a choice among their products. The two differences have important motivational and informational implications. The ordinary consumer choice in the automobile market is an individual choice among the products of competing expert-producers. There is no requirement—though, to be sure, it may conceivably be the factual outcome—that everybody in the relevant community purchase the same model. Further, the benefits as well as the costs of choice are fully sensed by the individual. The situation would clearly be different if the choice among models were made collectively—that is to say, if the community as a collective would decide by vote which model to choose. As for the difference between choosing among experts and choosing among their products, ordinary consumer choice in the market does not require any assessment of the producer's competence in any direct sense. For an informed choice no more is required than a comparative assessment of relevant working properties of the products, an assessment for which relevant information can be assumed to be much more readily available.

Analysis suggests, then, that the electoral choice among constitutional experts is likely to reveal significantly less responsiveness to constituents'/consumers' interests than the market choice among products. This is for two reasons: (1) because it operates through collective rather than individual choice and (2) because the choice among the experts themselves is likely to involve stronger informational requirements than the choice among their products. Of course, the question that now suggests itself is whether, within the realm of constitutional choice, we may conceive of a procedure that incorporates more of the working properties of the market model (i.e., a procedure that allows for a greater role of *individual choice among constitutions* instead of *collective choice among constitutional experts*).

There is, in fact, something like a "constitutional analogue" to the ordinary market role of experts. Any entrepreneur who organizes cooperative arrangements of whatever sort is, in a real sense, also a constitutional entrepreneur, even if the legal fixation of a set of predefined contractual-legal forms (partnership, joint-stock company, etc.) has narrowed down the range of potential variation. In setting up and managing an ongoing cooperative arrangement, an entrepreneur establishes and maintains a constitutional order among all those who take part in the joint venture, whether as investors or as contributors of labor, skills, and know-how. These other participants are typically in a position to choose individually and separately among alternative constitutional-organizational arrangements—as stockholders, to invest in company A rather than B; as employees, to contract with firm C rather than D—and typically they will base their decision on their assessment of what are to them relevant working properties of alternative cooperative arrangements. In other words, these participants will assess the product, rather than the entrepreneur-expert's competence per se. And the entrepreneur's prospects for success or failure will depend on his or her ability to produce a constitutional-organizational order with working properties that, in an environment of competing alternative options, are sufficiently attractive to those whose cooperation has to be secured. Similar arguments apply to other kinds of social-organizational arrangements (e.g., clubs or associations) that are voluntarily formed in a competitive environment.

If a comparable role for individual choice among existing alternative constitutional arrangements could be realized at the level of polities, this would have obviously significant implications. As one moves from collective choice among alternative constitutions to collective choice among constitutional experts to, finally, individual choice among alternative constitutional arrangements, not only are the informational requirements for an intelligent choice dramatically reduced, but the individual's incentives for making an informed choice significantly increase. While it may be very difficult to predict reliably the working properties of alternative constitutional rules, and also difficult to assess the true competence of constitutional experts, individuals will have much less difficulty assessing the relevant working properties of actually operating constitutional systems. Moreover, as they individually and separately choose their own "constitutional environment," they also have much more reason to make an informed choice, compared with their participation in a collective choice among constitutional rules or among constitutional experts.

Constitutional Choice and the Limits of Reason

So far, our discussion of the knowledge problem in constitutional choice has been confined to those aspects that can be viewed as a consequence of the "rational-ignorance problem." If we assume that "perfect constitutional knowledge" is in principle available, and that the only problem is to provide appropriate incentives for "experts" to acquire it, the previous line of argument could remain unchanged. The problem takes on a wholly new dimension, however, once we recognize that such perfect knowledge is not attainable and that there are no perfectly knowledgeable experts who would rationally be able to design a perfect constitutional system. The claim to such knowledge is part of the mind-set that F. A. Hayek (1967) has criticized as *constructivist rationalism*.

Hayek's critique, in fact, is directed against two distinguishable, though interrelated, versions of the "pretense of knowledge" that he sees in constructivist rationalism. The two versions correspond to two dimensions of the "knowledge problem" which we may distinguish as "horizontal" or "cross-sectional," on the one side, and "intertemporal" on the other. The first, or "horizontal," dimension is the principal issue in Hayek's critique of the notion of central planning. It is impossible, he argues, for any planner or planning agency to know, and make use of, that particular knowledge about locational and temporal contingencies that exists fragmented and dispersed among the individual contemporaries in society. As mentioned above, Hayek concludes that such dispersed knowledge can best be utilized in markets where individuals are free, within the constraints of general rules of conduct, to make their own choices and to trade freely with each other.

Of particular importance in the present context, however, is not the first dimension, but the second, "intertemporal," dimension of the knowledge problem. While the first explains, in Hayek's account, why we have to rely largely on general *rules*, rather than commands, in order to coordinate our efforts efficiently, the "intertemporal" dimension concerns the issue of how we can recognize *good rules*. What Hayek criticizes as "pretense of knowledge" in this regard is the claim that, based on abstract reasoning, we can rationally design an appropriate framework of rules, a desirable institutional order. Such a claim, he argues, ignores the fact that our cognitive limitations prevent us, first, from having reliable *ex ante* knowledge of how imagined alternative rules work out in practice and, secondly, from being able to determine by *ex ante* reasoning which system of rules will generate the most desirable socioeconomic order.

If, as Hayek suggests, we liken rules to "tools" (Vanberg 1992b, 107ff.), in the sense that they serve to solve recurrent problems, and accordingly if we view social rules as "tools" for solving recurrent social-interaction problems, then the "limits of reason" argument can be restated as saying that, on pure rational grounds and through logical deduction, we cannot discern *ex ante* what the best "tools" are. We are unable to do so because we simply do not possess as explicit knowledge the accumulated experience that underlies the system of rules and institutions in which we live. And we are unable to do so for two more reasons: (1) because our knowledge changes over time, and thus we cannot know today what we will know tomorrow, and (2) because our problems, or our perception of them, change as well, and we cannot know today what tomorrow's problems will be. Our search for *good rules*, therefore, has to be guided by the kind of experience that accumulates in an ongoing, open-ended process of trial and error.

It is in this sense that Hayek emphasizes the necessity for us to rely, in matters of constitutional choice, on the experiences that have been made by previous generations and that have become incorporated in time-tested traditions. And it is in this context that he introduces the notion of cultural evolution as a spontaneous process of "winnowing and sifting" that supposedly selects for efficient rules, a notion that is subject to criticism. Yet, even if one rejects a Hayekian acquiescence in cultural evolution as poor guidance in constitutional matters (Buchanan 1985), it has to be acknowledged that in our efforts at deliberate constitutional construction we cannot but operate on the basis of *conjectural* and *hypothetical* knowledge, and that we can never predict with certainty how potential constitutional alternatives will work out under ever-changing circumstances. From this perspective, competition among constitutional experts and competition among alternative constitutional arrangements are not only important for the motivational and informational reasons discussed earlier; they are also important in their role as a "discovery procedure" for finding desirable constitutional arrangements (Hayek 1978). That is to say, they are important because of their *dynamic* role, as *constitutional exploration,* for the inventing of and experimenting with new solutions to constitutional problems.

In regard to the issue of constitutional exploration, it is useful to remember the previously discussed differences between an electoral competition among constitutional experts and the market-type competition among alternative constitutional arrangements. In the constitutional realm, as elsewhere, it is not the fact of competition per se that is of interest, since all human social activities take place under *some* kind of competition. The critical issue is *what* kind of constitutional competition can be expected to operate in a desirable way, where "desirable" suggests some sort of normative criterion by which the performance of a constitutional order is to be judged. If responsiveness to constituents' wants and interests is what we deem desirable, it should be obvious that (where feasible) a market-type constitutional competition is superior to electoral competition.

As for the feasibility of market-type constitutional competition, there is, to be sure, a critical difference between constitutional arrangements at the level of polities and the kind of voluntary organizational-constitutional arrangements that we described above, a difference that limits the feasibility of individual constitutional choice at the polity level. Polities typically have a "territorial base," and membership in political communities is, therefore, essentially defined in residential-territorial terms, such that a change in membership affiliation typically requires a corresponding change in residency.[7] To the extent that such residential implications increase the individual's costs of separately choosing among alternative constitutional arrangements, the responsiveness of those arrangements to constituents' wants will tend to be reduced or, in Albert O. Hirschman's terms (1970, 1981), more dependent on the exercise of "voice." The interest of rational constituents in securing responsiveness to their constitutional interests, therefore, should suggest that the "cost of exit" itself becomes a matter of concern for constitutional considerations. Securing low-cost options for individuals to choose separately among alternative constitutional regimes may provide a remedy that goes beyond the problems associated with "rational ignorance" and the "limits of reason." By allowing for constitutional diversity and the "sorting out" of divergent constitutional preferences, it may also alleviate problems that result from differences and conflicts in constitutional interests.

A Metaconstitution for an Open Society

Rational actors who are aware of the fallibility of their efforts in constitutional construction, who know that they cannot know in advance what the best solution to their constitutional problems are—nor, as a matter of fact, what they will perceive as constitutional problems in the future—can be expected to have an interest in providing for the possibility of *constitutional learning*, for the possibility of correcting and developing further their constitutional arrangements in the light of new experience.[8] The "experimentation" that such learning requires is, to be sure, that which takes place in a competitive environment where individuals can compare, and act upon, the performance characteristics of alternative constitutional provisions. In cannot be expected to result from the global and sequential reorientations that have been characteristic of the way in which the centralist-socialist "experiments" of this century have been carried out.

It is in this context that the Hayekian notion of cultural evolution can be usefully reintroduced (in a modified sense). The essential problem with Hayek's use of this notion is his failure to specify the condi-

---

7. We ignore here the complexities that are introduced by the possibility of a dissociation of citizenship and residency, because it does not seem to us to have any relevant implication for the central concern of our argument.

8. Wiseman (1990, 105): "If the future is unknowable, not only will individuals make mistakes . . . but such mistakes will be expected. . . . [I]ndividuals will wish to 'build in' to any system of social arrangements provisions for the correction of previous error (as revealed by the divergencies between the expected and the actual outcome of plans)."

tions under which a process of rule evolution can be expected to select for rules that are "desirable," if we take the wants and interests of those who are to live under those rules as the proper measuring rod.[9] Hayek is certainly right in his emphasis on the limits of rational constitutional design and on the need to rely on experience which emerges from the trial and error of a competitive evolutionary process. Yet, as our earlier remarks on "kinds of competition" imply, not just any competitive evolutionary process can be expected to select in favor of rules that are "desirable" in the above sense. To the contrary, whether such selection will or will not occur depends critically on the terms of evolutionary competition, specifically on the role that the constituents' interests and desires play in the selection process. Conditions conducive to such a role cannot be presumed to prevail spontaneously, but are likely to require deliberate constructive effort.

The above arguments can be translated into the conjecture that rational actors who are aware of the fallibility of their constitutional constructions, and who therefore want to employ the explorative potential of an evolutionary competitive process, should have an interest in adopting a *metaconstitution* that is designed to secure favorable conditions for a constitutional competition that is responsive to constituents' interests.[10] A fundamental principle informing such a metaconstitution would be to favor those provisions which tend to reduce the costs of individual choices among constitutional alternatives.

An obvious minimal requirement, in this regard, would be the removal and prevention of deliberately imposed "exit barriers" which have been—and, in some places, still are—a common feature of totalitarian regimes.[11] *Decentralization,* in two principal forms to which the concepts of *federalism* (Ostrom 1986; Wiseman 1990) and *consociationalism* (Elazar 1985) refer, is the general provision by which we can reduce "natural" costs of individual choice among alternative constitu-

9. In fact, despite the normative individualism of classical liberalism that is at the foundation of Hayek's system of thought, in his discussion of "cultural evolution" Hayek is not at all unambiguous about the normative standard, if any, against which he judges whether the forces of cultural evolution work "beneficially."

10. This amounts to what may be called *constitutionally constrained evolution,* a combination of deliberate design and evolutionary learning: specifically, the design of a framework of metarules within which efforts at constitutional construction are subject to a kind of evolutionary competition that promises to select in favor of rules serving the interests of the respective constituencies.

11. An interesting issue, though one that we cannot discuss in the present context, is the role of *entry* as opposed to *exit* barriers. Even though both create obstacles to individual choice among alternative constitutional arrangements, they are clearly different in their factual implications and in regard to the kind of arguments that might be advanced in their support.

tional arrangements. Under the rubric of federalism we subsume all provisions for *territorial decentralization:* provisions that are informed by the principle of allocating political tasks in such a way that, wherever feasible and reasonable, preference is given to local subunits over more inclusive polities. The concept of consociationalism includes provision for *nonterritorial, functional decentralization:* provisions that are based on the principle that political tasks should be allocated in such a way that, wherever feasible and reasonable, preference is given to nonterritorial units over territorially based polities. The principle of federalism or territorial decentralization is exemplified by measures that transfer political authority from more encompassing to smaller polities. The principle of consociationalism is exemplified by measures that transfer authority from territorially based polities to organizations in which membership is dissociated from the residential-territorial dimension.

The appropriate level for effective agreements on a *metaconstitution,* in the sense of the above discussion, will to some extent be the level of international accords. International agreements—in particular, those concerning the free movement of persons, resources, and ideas—can serve as commitments of nation-states to constrain their ability to interfere with their constituents' freedom of "constitutional choice."[12] But there may be other conceivable forms in which relevant metaconstitutional provisions could be laid down.

Constitutional Choice as a Creative Process

Recent discussions in the natural sciences, concerning the evolutionary self-organization paradigm that is associated with Ilya Prigogine and others, have reminded us of the understanding of human social interrelations embodied in the work of David Hume, Adam Smith, and others among the group usually referred to as the Scottish Moral Philosophers, from which economics emerged as an independent discipline.[13] These pre-Darwinian thinkers offered a theory of social order and human history that is evolutionary in the sense of emphasizing the open-endedness of a process in which the complex interactions of human efforts produce an order without being directed

---

12. No specialized enforcement agency need be created. Such commitments could be made effective, for example, by specifying rights that individual constituents could claim at domestic courts. Thus, a free-trade agreement could give any individual a legal claim against his government if the latter should legislate any measure that amounts to a protectionist privilege for a particular industry. On this issue: Tumlir 1983; Moser 1990; Vanberg 1992a.

13. On the nature of this paradigm and its relevance for economics, see Buchanan and Vanberg 1991.

toward any predetermined end. Similarly, our efforts at constitutional construction must not be seen as steps in a process that over time might approximate a "perfect" constitutional-institutional order. The notion of the "perfectibility of society" may be just as misleading as the misplaced notion of the "perfectibility of man" (Passmore 1970). There is no uniquely perfect constitutional order "out there," waiting to be revealed and discovered through trial and error, no "optimal solution" toward which we might gradually move. If there is no "pre-determined future" waiting for us, if instead we create our future by our choices, then the problems for which constitutional remedies may be needed are also a creation of our choices, as are the solutions that our imagination may bring forth. The gigantic and, retrospectively, absurd "socialist experiment" that so tragically shaped the twentieth century is a case in point, for it provides an ample demonstration of how problems are created by erroneous constitutional analysis and misguided constitutional construction.

For rational actors who are aware of the fallibility of their constitutional efforts and who recognize their embeddedness in an open-ended evolutionary process which is, in part, molded by their own choices, the fundamental problem of constitutional choice can be stated in the following question: How can we maintain a desirable constitutional order among ourselves, given that—at any and every point in the continuing process—we cannot know what will be known, invented, and created tomorrow, what potential solutions may be available to us, what problems we will face, or even what we will perceive as problems tomorrow? The only reasonable answer to this question is that such rational actors would have an interest in providing for the possibility of continuous learning, for adaptability to changing and unforeseen problem scenarios. In other words, they should have an interest in a metaconstitution for an open society.

REFERENCES

Aranson, Peter. 1989–90. "Rational Ignorance in Politics, Economics and Law." *Journal des Economistes et des Etudes Humaines* 1:25–42.

Buchanan, James M. 1985. "Cultural Evolution and Institutional Reform." In *Liberty, Market and State*. New York: New York University Press.

———. 1988. "The Relatively Absolute Absolute." In *Essays on the Political Economy*. Honolulu: University of Hawaii Press.

————. 1991. "The Ethics of Constitutional Order." In *The Economics and the Ethics of Constitutional Order.* Ann Arbor: University of Michigan Press.

Buchanan, James M., and Gordon Tullock. 1962. *The Calculus of Consent—Logical Foundations of Constitutional Democracy.* Ann Arbor: University of Michigan Press.

Buchanan, James M., and Viktor Vanberg. 1989. "A Theory of Leadership and Deference in Constitutional Construction." *Public Choice* 61 (2):15–28.

————. 1991. "The Market as a Creative Process." *Economics and Philosophy* 7:167–86.

Elazar, Daniel J., ed. 1985. "Federalism and Consociationalism: A Symposium." *Publius—The Journal of Federalism* 15(2).

Gauthier, David. 1986. *Morals by Agreement.* Oxford: Clarendon Press.

Hayek, Friedrich A. 1948. "The Use of Knowledge in Society." In *Individualism and Economic Order.* Chicago: University of Chicago Press.

————. 1967. "Kinds of Rationalism," in *Studies in Philosophy, Politics and Economics.* Chicago: University of Chicago Press.

————. 1978. "Competition as a Discovery Procedure." In *New Studies in Philosophy, Politics, Economics and of Ideas.* Chicago: University of Chicago Press.

Hirschman, Albert O. 1970. *Exit, Voice and Loyalty—Responses to Decline in Firms, Organizations and States.* Cambridge: Harvard University Press.

————. 1981. "Exit, Voice and the State." In *Essays in Trespassing—From Economics to Politics and Beyond.* Cambridge: Cambridge University Press.

Kuran, Timur. 1989. "Sparks and Prairie Fires: A Theory of Unanticipated Political Revolution." *Public Choice* 61(1):41–74.

Moser, Peter. 1990. *The Political Economy of the GATT.* Grüsch, Switzerland: Verlag-Rüegger.

Ostrom, Vincent. 1986. "Constitutional Considerations with Particular Reference to Federal Systems." In F. X. Kaufmann et. al., eds., *Guidance, Control and Evaluation in the Public Sector.* New York: Walter de Gruyter.

Passmore, John. 1970. *The Perfectibility of Man.* London: Duckworth.

Rawls, John. 1971. *A Theory of Justice.* Cambridge: Harvard University Press.

Tumlir, Jan. 1983. "International Economic Order and Democratic Constitutionalism." *ORDO* 34:71–83.

Vanberg, Viktor. 1992a. "A Constitutional Political Economy Perspective at International Trade." *ORDO* 43:375–92.

————. 1992b. "Innovation, Cultural Evolution and Economic Growth." In Ulrich Witt, ed., *Explaining Process and Change—Approaches to Evolutionary Economics.* Ann Arbor: University of Michigan Press.

Vanberg, Viktor, and James M. Buchanan. 1989. "Interests and Theories in Constitutional Choice." *Journal of Theoretical Politics* 1 (January): 49–62.

————. 1990. "Rational Choice and Moral Order." In J. H. Nichols and J. H. Wright, eds., *From Political Economy to Economics . . . and Back?* San Francisco: ICS Press.

Wiseman, Jack. 1990. "Principles of Political Economy—An Outline Proposal, Illustrated by Application to Fiscal Federalism." *Constitutional Political Economy* 1(1):101–24.

CHAPTER THREE

From Irrationality to Autonomy: Two Sciences of Institutional Design

JOHN S. DRYZEK

POLITICAL INSTITUTIONS CAN be constituted only by people as they are, or as they might become. And human capacities to comprehend, cogitate, calculate, communicate, criticize, strategize, sympathize, predict, experience, and interpret do of course have their limits. How, then, might political innovation and constitutional inquiry take such limits into account?

I shall argue that the main task of institutional design under such conditions involves an enhancement of the ability of citizens to choose for themselves which competences institutions should promote, and so act as citizen-designers. In this light, institutional design is an open-ended, participatory, and democratic project, far removed from any notion of institutional engineering. The appropriate methodology is critique: ideas for new institutions should be sought through criticism of old ones, especially in terms of how the latter promote some competences and repress others.

I reach these conclusions through contemplation of two sciences of institutional design that are sensitive to limited human rationality. The first works within a paradigm of instrumental rationality, and it deploys behavioral decision theory as a corrective to the microeconomic faith in unlimited individual reason. The second, which I believe to be ultimately more defensible, is a reconstructive science that begins by describing the variety of human competences that are at issue in any context of institutional reconstruction. The argumentative trajectory through these two sciences begins with a definition of ratio-

For their advice and criticism I am grateful to Deborah Baumgold, Jeffrey Berejikian, and John Orbell, to the participants in the PEGS conference held at Yale University in January 1991, and especially to Jeffrey Isaac.

nality as strategic action. This narrow definition is then dissolved in a welter of competing rationalities and subjectivities. The story ends by restoring rationality redefined as autonomy, understood in turn as the capacity to make good judgments across different kinds of competences, and to know when and how to bring particular competences (e.g., strategic, communicative, or dramaturgical ones) to bear.

The basic topic of institutional design in the context of limited human capacities is very old. From St. Augustine through to medieval times, the question of how to design institutions in light of the manifest imperfection of human beings was arguably *the* perennial issue of political philosophy. For Augustine, original sin meant that the classical faith in (some) human rationality was mistaken; ordinarily, people could not control their wickedness or surmount ignorance.

Only with Hobbes do we begin to find the suggestion that "everyman" might be rational in some broad sense, and this suggestion soon helped define the core of the liberal tradition. Yet challenges to this paradigm of rational personhood persist, both from within the liberal tradition and outside it. Challenges from within include F. A. von Hayek's lonely attempt to reconstruct liberalism on the basis of a postulate of individual ignorance, rather than individual rationality, and some social science findings which I shall introduce shortly. Challenges from without are made by classical conservatives, who from Edmund Burke on have preferred to depend on the experience of the few, rather than the rationality of the multitude; by feminists, for whom instrumental rationality (especially when combined with egoism) is very much a model of *man;* by poststructuralists, who regard individuals as for the most part creations of the (generally repressive) discourses in which they move; and by critical theorists, who recognize a variety of social forces that act to limit individual autonomy.

The issue of how to design institutions in the light of limits to human rationality is not, then, a novel question. But if the question is a very old one, why not simply raid the history of political thought for some very well thought out answers? The answer may be that today we live in unprecedentedly democratic times. Not only must institutional products meet democratic criteria; redesign itself must be a democratic process, in the minimal sense of not being confined to an uncontrolled elite of engineers and advisers.

There is another (perhaps more controversial) reason for not simply turning to the ancients and greats here. Modern social science has told us a great deal about the character of, and limitations upon, individual and collective rationality that was not available to premodern or even antimodern political philosophers. Can we deploy these social sciences while retaining a commitment to democracy? I suggest that social science findings can indeed be pressed into the service of institutional design. How this might be done, and to what effect, varies substantially across different approaches to institutional design. Stephen Linder and B. Guy Peters (1994) have recently described two such traditions: the decisional and the dialogical. Design in the decisional category is a matter of institutional engineering in pursuit of ends given by some policy elite or by liberal moral philosophy (be it Kantian or utilitarian). The dialogical tradition sees design as a matter of facilitating open-ended and participatory institutional reconstruction. I argue that both traditions can be home to sciences that take into account the limits of human rationality. But any such science can most clearly contribute to a democratic negotiation of these limits within the dialogical tradition.

The decisional tradition is home to what may be termed a thin science of the limits to human rationality, "thin" because its paradigm of personhood is the strategic individual, albeit limited by some generalizable deviations from effective utility maximization.[1] A thin version of rationality is sometimes equated with *Homo economicus,* who is of course *un*limited in his calculating capacities. For the purposes of this essay, "thin" means the confinement of rationality to the strategic choices of individuals, however much they depart from the assumptions of microeconomics and public choice. Thus, the thin science can be constructed in light of the heuristics and biases identified by behavioral decision theory.

The science appropriate to the dialogical tradition has to be more inclusive, "thicker" if you will, making no prejudgment as to the essence of personhood. It is a reconstructive science, and as such seeks first of all to describe the various competences of individuals or grammars of human interaction. Building upon such reconstruction, this second science can then consider how different institutions might evoke or repress different kinds of competences, only one of which is captured by a thin account of rationality. Neither science is yet well developed, so both are sketched here in programmatic terms.

Before proceeding, a word of caution is in order. Limits relevant to institutional design do not exist only at the level of individuals. For structural factors impose rather severe constraints on the possibilities for political innovation (Dryzek 1992a). Notably, all states must secure a growing economy, legitimate their political systems, curb the instabil-

---

1. I was tempted to refer to this activity as a "liberal science" of institutional design, but that label would stress ideology rather than methodology, and so cloud the terms of comparison with the other science. Moreover, liberalism's categorical boundaries are today so elastic that to label something "liberal" communicates very little.

ity of markets, keep order, and compete internationally. These imperatives limit not just policies, but also institutional structures (e.g., the size and scope of the welfare state). Such concerns are set aside for the purposes of this essay, though it should be noted that the two sciences sketched here can achieve practical import only in the spaces for freedom in political innovation that remain after these structural constraints are recognized.

A Thinly Rational Science of Institutional Design

Microeconomics and its progeny posit no limits to the ability of individuals to comprehend, calculate, and maximize. If we are to locate a science sensitive to the limits of rationality, then this heroism must be abandoned (though, for the purposes of the first science, the basic idea that rationality is a property of individuals in strategic pursuit of their ends must be retained).

Now, there are those who would argue that this thin rationality assumption is itself highly, perhaps fatally, incomplete, in that it assumes that the capacity to devise, select, and effect good means to clarified and consistent ends is all there is to rationality. In assuming that rationality is only instrumental and, for the most part, egoistic, one misses a rich variety of motivations that might also claim rationality—and, above all, one misses the individual's rational capacity to decide which kind of motivation it is proper to invoke, and when. Later, I shall return to these richer possibilities in my second science of institutional design, but let me set them aside for the purposes of the first science.

The prospects for this first, thinly rational, science are clouded somewhat by the fact that the best-developed analysis of institutions grounded in strategic rationality is currently found in public choice that, as an offshoot of microeconomics, is inattentive to the limits of human rationality. Its assumptions about individuals are therefore empirically unfounded. Friedman (1953) argues that the realism of these assumptions does not matter, provided that testable hypotheses can be derived from them. A defense of public choice on Friedman's grounds would be more convincing if (1) public choice models more often generated hypotheses capable of being put to the empirical test (Kramer 1986, 17), (2) practitioners actually put these predictions to the test, and (3) the models were more often corroborated when this is done (Johnson 1991).

A literature that is stronger than public choice on empirical results about the limits to individual rationality, but weaker in analyzing (let alone designing) institutions, may be found in empirical decision theory (Kahneman, Slovic, and Tversky 1982; Dawes 1988). This field has found that individuals depart from the precepts of instrumental maximization in common and predictable ways. They respond differently to formally identical choices, depending on whether the decision is framed in terms of potential gains from some baseline rather than in terms of potential losses, and they become far more willing to take risks when losses seem to be at issue (prospect theory). Rather than use the entirety of the information available, people make use of vivid memories of dramatic events (the availability heuristic). They oversimplify alternatives and attend to only a few aspects of utility. Actions are often selected on the basis of analogy rather than through an assessment of the range of alternatives. Actions may also be chosen because they are diagnostic of a desired state of affairs, even though they may have no conceivable causal influence on that state of affairs.

To date, the compelling results of this field have found little use in the analysis and design of institutions. But, taken to heart, they suggest that the whole of microeconomics and public choice should be recalled, just as an automobile manufacturer might recall a line of cars with defective parts. Once recalled, all these analyses would be reworked using behavioral decision theory's findings about the bounds of rationality. This project is worthwhile and will doubtless build the careers of a good many social scientists; thus far it has not been done, however, and there is no way I can do so within the confines of this paper.

It is possible, though, to work through an illustrative example. Consider how one might frame budgetary allocations. A zero-based budgetary process necessarily frames allocations in terms of potential gains from zero; so individuals representing agencies seeking money will settle for modest budgets, perhaps even decreases from the previous year, rather than take the risk of coming up short by gambling for bigger budgets. As Wildavsky notes (1984, 21–22), if you come in with too high a request, you may lose big, so there is a risk involved in asking for too much. This is true in any kind of politicized budgetary process, whether zero-based or incremental, though Wildavsky's own discussion relates solely to the latter.

In contrast to zero-based budgeting, an incremental process frames decisions in terms of potential losses from some baseline—last year's allocation plus x percent, with x depending on general economic and political conditions. Thus, risky decisions on the part of budget-seeking bureaucrats are more likely. Rather than take a small but certain loss (framed in terms of the baseline), they will come in high and take the risk of a big loss in order to have a chance at maintaining the baseline. Sometimes they will win, sometimes they will lose; but the net result of this risk-taking behavior is that total budgetary requests are going to be higher than under a zero-based system. This means that budgets probably will grow bigger and faster than under a zero-based system.

Note that this prediction arises for exactly the opposite reason than that advanced by proponents of zero-based budgeting and like techniques. These proponents see such techniques as enabling a centralized, rational, comprehensive scrutiny of budgets which will cut out the "fat." As a result, efforts to implement zero-based schemes always collapse under excessive burdens of calculation. In contrast, an analysis in terms of the framing effect suggests that zero-based budgeting will indeed produce smaller budgets, albeit because of a generalizable deviation from effective maximizing (but still instrumental) rationality. To realize these results, though, the process has to involve political bargaining, rather than the purging of politics with which zero-based budgeting is normally associated. Wildavsky believes zero-based budgeting imposes impossible demands on the human ability to calculate; but his conclusion holds only if zero-based schemes are tied to centralized, comprehensive, goal-oriented calculation, as opposed to political interaction. There is no reason why this linkage has to obtain, even if all zero-based schemes to date have emphasized it.

In this deficit-ridden age, the moral of the above example might seem to be that framing situations in terms of potential losses produces collectively undesirable behavior. However, the same kind of framing may prove beneficial in other circumstances. Successful collective action requires that individuals renounce opportunities to take free rides on the efforts of others. If potential gains to the individual from collective action are at issue, then they may well appear small in relation to a reference point of no contribution and no benefit. But if instead it appears to the same individual that the (formally identical) issue involves potential losses in relation to a reference point that will persist if no successful collective action is undertaken, then the net utility to the individual of successful collective action will be greater. In the latter case, the individual will be more likely to contribute to the public good in question, and less likely to seek a free ride. The trick here is to frame the status quo as a situation of actual or potential loss from some baseline, rather than to frame it as the baseline itself. Thus, for example, in order to mobilize support successfully, revolutionary political ideologies must frame the status quo as an unacceptable deviation from some reference point (Berejikian 1992). This is not the same as saying that people who have nothing to lose are more likely to accept the risks of revolutionary participation than people with something to lose. (The conclusion of the *Communist Manifesto*, rooted in unmodified economic rationality, already tells us that.) Rather, the matter is one of convincing people that they have lost something which they once had.

Institutions, too, might be designed so that they frame decisions in terms of potential losses rather than potential gains, and thus elicit contributions to public goods. This might explain why we have Departments of Defense, or Ministries of Defense, rather than Departments of Offense, or Ministries of War. "Defense" implies loss avoidance, and so may elicit national solidarity on its behalf, not to mention cannon fodder, more readily than a name with gain-seeking connotations. Similarly, framing the welfare state in terms of social insurance rather than social assistance suggests a baseline against which losses are calculated (and insured), thus eliciting individual willingness to pay the taxes to finance it.[2] Words matter, and political rhetoric can have real consequences.

The Limits of Instrumental Rationality

Even if a project built on behavioral decision theory were brought to fruition, that theory would not necessarily constitute the philosopher's stone of institutional design. For despite its sophistication, behavioral decision theory deals in instrumental rationality and nothing more. As such, it may share some of the defects of public choice as a science of institutional design grounded in a constricted view of human rationality. Let me therefore take a look at those defects and attempt to ascertain whether or not a more empirically sophisticated thin science of institutional design must necessarily share them.

The first such defect is a paradox: institutional engineering informed by public choice is possible only to the extent that public choice behavioral assumptions are violated. For such engineering assumes the presence of a public-spirited engineer. If this engineer is an individual, then he or she can be strategically rational, but not egoistic. Though an unwelcome figure in public choice, a rational non-egoist is conceivable in that world. The problems are greater if the institutional engineer is conceptualized more realistically (at least in this democratic age) in collective terms.[3] For this collective engineer will be subject to the cycles, paradoxes, and irresponsibilities in collective decisionmaking which the field has so carefully explicated (see, e.g., Barry and

2. Like any kind of insurance, social insurance can also be explained in terms of strict individual maximization, as risk sharing. But any such explanation will hold whether it is called social insurance or something else; it does not explain why welfare is *framed* as insurance.

3. Collective yet nondemocratic institutional engineering is also conceivable, as in the Hobbesian social contract.

Hardin 1982). If, as Riker (1982) among others demonstrates, a wide variety of collective outcomes is possible based on any given distribution of preferences across individuals, then this result is no less true for preferences about institutions.

Whether or not the chastening results of social choice theory will still exist in the world as reinterpreted by behavioral decision theory is, for the moment, an open question, so it is not clear whether the first science will be as paralyzed as public choice on this score.

A second problem cuts deeper. As a result of its overload on one dimension of rationality, public choice can tell us only what happens when institutional contexts are conceptualized in these terms. It does not tell us when, or if, such contexts will be so conceptualized by the actors involved or, conversely, whether other dimensions of rationality might come into play.

At this juncture, one might object that there is nothing wrong with such an exclusive focus. But public choice itself has demonstrated that the relentless pursuit of instrumental rationality through political institutions has all kinds of negative effects. Indeed, a large part of the literature constitutes horror stories along these lines, ranging from the cycles and paradoxes inherent in collective choice to denunciations of majority rule, populism, bureaucratic budgetary excesses, distributional coalitions, iron triangles, rent-seeking politics, and legislative perversity. Democracy in particular starts to look very unattractive, as democratic politics of *any* sort is rife with irresponsibility, rent seeking, and instability and arbitrariness in preference aggregation. The moral drawn by most of the field's practitioners, not just those of the Virginia school, is that the scope of government and politics should be limited, and that of the market maximized.

But there is no reason why one should not draw a different moral: that rational egoism in politics should be neutralized or brought under the control of a different sort of proclivity. Interpreted in these terms, public choice theory, by elucidating the often perverse results of strategically rational behavior, is helpful in describing the limits to strategic rationality. In this light, public choice can be reinterpreted as contributing to a critical theory of political institutions by exposing the dire consequences of relentlessly instrumental rationality. Such a critical theory would point to alternative rationalities that would meet better the needs of the inhabitants and victims of institutions, and produce less pathological collective results (Dryzek 1992b). This interpretation would press public choice into the service of the dialogical tradition in institutional design—but as a source of warnings, not guidelines.

If public choice were reworked using the findings of behavioral decision theory, would this battery of chastening political results stand? As I have already said in the context of social choices about institutions, I do not know—which is why this first science merits development, rather than prejudgment.

At this juncture it may be concluded that a science of institutional design based on public choice merits rejection because it fails to take into account the limits of human rationality, because it is a deeply paradoxical enterprise, and because its hostility to democracy in institutions and their design is unremitting. A science grounded in the findings of behavioral decision theory would meet the first of these three objections, and is less obviously damned on the last two. On the other hand, such a science does not possess any obvious means of addressing these latter two objections. So let me now move from the decisional to the dialogical tradition to see if we might do better there.

Proliferating Rationalities

Institutional design starts to look a bit different—and more intractable—once we begin to recognize the contested character of rationality as a concept. Rationality can indeed cover the capacity to act instrumentally with individual goals in mind. However, other kinds of competences merit categorization as rationality, including the capacity to act communicatively (in seeking reciprocal understanding with others), socially (in recognition of a place in an established normative order or web of relationships with other persons), self-referentially (in affirmation or re-creation of personal identity), dramaturgically (as an expressive subject), or ecologically (in recognition of a place in relationships with nonhuman entities).[4]

If rationality as an ideal is contested, then deviations from any baseline become of contested significance. For the institutional engineer accustomed to working from a baseline of instrumental rationality, behavior that does not accord with the axioms of instrumentality may appear problematical; as something to be lamented, corrected if possible (perhaps through the use of decision analysis), and accommodated in institutional design if it cannot be adjusted. From the perspective of those accustomed to working with different conceptions of rationality, the same deviations may be a cause for celebration rather than regret, something to take advantage of rather than bemoan.

4. See Dryzek 1990b for an indication of what a distinctively ecological rationality, or noninstrumental way of relating to the natural world, might look like. For a somewhat less inclusive catalog of varieties of rationality, more strongly rooted in instrumental choice, see March 1978, 591–93. My list here extends that of Habermas (1984, 87–93), who when speaking of varieties of rationality includes instrumental, social, and dramaturgical aspects.

To illustrate this point, consider one particularly disastrous piece of institutional engineering: the Alaska Native Claims Settlement Act, passed by the U.S. Congress in 1971. The act settled Native American land claims in Alaska by transferring land and cash to thirteen for-profit regional corporations with ordinary Indians and Inuit as shareholders. The assumption was either that *Homo economicus* already populated the tundra or that institutional engineering would also be social engineering, an acculturation of Alaskan Natives into mainstream American patterns of thought and action.

Economically and socially, the corporations have failed, and all are on or over the edge of bankruptcy. Moreover, they are generally run by non-Native managers. The reasons for failure are complex, but one that looms large is the centrality of normative order and social integration in Native life. The corporate form may be suited to a society, or at least an economy, where rational egoism is standard behavior. It is unsuited to a society where rational egoism is exceptional, even deviant. It is doubly unsuited to such a society given that the corporations were expected to play social and political roles in the development of Native Alaskan society, not just a narrowly economic role. The failure of Indians and Inuit to act instrumentally and egoistically, even when provided with a corporate context that rewards such behavior, has undermined the schemes of the economistic institutional engineers, who can only lament this mass departure from rational egoism. But this same departure has enabled both Native resistance on behalf of traditional ways of life and the articulation of alternative political and economic models (such as reinvigorated tribal governments) that would accord better with the kinds of rationality actually found in Native society (see Berger 1985 for more details on this case).

A Reconstructive Science of Institutional Design

The multiplication of rationalities might seem to bode ill for any parsimonious science of institutional design sensitive to the limits to human rationality, and not just for the thin science of the kind discussed earlier. Indeed, we stand here on the verge of postmodern relativism and self-reference in which absolutely any kind of action principle can be described as rational, depending on its context. And if rationality can mean anything, then ultimately it means nothing.

The alternative is to reject postmodernism, while recognizing the proliferation of competences, by redefining rationality as the competence to decide when it is appropriate to bring which of the alternative action principles into play.[5] Thus, instead of conceiving of individual rationality in terms of multiple ideals and multiple deviations from them, we can speak of a multifaceted individual subjectivity. Overarching these facets is the power of judgment that helps constitute us as social beings who know when and how to bring particular principles to bear in social interaction—which is what rationality means in the dialogical tradition of institutional design introduced earlier.

The idea that individuals are not all of one piece is at least as old as Plato. More recently, "the multiple self" has been celebrated (or at least investigated) by the contributors to Elster's (1986a) volume. Therein may be found accounts of self-deception, weakness of will, Freud's id and ego, split brains, inconsistent programmed subroutines, daydreaming parallel selves, contradictory beliefs, and hierarachical selves with metapreferences. These phenomena conspire to make the social scientist's lot an unhappy one, suggesting that any simple science of selfhood relevant to institutional design may be beyond our reach.

Let me suggest that we can indeed have such a parsimonious science of subjectivity, though its character must be "reconstructive." Reconstructive inquiry finds its categories in its subjects, rather than relying on the theorist to construct and impose categories. The term is used by Jürgen Habermas (1979, 11–15), whose own candidates for reconstructive sciences are some dubious moral, educational, and linguistic theories associated with the names of Lawrence Kohlberg, Jean Piaget, and Noam Chomsky. Reconstructive science is concerned with the "cognitive, linguistic, or interactive competence" of individuals (Habermas 1979, 14). Such competences represent generative grammars of human interaction, and one can accept the idea of reconstructive science while being skeptical of Habermas's particular candidates.[6]

This language of subjectivity is both more neutral and more inclusive than what we started with. It is more neutral because each facet of subjectivity is not preevaluated by being measured as an ideal or as a deviation from an ideal. It is more inclusive because it makes no prejudgment as to what kinds of action principles merit description as

5. This is one aspect of what Habermas (e.g., 1979) refers to as communicative competence (see also White 1987, 117).

6. Johnson (1991) suggests that game theory is a reconstructive science. In this light, game theory is not positive social science theory, so prediction and empirical testing of hypotheses are irrelevant to its claims. Rather, game theory tells us what rationality *is* in particular situations; in so doing, it reconstructs the strategic competence of actors. The reconstructive science of subjectivity which I describe seeks to encompass a broader variety of competences.

rational; the list of competences is open-ended.[7] For example, consider the individual acting on a diagnostic basis. Quattrone and Tversky (1986) give the example of strict Calvinists who accept the doctrine of predestination, but who nevertheless take great pains to lead a moral life, on the grounds that such behavior would indicate they do in fact belong to the elect. Is such behavior rational or pathological? If we think in terms of subjectivity rather than rationality, we need not even ask this question, let alone answer it. We can simply say that Calvinists choose to invoke diagnostic subjectivity. All that now remains of the idea of individual rationality is the competence to choose among the various facets of subjectivity available to a person.

This inclusive approach to categorizing competences means, too, that many of the rationality debates that have preoccupied social scientists and philosophers can be short-circuited. For example, the essays collected by Wilson (1970) constitute an extended and ultimately inconclusive dispute on the degree to which magic, ritual, religion, and "traditional thought" can be described as rational. Reconstructive inquiry can simply allow that these modes of belief and action constitute different kinds of subjectivity. And again, rationality in this context can be interpreted as the ability to know when and how to invoke different competences and subjectivities.[8]

The connection back to institutional analysis and design can be made here inasmuch as different institutions can be expected to evoke different aspects of subjectivity.[9] Buchanan (1986) recognizes this point when he justifies constitutional inquiry through reference to the idea that institutional designs "can and do influence the relative importance of separate motivational elements." Some institutions (perhaps markets and legal systems) might evoke strategic, adversarial dispositions. Some (perhaps alternative dispute-resolution processes oriented to consensus) might evoke sociability. Some (perhaps hierarchy) might evoke fatalism and resentment. Some (perhaps participatory democracy) might evoke civic virtue.

Of the many—perhaps innumerable—aspects of subjectivity, which should the institutional designer try to evoke, and when? Who

---

7. This open-endedness is a significant departure from Habermas's formulation.

8. The basics of a science of subjectivity already exist in the form of Q methodology (Brown 1980).

9. Another way of stating this point, more applicable to the intersubjective and social level of analysis, is that different institutions draw upon and reinforce different discourses. For the development of a discursive logic of institutional design along these lines, making use of Q methodology, see Dryzek 1995. The discursive logic is compatible with the reconstructive approach described here.

gets to decide? What can we say about *their* subjectivity and *its* influence on the course of institutional design they choose?

The only defensible answer here, at least in this democratic age, is that it is up to the individuals who will be involved with an institution to decide reflectively for themselves what kinds of subjectivity shall be invoked. In a reconstructive science of institutional design, as I suggested earlier, rationality is best conceived of as the capacity to make competent choices about which kinds of subjectivity to apply in any given context. Thus, limits to individual rationality become psychological or social barriers to this capacity.

Rationality and Autonomy

Rationality in this sense is very close to what we generally mean by autonomy. Lane (1978, 5) suggests that "today autonomy is everyone's candidate for the preferred model of political (or other) man." He may be right (though poststructuralists and ecofeminists might disagree), but only because autonomy is a very flexible ideal. In its thin sense, autonomy refers to the capacity of an individual to make good, informed, goal-directed choices. This is the autonomy of thinly rational economic man, and so, as Lane notes, it is promoted by market society, which abolishes the constraints of traditional groups (tribe, kinship, community, etc.), and provides many occasions and the necessary resources for the exercise of choice.

Autonomy in a somewhat thicker sense involves, in addition, reflective and competent selection of ends. As Dahl (1989, 91) puts it, "By a morally autonomous person I mean one who decides on his moral principles, and the decisions that significantly depend on them, following a process of reflection, deliberation, scrutiny, and consideration."[10] For the sake of his democratic theory, Dahl takes this as an empirical assumption (though not as a demonstrated truth). Dahl's (1989, 99) "presumption of personal autonomy" is that people are indeed the best judges of what results are in their own best interests (though not necessarily of the best means or policies for securing those results).

A thin conception of autonomy has direct institutional implica-

10. Translating this idea into the language of social choice theory, a morally autonomous individual may be said to act upon her or his metapreferences. Such a metaranking, M, might be over rankings A, B, and C, which in themselves rank alternatives x, y, and z. Sen (1977), for one, believes such metarankings exist. As Elster (1986b, 13) notes, metarankings may come into effect inasmuch as the individual might strive to ensure that M comes out on top, aware that weakness of will might lead to some order other than M triumphing.

tions; if it is promoted by the market, then the market is to be preferred. But the market is no help when it comes to Dahl's thicker notion of moral autonomy; as Lane (1978, 22) notes, in market society a "sense of purpose and hold on non-economic values are sharply diminished." Lane's metaphor is that of a high-performance vehicle with a good driver but no place to go.

Dahl's presumption of moral autonomy also has direct institutional implications: it is one cornerstone of his defense of democracy, though just what kind of democracy this presumption underwrites is less clear. The argument here is not quite homologous with that of thin autonomy and market society, for Dahl's argument does not require that democracy promote moral autonomy; rather, if one presumes, as Dahl does, that moral autonomy already exists, then democracy becomes the most appropriate institutional accommodation for competent individuals. Dahl, of course, is aware of developmental theorists of democracy from J. S. Mill on who argue that the experience of political participation does indeed promote autonomy, but his own argument does not rely on such empirical claims.

For Dahl, the institutional choice here is stark. One can either presume personal autonomy, in which case one prefers democracy; or one can presume that individuals are not the best judges of their own interests, in which case one prefers paternalistic authoritarianism. Let me suggest a third alternative, which Dahl does not recognize. This third alternative builds on a still-richer conception of personal autonomy but does *not* presume that such autonomy actually exists.

Recall that thin autonomy refers to competent choice of means, whereas moral autonomy refers to competent choice of ends. However, both conceptions are alike in working with an instrumental conception of action, in which individuals first choose ends and then choose means. I noted earlier that a competent individual may choose not to act instrumentally. Dramaturgical, communicative, socially integrative, playful, emotional, intuitive, and ecological principles of action are also available. In this light, autonomy refers to the capacity to decide reflectively which kind of principle—or which aspect of the self—to invoke, and when (so it cannot be reduced to metarankings or metapreferences across alternatives as outlined in Sen 1977).

Unlike thin autonomy and Dahl's moral autonomy, autonomy in this third and last sense—let me call it *full autonomy*—has no immediately obvious institutional implication. Such a connection, however, can be made once one recognizes that full autonomy rarely exists but that deviations from it can be of greater or lesser degree. The point becomes not only to identify those institutions that would facilitate autonomy, but also to criticize institutions that repress it, or which bring out one kind of subjectivity and exclude others. Of these two tasks, the latter is easier; it is quite straightforward, for example, to develop a critique that shows how the market brings out the instrumental aspect of subjectivity and suppresses alternatives (see, e.g., Lane 1978; Marcuse 1964). It is equally easy to criticize bureaucracy for its creation of subservient and/or manipulative "organization man." Rhetoric on such issues is plentiful; data are scarce.

The Critical Theory of Institutions

In short, what we need here is not an empirical theory or even a normative theory of institutions, but a critical theory. A critical theory is by definition directed at an audience of sufferers, designed to make plain the contingent, ideologically perpetuated causes of suffering, and is indicative of measures that can be taken by the audience to relieve suffering. So the second science is critical as well as reconstructive. This critical theory would (1) show how particular institutions evoke particular kinds of subjectivity and repress others, (2) demonstrate that any such situation is not immutable, and (3) intimate institutional alternatives. Critical theorists have generally paid little attention to political institutions, except in very sweeping terms, and hence part (3) is currently underdeveloped (but see Forester 1989; Dryzek 1990a).

Part (3) in this scheme certainly cannot be ignored. For one aspect of full autonomy is surely the ability to utilize and if necessary create one's own concepts, and so one's own language. Otherwise, one enters the world as portrayed by Foucault and other poststructuralists, in which individuals are imprisoned by the discourses (about economics, criminality, sex, mental health, etc.) in which they move. In the Foucauldian world, there is no escape. In the critical theorist's world, in contrast, escape is indeed conceivable—but only if the *social* situation exists to make it possible. Concepts and language cannot be created, appropriated, reinterpreted, and redesigned by an isolated individual; this can be done only in association with others. In the counterfactual world of Habermas, the location for such processes is the ideal speech situation. This situation features uncoerced, unlimited communication among fully competent individuals, free from deception, self-deception, strategy, or hierarchy. While that situation is of course an unattainable ideal, we can utilize it to criticize real-world institutional arrangements and even (more controversially) to inspire participatory design of such arrangements. Thus, to think about the promotion of full autonomy in the real world, we have to think about institutions.

Considering this conclusion in light of Dahl's institutional dichotomy, I think it is obvious that he proposes a false choice. According to Dahl, we either presume personal autonomy, and so choose democracy, or we choose paternalism and authority. I suggest that instead we can start from the (more realistic?) assumption that people are not necessarily the best judges of their own interests, but then add that people can become better judges. The challenge for institutional design, therefore, becomes that of facilitating autonomy; and for that, only a critical theory of institutions will do.

The job of the good-society theorist, then, becomes not institutional engineering with different aspects of subjectivity in mind, but promotion of the capacity of individuals to decide for themselves what it is that institutions should try to bring out and, consequently, how they might be designed. Otherwise, the theorist is judging people by the theorist's own baseline of what constitutes appropriate subjectivity and deviations from it.

The Limited Rationality of Institutional Designers

Let me now try to show how a reconstructive science of institutional design deals with a perennial problem: the limited rationality of institutional designers themselves. Recognizing this limitation, the question "How shall institutions be designed to adapt them to the limits of human rationality?" should not reduce to determining how the omniscient institutional engineer might adjust his or her scheme to take into account the imperfections of the masses. Instead, everyone involved in processes of institutional reconstruction—participants, voters, institutional denizens, victims, or luminaries of the Committee on the Political Economy of the Good Society—may be assumed to be less than perfectly rational. Taken to an extreme, institutional reconstruction might be a project for a "democracy of dunces," whose first task would be to ponder where, if at all, the requisite knowledge and capabilities might be located.

Or perhaps a project for nobody. Hayek, for one, argues that we simply do not know enough to undertake effective institutional design. Only misguided social constructivists have the hubris to believe we do. Taking Popper's (1966) critique of dangerous "holistic planners" a step further, Hayek suggests that all attempts to change social, economic, and political reality (socialism in particular) end only in repression, and never in anything resembling the intentions of institutional engineers. It is far better, according to Hayek (1979, 65–97), to allow the evolution of decentralized "catallaxies"—of which the free market is the best example—to aggregate and make sense of fleeting and fragmentary bits of knowledge in the hands of many individuals.

The paradox inherent in a Hayekian approach to institutional nondesign, of course, is that to get to the kind of catallaxy he admires we would today need to engage in some very deliberate institutional engineering. *Contra* Hayek, this was even true historically, when the "great transformation" (Polanyi 1944) heralding the inception of the market order occurred with a series of very complex constitutional and legislative choices that redefined rights, established the boundaries of government, destroyed feudal economic relations, and generally laid the framework for commercial society. Today, the complexities of the mixed economy and welfare state could be dismantled only by some very extensive and complex action, which itself would violate the social conditions of human intelligence so carefully described by Hayek.

The Hayekian contradiction highlights what is in fact a universal problem for all would-be institutional redesigners in a world of limited rationality. But in designating full autonomy as the primary concern of institutional design in the light of limits to human rationality, the second science avoids the hubris to which even Hayek is prone. For in the reconstructive science of institutional design there is no disjunction between process and target, means and end: autonomy and competent dialogue are both path and prize.

Conclusion

Institutional design is not a matter of the theorist devising blueprints and then seeking to effect them. Instead, the second science points to an open-ended, discursive, and quintessentially democratic process in which everyone involved can be designer and subject. Moreover, it allows for difference, diversity, and full autonomy in terms of who we are and how we reason. Thus I believe that the *reconstructive* science of institutional design is ultimately a more worthwhile project than the thin science. The thin science does have value, but any such value is contingent upon the degree to which instrumental or strategic rationality is reflectively deemed appropriate in a situation, and that is itself a matter for reconstructive inquiry to determine.

REFERENCES

Barry, Brian, and Russell Hardin. 1982. *Rational Man and Irrational Society? An Introduction and Sourcebook.* Beverly Hills, Calif.: Sage.

Berejikian, Jeffrey. 1992. "Revolutionary Collective Action and the Agent-Structure Problem." *American Political Science Review* 60:647–57.

Berger, Thomas R. 1985. *Village Journey: The Report of the Alaska Native Review Commission.* New York: Hill & Wang.

Brown, Steven R. 1989. *Political Subjectivity: Applications of Q Methodology in Political Science.* New Haven, Conn.: Yale University Press.

Buchanan, James M. 1986. "Then and Now, 1961–1986: From Delusion to Dystopia." Paper presented at the Institute for Humane Studies, Fairfax, Va.

Dahl, Robert A. 1989. *Democracy and Its Critics.* New Haven, Conn.: Yale University Press.

Dawes, Robyn M. 1988. *Rational Choice in an Uncertain World.* New York: Harcourt Brace Jovanovich.

Dryzek, John S. 1990a. *Discursive Democracy: Politics, Policy, and Political Science.* Cambridge: Cambridge University Press.

———. 1990b. "Green Reason: Communicative Ethics for the Biosphere." *Environmental Ethics* 12:195–210.

———. 1992a. "The Good Society versus the State: Freedom and Necessity in Political Innovation." *Journal of Politics* 54:518–40.

———. 1992b. "How Far Is It from Virginia and Rochester to Frankfurt? Public Choice as Critical Theory." *British Journal of Political Science* 22:393–417.

———. 1995. "The Informal Logic of Institutional Design." In Robert E. Goodin, ed., *The Theory of Institutional Design.* Cambridge: Cambridge University Press.

Elster, Jon, ed. 1986a. *The Multiple Self.* Cambridge: Cambridge University Press.

———. 1986b. "Introduction." In Jon Elster, ed., *The Multiple Self.* Cambridge: Cambridge University Press.

Forester, John. 1989. *Planning in the Face of Power.* Berkeley and Los Angeles: University of California Press.

Friedman, Milton. 1953. *Essays in Positive Economics.* Chicago: University of Chicago Press.

Habermas, Jürgen. 1979. *Communication and the Evolution of Society.* Boston: Beacon Press.

———. 1984. *The Theory of Communicative Action I: Reason and the Rationalization of Society.* Boston: Beacon Press.

Hayek, Friedrich A. von. 1979. *Law, Legislation, and Liberty III: The Political Order of a Free Society.* Chicago: University of Chicago Press.

Johnson, James. 1991 "Rational Choice as a Reconstructive Theory." In Kristin Monroe, ed., *The Economic Approach to Politics.* New York: HarperCollins.

Kahneman, Daniel, Paul Slovic, and Amos Tversky. 1982. *Judgment under Uncertainty: Heuristics and Biases.* New York: Cambridge University Press.

Kramer, Gerald H. 1986. "Political Science as Science." In Herbert F. Weisberg, ed., *Political Science: The Science of Politics.* New York: Agathon.

Lane, Robert E. 1978. "Autonomy, Felicity, Futility: The Effects of the Market Economy on Political Personality." *Journal of Politics* 40:2–24.

Linder, Stephen H., and B. Guy Peters. 1994. "The Two Traditions of Institutional Designing: Dialogue versus Decision?" In David Weimer, ed., *Institutional Design*. Boston: Kluwer.

March, James G. 1978. "Bounded Rationality, Ambiguity, and the Engineering of Choice." *Bell Journal of Economics and Management Science* 9:587–608.

Marcuse, Herbert. 1964. *One-Dimensional Man*. Boston: Beacon Press.

Polanyi, Karl. 1944. *The Great Transformation*. Boston: Beacon Press.

Popper, Karl R. 1966. *The Open Society and Its Enemies*. London: Routledge & Kegan Paul.

Quattrone, George A., and Amos Tversky. 1986. "Self-Deception and the Voter's Illusion." In Jon Elster, ed., *The Multiple Self*. Cambridge: Cambridge University Press.

Riker, William H. 1982. *Liberalism against Populism: A Confrontation between the Theory of Democracy and the Theory of Social Choice*. San Francisco: W. H. Freeman.

Sen, Amartya K. 1977. "Rational Fools: A Critique of the Behavioral Foundations of Economic Theory." *Philosophy and Public Affairs* 6:317–44.

White, Stephen K. 1987 "Toward a Critical Political Science." In Terence Ball, ed., *Idioms of Inquiry: Critique and Renewal in Political Science*. Albany: State University of New York Press.

Wildavsky, Aaron. 1984. *The Politics of the Budgetary Process*. 4th ed. Boston: Little, Brown.

Wilson, Bryan R., ed. 1970. *Rationality*. Oxford: Basil Blackwell.

CHAPTER FOUR

Institution Building and Human Nature

KAROL EDWARD SOŁTAN

MADISONIAN POLITICAL SCIENCE is back. We see it advocated under the name of "new institutionalism" (Smith 1988), "new constitutionalism" (Elkin and Sołtan 1993), or "institutional design." Proponents commonly reject mainstream social science, emphasizing politics as an art form, a creative enterprise centering on reflection and choice (Mansfield 1990). They want to keep close to the format established in *The Federalist* and are hostile, or at best indifferent, to science as a form of knowledge that constructs and tests abstract models of the causal mechanisms underlying social reality.

I believe they are making a mistake. A Madisonian political science can be strengthened only if it takes advantage of the usual toolbox of science, including mathematical models and empirical research. A rich source of relevant precedents on this issue can be found in a place not much consulted by political scientists: the history of the development of generative grammar (see Chomsky 1965). Chomsky based his new research program in linguistics on a distinction between (linguistic) performance and competence, generative grammar being a science of competence. The result was a theoretical breakthrough and a period of rapid scientific progress, moving away from older behaviorist assumptions in linguistics. The models of generative grammar did not predict linguistic behavior (performance); instead, they gave an abstract and rigorous description of the rules used in making grammatical evaluations. They were accounts of competence, of the skills that good performance required. In opposition to the various kinds of behaviorism and determinism, here was a form of social science compatible with human creativity and unpredictability.

We have yet to assimilate fully the methodological revolution Chomsky started. The work of Habermas (1979) is, as far as I know, the only systematic attempt to do so.[1] But his theory of "communicative competence" remains narrowly focused on communication skills, which are somewhat tangential to the central concerns of the social sciences. Habermas's account of communicative competence is, in any case, closer in intellectual style to certain branches of analytical philosophy, and to philosophical forms of "rational reconstruction," than to empirical science. The spirit of generative grammar is lost in translation.

A reformulated Madisonian political science can do better. Its task would be to give an account of the political competence of an ideal citizen, parallel to Chomsky's account of the grammatical competence of an ideal speaker/hearer. This political competence consists of the skills required for the design and reform of institutions. An account of those skills will provide us (among other things) with an understanding, scientific in style, of the microfoundations of institutions as relevant to institutional reform. To develop his notion of communicative competence, Habermas turned to linguistic philosophy; the alternative strategy I am suggesting would turn instead to the constitutionalist tradition as one of its main sources. It will contribute, I hope, to a revival of a "Madisonian" political science. Within this Madisonian political science, it will also engage in a set of polemics about both *method* and *substance*.

On the subject of *method,* my polemic can be summarized in two slogans. First: Let Us Not Be Woolly-Headed. Madisonian political science seems to me a nonstarter as an alternative to social science. It is simply a *form of* social science. This means, among other things, that we do not turn away from mathematical models, or empirical tests, or rigor (when these are possible, and they are often possible). We do draw on traditional constitutionalism, but what we produce need not look like *The Federalist.* We also draw on scientific precedents: on the family of rational-choice models or on Chomsky's idea to replace the study of performance with the study of competence.

My second methodological slogan is related to the first: Do the Detail Work, Don't Just Paint the Big Picture. We need more than sketches of general political programs, or regime analyses, or conceptions of a good society. I do not mean to say that these things are not necessary: they are simply not sufficient. Without scientific detail work, our accounts of the big picture will have a strong tendency to sound familiar. They are overwhelmingly likely to be repeating some sample of old truisms.

On more *substantive* questions, it is also worth making some sharp

1. But see also Chapter 4 (Dryzek) in the present volume and J. Johnson 1991.

and clear initial choices. Our goal should be to find a conception of human nature and human circumstances that is most likely to produce successful politics. Political practice is *a* test of theory (this much is common ground for Marxists, Aristotelians, pragmatists, and constitutionalists of various stripes). And we can quickly narrow the range of plausible, practically oriented forms of social science.[2] These should be, above all else, instruments for the elimination of wasteful utopianism. They should take most seriously the lessons of practical success and failure. They must consider *what works*—not because of some silly notion that everything that works must be good, but because everything that does not work is a waste of time and energy.

A practically oriented social science will be tested in part by the political action and political program it suggests. Success or failure of different styles of politics is relevant to the adequacy of their underlying theories. Thus, a few summary judgments concerning success or failure can help us dramatically narrow the list of candidates for the style of thinking and theory that can most effectively guide practice without wasting moral resources. Here is a list of such judgments that I am willing to defend:

1. Marxism is a complete failure in political practice, despite the fact that Marx and Marxists emphasized more than others the importance of the practical test of theories (Second Thesis on Feuerbach: "The question whether objective truth can be attributed to human thinking is not a question of theory but is a *practical* question. In practice man must prove the truth, that is the reality and power . . . of his thinking." [Marx, (1845) 1977: 156]). Marxism as a purely academic exercise has had, by contrast, a long string of successes.

2. Madisonian constitutionalism is a success, as measured by two hundred years of almost continuous republican government and evolution toward democracy in the United States. Success of various closely related traditions of constitutionalism elsewhere, of course, also counts in its favor.

3. Revolutionary *movements* are a complete failure. Revolutions are sometimes successful, but not the movements that propose and organize revolutions. They can gain power, certainly, but they hardly ever achieve their ends, except in very limited ways. Despite this, as Hannah Arendt has noted, revolutions have been a great intellectual inspiration in social and political thought, while constitutionalism has not. Perhaps we should not be sur-

2. The following paragraphs draw on Sołtan 1992.

prised at the troubles of the Enlightenment tradition, which finds so intellectually attractive what is politically disastrous.

4. Self-limiting social movements of reform (Gandhi in India, Martin Luther King in the United States, Solidarity under Communism in Poland) are a dramatic success, in fact perhaps the greatest invention of twentieth-century politics.

5. Capitalism is a great success: not in its early form (small entrepreneurial firms, the night-watchman state, laissez-faire policies), but in a more organized form with a large, activist state and large multinational corporations.

6. Socialism as an alternative to capitalism is a complete failure. Some will protest here that the "right" form of socialism has never been tried. This is no doubt true, but it is also irrelevant. We will not wait until all plausible forms of socialism have been tried. One could say, after all, that feudalism was also abandoned without really having been tried. At some point, we just have to move on.

7. Socialism as a program for reforming capitalism has been a great success. Some version of the welfare state, a product in large part of reformist socialist efforts, is now indispensable to capitalism.

From these practical lessons in success and failure I draw two main conclusions. First, let us not waste our time with alternatives to capitalist democracy. Forget about the Third Way! We need to concentrate our attention on fixing and improving capitalist democracies. Second, since it is wise to build on success, we should build a program for reform of capitalist democracy that derives from both Madisonian constitutionalism and the political strategies of self-limiting social movements, from a marriage of Gandhi and Madison, of *satyagraha* and the rule of law. This would be a form of constitutionalism based on a commitment to rational deliberation and self-limitation in the pursuit of some form of objective political ideal, expressed in the metaphors of nature (as in natural rights and natural law) and truth (as in *satyagraha*, or "truth force").

What kind of *detail work* will this perspective require? I see two central tasks. First, in order to avoid the waste of moral energy characteristic of utopianism, we must develop fully our understanding both of the common impediments to successful human action and the strategies for handling them, including strategies of self-limitation. In the language I used in the Introduction above, this requires development of the instrumental component of political competence. But attention to the difficulties that face us should not undermine hope; it should not prevent institutional reform from tapping into strong sources of moral energy, perhaps even new sources. Wishy-washy and tired post-modernist talk certainly will not do. Why not look instead, against the spirit of the age, for an objective moral order, for something like *nature* and *truth* as moral sources?

Detail work is best seen—well—in the details. Hence the rest of this paper will focus on details. A tension between the aspiration to objectivity and a recognition of human limits, and the various impediments to human success, is central to the constitutionalist tradition. The effect of some of those impediments (scarcity, the power of narrow interest, uncertainty and risk) is relatively well understood. I will consider two other impediments, whose effects are less thoroughly studied but which have been considered central in the constitutionalist tradition. First, human beings are fallible and error-prone. Much of the constitutionalist tradition can be seen as the development of strategies for error avoidance (e.g., the precommitments modeled on Ulysses' self-protection against temptation by the sirens) or error correction (e.g., the Popperian open society). Second, human beings are not fully autonomous: they make their decisions not independently but within a field of mutual interdependence and power. Much of the constitutionalist tradition can also be read as developing strategies for limiting power and promoting autonomy.

The most distinctive moral foundation for the constitutionalist tradition can be found in various accounts of natural rights and natural law, each making a claim to a particular kind of moral objectivity. These claims have been put in question since the revolutionary high point of constitutionalism at the end of the eighteenth century, but they seem to me essential if we are to give constitutionalism a scientific turn *or* if we want to make of it again an activist and politically creative tradition.

I will focus, then, on persons as fallible, interdependent creatures capable of creative innovation and aspiring to objectivity. We *are* fallible and prone to error, governed by selfishness and impulse, making our choices in a field of mutual interdependence. Yet we also aspire to be creators, not just passive observers, of the world around us, and we aspire to a kind of objectivity that has been traditionally expressed in metaphors of *truth* (as in Gandhi's *satyagraha* or Václav Havel's "living in truth") and of *nature* (as in natural law and natural right).

Imperfection

In social science the recognition and acceptance of our imperfection and error-proneness has specific theoretical consequences.

Among the signs of human imperfection are the effort and time we put into our decisions (decision costs) and the departures from perfection that nonetheless result. We can refer to these generally as "errors." Given this fallibility, human rationality or competence cannot require simple case-by-case optimization; it must include efforts to develop a decisionmaking "technology" which either improves decision quality (without necessarily attaining the optimum) or decreases decision costs, or both. We can distinguish three important strategies. The first I will call "rational caricature," borrowing from the philosopher Leszek Nowak (1977). The second consists of the use of substitute measures and indices. The third is the simple division of decisions (for a similar list, see Simon 1979).

Rational Caricature

Within most of the rational-choice tradition across the social sciences, decisionmaking is seen as maximizing expected utility (this is the "MEU model"). MEU is still the standard model despite the massive amount of evidence that human beings do not in fact behave in that way (Kahneman and Tversky 1979). This evidence, however, has led to the development of many alternative theories, among the most serious of which have been prospect theory (Kahneman and Tversky 1979) and regret theory (Loomes and Sugden 1982). Both incorporate various forms of editing and distorting of the decisionmaker's utility and of the information on which he or she acts. Much of this editing and distorting can be seen, I would argue, as a rational adaptation to human error-proneness. This is not how others see it. In prospect and regret theories (for example) the various abstractions (editing) and distortions are for the most part taken as a psychological fact, not further explained.

We can do better by borrowing from the work of Leszek Nowak in the philosophy of science. Nowak (1977) emphasizes the highly idealized and abstract quality of scientific theories, and he shows the distorted and partial nature of scientific descriptions of events when compared with commonsense descriptions. To dramatize the nature of the contrast between science and common sense, Nowak refers to science as caricature in the service of explanation. Scientific descriptions, like caricatures, are both highly abstract and distorted; some features are enhanced, others neglected. But the caricaturing has a rational purpose: it is an instrument of *explanation*.

We can extend the idea from rational explanations to rational decisions. Decisions, like explanations, require both abstraction and the distortion of descriptions. Thus, rational choices are based on a description of the situation that is distorted when compared to some "choiceless" baseline. The distortions, however, are not arbitrary. They are rational adaptations to human imperfection. The description of a decision situation, then, will differ systematically, depending on whether the describer is purely an observer ("choiceless" description) or a participant and decisionmaker. And the changes or "distortions" owing to the decisionmaker's perspective will, at least in part, be instruments of rational decision, aiming to improve the quality or lower the cost of decisions.

Descriptions will not be passive reflections of the situation (they will not be simple "mirrors of nature"); they will be actively chosen means to an agent's end, instruments to combat human imperfection. This suggests there are two ways of viewing caricature in the service of rational decisions. We can think of caricature, first, as distortions applied to a "choiceless" description by a pure observer. And we can think of it also as distortions applied to the descriptions used by a perfect decisionmaker. Much of the stock-in-trade of the critics of MEU theory (regrets, rule following, decision baselines and reference points, satisficing) can be seen, I believe, as consequences of this form of caricature in the service of rationality.[3]

Substitute Measures

Indices for goals play a double role in decisionmaking. They can provide us with an approximate measure of success when the underlying goals are vague, only roughly known or difficult to observe. We can also use them to understand better the nature of our goals. For either purpose, we can replace direct measurement of goal achievement with indirect measurement. This is done frequently, and it is well documented in the literature on behavioral decision theory (e.g., Simon 1982). It serves us well, when we do not really know what we want, as often happens.

An important example is the promotion of human welfare, a widely accepted goal, but one whose achievement is not easy to measure. We cannot observe people's welfare directly. Nonetheless we can use as an indirect measure their willingness to sacrifice what they value. The "willingness to sacrifice" standard can take a number of forms. In public policy evaluation, and increasingly in American law, it takes the from of the "willingness to pay" standard, the willingness to sacrifice *money*. We take advantage of the existence of money as a

---

3. I hope to have this worked out in more detail in a book manuscript I am working on. The book's title will probably be *The Ideal Citizen*.

convenient measure of value: the more I value something, the more I will be willing to pay for it. Willingness to pay is relatively easy to measure and, unlike many indicators of preference or welfare (Arrow 1963), it can be aggregated. A group's willingness to pay is simply the sum of the amounts all the individuals in that group are will to pay.

But the willingness-to-pay standard is not the only possible index that uses willingness to sacrifice as a measure of well-being or value. An important alternative is the willingness to risk one's life. The promotion of human welfare has come to be associated with economic thinking and economic institutions. As a result, we now find the wealth-maximization indicator more natural. To understand what it means to promote human welfare, however, we should consider a variety of indicators. This is especially important when the indicators give us very different results, as these do.

Thanks to the development of modern economics, we know something about which institutions and policies are likely to maximize wealth and about how to find out which institutions and policies do maximize wealth. With the maximization of the willingness to die, we are far more in the dark (but see Kellett 1982). A few things can be said, though.

First, *all* indicators using willingness to sacrifice, not just the willingness-to-pay standard, are likely to be distorted by differences in how valuable the object sacrificed is to those sacrificing it. Thus the rich, on average, will be willing to pay more, simply because each dollar means less to them. Similarly, people are more likely to risk their lives in defense of what they value when they believe that this earthly life is nothing compared to the bliss that awaits the martyr after death. The situation will be different for those who value this life more than they value life after death (especially once we discount for either the probability that it does not exist or the probability that it will be spent in hell). Because of these differences, one cannot simply count martyrs in order to compare institutions.

Second, at least under some circumstances, differences in suicide rates between institutional contexts can be taken as evidence of differences in the availability of anything worth dying for. In settings that provide something worth dying for, suicide is less likely, since life in those settings will be valued not just for its own sake but also as a possible sacrifice for some larger cause. Thus the extensive research on variation in suicide rates as a function of institutional context (see, e.g., B. D. Johnson 1965; Lester 1989; Girard 1993) has at least some relevance to the evaluation of institutions by the willingness-to-die standard.

Third and finally, the admittedly limited evidence points in some well-defined directions. We can distinguish, for example, two types of goods that institutions can provide. Consumption goods are what we like to consume, and markets are effective in providing them. They are the goods for which we typically pay. Identity-constitutive goods, by contrast, make us what we are (and so we better *not* consume them), and they clarify (to us) what makes it worthwhile to be what we are. Our identities are composed of different aspects: nationality, family, religion, gender and species, among others. The institutions that help us articulate and honor these various aspects of our identity provide us with identity-constitutive goods. These are among the goods that many people are willing to die for. And institutional contexts that do not provide them, or that provide fewer of them, appear to be more conducive to suicide (as in Durkheim's [1951] anomic suicide).

Using the two substitute indices ("willingness to pay" and "willingness to die"), we can measure (at least approximately) our success in the promotion of human welfare. But their availability also shows the internal complexity of human welfare as an end. We can see more clearly the potential contradictions hidden within the seemingly straightforward utilitarian standard.

Division of Decisions

Perhaps the most common rational response to human limitations in the making of decisions is the strategy of dividing large and complex decisions into many smaller and simpler ones. This can be done in two very different ways, which I will call division into *parts* and into *stages*. Division into parts splits a task into separate components which can be performed more or less autonomously. This kind of division has been central to the development of institutions and cultures we recognize as "modern." We know it as the division of labor, social differentiation, and specialization. It has been one of the most important mechanisms of economic growth (as Adam Smith saw), but it has also produced fundamental transformations in a broad range of human institutions (see Durkheim [1893] 1964; Parsons 1971) as well as in human consciousness.

The division into stages is best explained by way of a homely example familiar in the academic setting. When we write papers, we divide our task into stages we call drafts. Each draft is a draft of the whole paper (though it may be incomplete). Thus we distinguish two kinds of divisions of a task. We can separate a paper into parts, and then work on each part separately, but we can also divide the writing into stages. The first draft of a paper, even if it is "complete" in that it includes all the parts, will typically mark only the end of an initial stage. There are likely to be many subsequent stages.

Both these ways of dividing decisions are powerful instruments of human progress. They can be effective, however, only to the extent that we have at our disposal appropriate means for recombination or reassembly of the divided decisions. In the case of division into parts, the recombination and coordination is achieved mainly through *hierarchy* and *exchange*. Division of labor can be made more effective in situations where either hierarchy or exchange is available as a possible coordinating mechanism. Hence, modern politico-economic systems are largely complex combinations of hierarchies and exchanges, organizations (enterprises, corporations, states), and markets (Williamson 1975 and 1985; Lindblom 1976). And one important path of development of such systems has taken us through a sequence of institutional inventions that reduce the cost of either exchange or hierarchy (North 1981 and 1990; Williamson 1975 and 1985). We are also used to characterizing different types of politico-economic systems by their degree of reliance on exchange and on hierarchy (Lindblom 1976) as well as by the extent of separation or fusion between these two coordination mechanisms (Kaminski 1991). Thus, in a number of ways, these coordination mechanisms play a central role in progressive rationalization of societies, in economic development, as well as in our understanding of these processes.

The situation is quite different with coordination mechanisms that allow the division of decisions into stages. For these are neither as well developed nor as well understood as exchange and hierarchy. These are the mechanisms thanks to which each stage of a task (after the first) can be recognized as a subsequent stage of the *same* task, rather than something completely new.

The effect is relatively easy to achieve when the same person is in charge of all the stages (as when I am writing a paper); it becomes difficult when different people take over at each stage. The exercise, then, looks like a modified version of the chain novel that Dworkin (1985) used to clarify the nature of legal reasoning. Dworkin's chain novel is written as a group effort. One person writes the first chapter and gives it to the second person, who must write the second chapter, constrained (of course) by the nature of the already written chapter. Each subsequent chapter is written by a different person, but each must be a chapter of the *same* novel. Hence the chapters already written constrain what can be written at later stages. Even as an exercise to clarify legal reasoning, a modified version of this story seems more appropriate. The writing is still a group effort, but the first person writes an outline or a sketch of the whole text, not just the first chapter.

Each subsequent author adds, clarifies, and develops until the text is ready. The earlier stages constrain the later ones, yet they do so not as components or parts (chapters), but as drafts of the whole text.

The integrity of a sequence of stages can be maintained in a variety of ways. We can do so by establishing a strict hierarchy of authority, with the initial author at the top. We can also follow something like a strategy of "disjointed incremetalism," in which the integrity of the sequence is maintained because each stage involves only a small step. Neither of these, however, is indispensable to the integrity of a decision sequence. Two features *are* indispensable. First, we must learn to evaluate not individual decisions separately, but decision *sequences,* with the value of the individual decisions fully dependent on their place in such sequences. Second, to provide the basic glue that will keep each successive stage connected to the previous ones, we must learn to take an internal point of view on decisions-in-progress (which often means: on institutions in the process of development).

An internal point of view (Hart 1961; Finnis 1980; Dworkin 1985 and 1986) combines expertise with appreciation. It allows us to continue the sequence of decisionmaking stages, because we are knowledgeable about what has been done in that sequence already, and because we value it sufficiently. At each successive stage we must, to borrow Dworkin's terminology (1985, 1986), make the decision sequence *the best it can be.* To the extent we can *rely* on the internal point of view to maintain the integrity of the sequence, we will need neither the authority of the original author nor incrementalism. Thus, for example, the practice of social criticism (as described by Walzer [1985], among others) depends on the critic taking the internal point of view toward the institutions and traditions of the critic's society. But the critic is not constrained by either hierarchical authority or a conservative commitment to incrementalism. The division of decisions into stages is consistent with radical disjunctions between stages.

Perhaps the most fully understood example of decisions divided into stages is the development of scientific theories. A scientific research program is a sequence of scientific theories (Lakatos 1978). Each successive theory builds on the previous one. Each theory must be evaluated not in isolation, but on the basis both of its place in the sequence and the nature of the sequence. A research program usually develops incrementally, in what Thomas Kuhn has called "normal science." Sometimes, however, it undergoes a radical transformation (a scientific revolution) while maintaining a certain amount of continuity (hence, Newtonian mechanics is preserved as an approximation to a special case of relativity theory).[4]

4. More precisely: Newtonian mechanics is reformulated to become an approxima-

A scientific research program is not exclusively a sequence of theories. A family of ideas ("heuristics," Lakatos calls them) develops in association with those theories. They help in the construction of successive theories and, therefore, also maintain the integrity of the sequence. The mastery of a research program involves more than the understanding of theories, requiring other explicit and tacit knowledge together with a conviction that the program is valuable. Thus, scientific education develops in the students a capacity to adopt an internal point of view on scientific research programs. And we can talk of scientific progress only when scientific theories begin developing in this way, in a sequence of stages. The division of decisions into stages, then, is a central feature of scientific rationality. It is much less systematically developed elsewhere, though it should be. It should be a feature of human rationality in the development of all institutions. Skill in the construction of decisionmaking sequences that build and improve institutions should therefore be an important element in the competence of an ideal citizen.

Dependence and the Pervasiveness of Power

If by spontaneous action we could achieve everything we wanted, then we would not need institutions, and the constitutionalist perspective would not have a subject matter. But we cannot achieve everything we want in this way. Modern economics emphasizes one reason for this situation: the scarcity of goods. Economics is known as the dismal science in large part because of its insistance on scarcity: we cannot have everything we want; to get one thing, we have to give up something else; everything has a price. This message is dismal, but not nearly dismal enough. It needs to be pressed further—not because of a masochistic desire to wallow in the most depressing aspects of the human condition, but because we need to understand our limits in order to appreciate the cleverness of what we have done with the cards we have been dealt, and in order to help us reform our institutions more intelligently. Understanding our limits helps us both to expand human opportunities and to gain a more respectful view of human achievement and potential.

Institutions are not needed when the going is easy. They make a difference in *difficult* circumstances. This is a familiar point illustrated by the famous "theorem" of Coase (1960): when transaction costs are zero, then the initial allocation of property rights does not affect the

tion to a special case of the new relativity theory. Some people read into Kuhn's *Structure of Scientific Revolutions* (1962) radically irrationalist claims which deny even this limited continuity in scientific revolutions. But whatever Kuhn said, or meant, *this* much continuity unquestionably does exist.

efficiency of the outcome.[5] In more difficult circumstances, however, when transaction costs are positive, the allocation does matter and the nature of property institutions makes more of a difference.

When we make decisions in social contexts, we face at least two kinds of difficulty which may prevent us from getting what we want. First, we may be unable to make enforceable collective agreements. Second, we may be unable to make autonomous individual choices. It is useful to keep these difficulties separate in our minds and, on that basis, to develop two complementary abstract models of decisionmaking and social interaction. One model, elaborated in noncooperative game theory, assumes that individual autonomy is easy (in these models it is simply assumed in the rules of the game), but collective agreements are impossible. The other model takes existing formal theories of bargaining and presses them further: it assumes that collective agreements are easy, but individual autonomy is impossible.

In noncooperative game models, such as Prisoners' Dilemma or Chicken, it is assumed that agreements are impossible to enforce and that individual autonomy is guaranteed. This is also the basic structure of the problem of providing public goods and, more generally, the problem of collective action:[6] a collective-action problem is any situation in which rational action by individuals *can* lead to a Pareto inferior outcome. This includes (but is not limited to) the standard games of Prisoners' Dilemma and Chicken and most situations involving the provision of public goods.

In these models it is *assumed* that individual autonomy is easy and that collective agreement is difficult. If we accept them as our only representation of social reality, it is hardly surprising that the problem of collective action comes to be seen as central, and that institutions come to be seen as instruments for the resolution of the problem of collective action.

Thus, for example, Michael Taylor (1987) believes the study of politics is a study of the ways to solve collective-action problems. Jon Elster (1976) thinks of politics even more narrowly as ways of transcending the Prisoners' Dilemma. The state and many other institutions are both explained and justified as solutions to the problem of collective action. And, for Taylor, the case for anarchy is decisively strengthened when it is shown that nonstate mechanisms can also be effective solutions to the problem of collective action. A form of coercive anarchy, best approximated (it seems to me) by the traditional village, is Taylor's

---

5. This is not quite true. See Aivazian and Callen 1981; Mueller 1989.
6. We can define a collective action problem in a number of ways, but Michael Taylor's (1987) conception, which I give here, seems to me most apt.

substitute for the Hobbesian sovereign state. It is a real-world example of a situation in which cooperation in a Prisoners' Dilemma can be sustained without external enforcement: the parties expect to continue to interact into the indefinite future, the size of the group is small, and the structure of the payoffs favors cooperation (see also Axelrod 1984; Oye 1986).

Not just security but also economic growth is at stake in finding solutions to the problem of collective action. Without such solutions our capacity for voluntary cooperation is diminished, and a certain amount of mutually beneficial trade is blocked. Thus, argues North (1990), solutions to the problem of collective action are a necessary prerequisite to economic growth. The availability of such solutions is hardly sufficient, however; for neither a Hobbesian absolute dictator-ship nor a tight-knit village is the best environment for economic growth. The reason is not far to seek: these are societies that cannot guarantee the individual autonomy necessary for economic growth, even as they make the enforcement of agreements relatively straight-forward. They do not allow individuals the space necessary to make their creative economic contribution or to protect their investments. Protection of autonomy is as important to growth as enforcement of agreements. Both property rights *and* freedom of contract are the basis of a successful market economy.

The belief that the problem of collective action is *the* central issue for the analysis and design of institutions, a belief we find in Elster, North, and Taylor, is thus seriously one-sided. In general, agreements and autonomy may both be difficult. As a counterpart to the various discussions of the Prisoners' Dilemma and the game of Chicken, we need to consider a model in which enforceable agreements are auto-matically, easily guaranteed but individual autonomy is difficult or im-possible. In the society represented by such a model, the central prob-lem for institutions is to protect individual autonomy, not to expand the sphere of cooperation. Instead of individual players each making their choice independently, simply because this is guaranteed in the rules of the game, we have a situation where bargaining and tacit bar-gaining pervade the players' lives, as in a village community. Auton-omy is then seen for what it so often is: a difficult achievement, requir-ing the creation and maintenance of very distinctive institutions.

When we assume that autonomy is easy, but cooperation difficult, we represent social interactions as noncooperative games. Naturally we then see the problem of collective action as *the* problem of politics. But this is only because of the abstraction we have made. Now consider the opposite abstraction: Assume that cooperation is easy, but auton-omy difficult. We live within a field of power, in a sea of mutual influences, of explicit and tacit *bargaining*, where "bargaining" includes all events of explicit mutual influence, whatever the method of this influence (argument on merits or haggling, "positional" or "principled" bargaining). Both visible and hidden power are the basic reality that human decisionmakers face, and faced with this reality our basic problem is not how to organize *collective* action, but how to make *separate* action possible.

This problem has political immediacy in the transition from communism. The ideal, communist society, as seen by Marx, was supposed to be above all a society in which *alienation* (a more elaborate version of separation) is overcome, mainly by abolishing private property. This feature of the ideal of communism had real consequences for actually existing socialist systems. We found in them two characteristic fusions: the economic-political fusion and national fusion (especially in the Soviet Union and Yugoslavia). The economic system was not separate from the political system, and individual nationalities were not kept separate from each other. One of the key tasks of transition from communism is to undo these fusions—to separate economics from politics, and to separate nation from nation—and the cost of performing these tasks has already been dramatic. In the face of this human drama we look for solutions to the problem of separate action, not to the problem of collective action. We need to practice the "art of separation," as Walzer (1984) called it.[7]

The capacity to separate is important to economic performance. Economic systems can operate well only when they are relatively independent from the political system, and stable and secure property rights are one good way of achieving such separation. But the capacity to separate is also a prerequisite to the achievement of many other valuable goals. It is central, for example, to the institutional design of liberal political systems (which include the separation of church and state, the separation of state and dynasty, and the separation of powers within the state).

In political thinking that developed in opposition to communism in Eastern and Central Europe, the concept of "civil society" was a central category. In the first instance, civil society requires separation of society from the state, the depoliticization of various spheres of social life. In some Western usage, it also means the separation of various spheres of social life from the economy, so that not everything in life is taken to have a money price, and not everything goes to the highest bidder. Many of the movements in opposition to communism were

---

7. In the following paragraphs I draw heavily on Walzer 1984.

also movements for national liberation, aiming to separate the national unit from the larger empire. Here, too, separation was a goal.

In Marxism, by contrast, separation is identified with alienation and is seen as the main impediment to the achievement of a good society. Marxists also neglect internal boundaries in existing capitalist societies. These societies are seen as tight causal networks, which cannot be changed piecemeal; only revolutionary change is possible. But revolutionary change, we now conclude on the basis of two hundred years of experience, is overwhelmingly likely to lead to disastrous consequences. The only change that is likely to produce improvements, to produce progress on some front, is piecemeal. This requires a social system divided up into spheres, each having some independence from the others. Separation is thus also a prerequisite for any successful reform and for progress.

What methods of separation are available to us? To separate ourselves from others, we need strategies and instruments for defense against the pressure of others. We need to be able to resist such pressure. It is helpful to think about methods of separation in the context of specific stories: an entrepreneur facing the pressure of the state, for example. He may be protected by clear and enforced boundaries surrounding what is his (property rights). If not, he may choose to invest in mobile resources instead of stationary ones (a truck rather than a factory), or he may choose something easy to hide (gold or Swiss bank accounts, rather than production machinery), or something immediately consumed (and not requiring long-term protection).

Alternatively, let us consider a more stylized theoretical story: the problem of separate action can be thought of as the obverse of the problem of collective action. The absence of what is required for collective action is what makes separate action easier: large groups, high monitoring costs (including the capacity to hide), and a short-term time horizon. A city, not a village, is the optimal locus for successful separate action. And a competitive market is possible when collective action (of one kind) fails: there is no collusion.

Separate action requires *defensive* weapons (or strategies for *protection*). Various kinds of walls are the best examples of purely defensive weapons, among them the Great Wall of China, coats of arms, the Maginot line, and various kinds of shields (including that proposed in the Strategic Defense Initiative). Projectiles can also be used for defense, of course, but not exclusively for defense. Walls, by contrast, are purely defensive. If we cannot build walls, we can do other things: we can flee, we can hide, or we can do without (making us resistant to the threats or promises of others).

The capacity to separate is enhanced by whatever diminishes the cost of geographic, social, or job mobility. Thus, for example, in post-communist societies the capacity for separate action is limited by the great shortages of shelter, which make geographic mobility difficult. And in all societies a similar effect results from the absence of retraining opportunities, which makes job mobility difficult, as do job-specific skills and assets. When people have valuable things, and cannot move them, they are likely to turn to other forms of protection. So when it is costly to quit, we are more likely to demand protection against being fired. These are defenses against external pressure which are partial substitutes for one another.

The capacity to separate is also enhanced through self-reliance, which can be achieved in two ways. You can modify your capacities, learning to produce everything you need or want. In the global economy this is the strategy of import substitution, whereby gains in economic independence (or separation) are achieved at the price of economic stagnation (this is the route of Albania, North Korea, and Burma). Or you can modify your preferences and goals, making yourself less dependent on others. For individuals this requires the development of two kinds of virtue: courage (to protect against the pressure of threats) and asceticism (either this-worldly, as in the Weberian hypothesis about the origin of capitalism, or other-worldly [see Kolm 1985]).

What we do is only rarely a product of independent individual choice. It is more commonly a product of tacit (or explicit) mutual influence and bargaining. Hence social interactions (in the sense of mutual influence, tacit politics, and power) pervade human activity. The human species is indeed a social or a political animal. Power and politics pervade all, as Foucault and his followers have argued at length. Both our action (if it is rational) and our institutionmaking must adjust to this relative heteronomy of human choice. We must see human choice in the context of a pervasive field of mutual influences and power. Action will then be seen as the product of a field of interaction of crosscutting capacities to influence, a field of power. But the degree to which we are subject in our action to the influence of others is *variable*. Separate action is possible. The degree to which we are prisoners of the field of power is not fixed. To defend ourselves against power, we can deploy a broad range of strategies and resources, and we can build institutions to make this easier.

Credibility and Objectivity

Objectivity matters for institutional design because it is what distinguishes moral ideals worthy of our sacrifices from distorted or narrow ideological thinking. If our moral conceptions are simply epipheno-mena, delusions, or partisan weapons, if they do not *in themselves* have any power over us, then they are not worthy of our attention—no mat-ter how coherent, complex, well integrated, or even self-evident they may be. Much of the worry about objectivity in moral philosophy is about other difficulties, about whether moral objects would be queer things if they existed (Mackie 1977) or about whether moral judgments can be true or false.

In some contexts, these are important questions. If we are to give force to moral ideals, however, then what matters above all is whether the ideals we promote are, or can be, anything but some form of dis-torted ideological thinking or ideological manipulation. To find mor-ally significant differences in the exercise of power, we must make sure that the moral standards we use to mark such differences are not themselves simply ideological weapons, manipulative in their effect just like other weapons. This is the crucial problem of objectivity.

Not everybody thinks objectivity matters. Dworkin, for example, thinks objectivity does not matter, even though he believes there are right answers to moral and legal questions. "Slavery is unjust in mod-ern societies" is one example of such a right answer (Dworkin 1985, 171). Dworkin has arguments that this conclusion is right. He believes that everyone has good reason to think so and, therefore, that every-one ought to oppose slavery. But he does not, he says, have any sepa-rate arguments for the *objectivity* of that judgment. He claims not to understand what form such arguments could take.

Let me suggest one answer to Dworkin's difficulty. We have two kinds of arguments for the injustice of slavery. Arguments of the first kind are direct arguments aiming to convince us of the injustice of slavery. Arguments of the second kind provide evidence that our eval-uation of direct argument is not likely to be distorted. They establish our *credibility* as evaluators. Without this second type of argument, there would be no way to know if our conclusion is not simply a prod-uct of some elaborate ideology serving the interests of a powerful class, or if it is nothing more than a by-product of a causal process (e.g., indoctrination) that has no moral relevance.

A person's commitment to his or her moral positions can be un-dermined by an explanation of how he or she came to hold that posi-tion. Suppose we show that Dworkin's liberalism is a product of indoc-trination serving the long-term systemic interest of capitalism. We have not countered any of his arguments, and our counterattack is ad homi-nem. Yet if that counterattack is done well (a very big if, to be sure), it can be quite effective, since it will undermine Dworkin's credibility. We will lose interest in the merits of his arguments, and we will begin to see what he says as a set of symptoms for something else. We will withdraw from direct conversation with Dworkin for reasons like those that would make us withdraw from a conversation with a schizophrenic. We come to be convinced that we should use our time and effort explaining the genesis of the position rather than appreciating the point of that position. Claims of objectivity, and the arguments that support them, are designed to prevent such a move—and it is a common move in modern cultures.

When challenged in this way, Dworkin could produce a number of responses consistent with his belief that objectivity does not matter. But he will have trouble getting us to pay attention in the right way. By then, after all, our trust in his reliability as a judge of the merits of an argument will have been undermined. He will need to rebuild that trust first. He needs arguments showing that his beliefs have been produced by a causal process that is relatively undistorting, or at least that they *could* have been produced in such a way.

Common patterns of moral reasoning, because they provide arguments of this type, suggest that objectivity matters. In addition to direct arguments *on* merits, we commonly use arguments that are more like *tests of* merits. These range from such simple injunctions as "Put yourself in the other person's shoes" to elaborate theoretical constructions such as those of Harsanyi (1982), Rawls (1971), or Ackerman (1980). The common use of such tests suggests a mistrust of simple and direct judgments of the merits of arguments. We have at least some inclination, often inchoate to be sure, to test the objectivity of our judgments. But objectivity requires more than these commonly used, simple, and informal mental tests, more than playing "moral musical chairs."

Methods for Testing Moral Force

Consider Rawls's famous method of reflective equilibrium, an attempt to be systematic and rational in our moral judgments. The method of (narrow) reflective equilibrium attempts to reconcile our considered moral judgments with general moral theory. We try to find a moral theory that best fits our judgments. Yet we also revise our judgments, as we come to be persuaded by the moral theories we consider (see Rawls 1971; Daniels 1979, 1980a, 1980b). Some have seen this method as closely analogous to the methods of science. Considered moral judgments are the data. We pick that moral theory which best fits the data. Others have noted, however, what seems to be a fundamental difference: scientific data are not revised to fit a theory in the way that considered moral judgments can be revised as we come to be convinced by a moral theory. The significance of this difference has in turn been questioned (e.g., Moore 1982) on the basis of a more sophisticated view of the theory-boundedness of observations in science. But the distinction can be restated in a way that allows for this more sophisticated view of science. Scientific observations are indeed dependent on theories, so a new theory may well force a revision in observations. Still, moral theories are *better* the more they can change the initial observations (the original considered moral judgments), and this is certainly not true in the case of scientific theories.

There is another view of the method of reflective equilibrium, based on an analogy not to science but to the methods for interpreting texts. This view takes the mutual adjustments of considered judgments and moral theories as simply one more instance of the hermeneutic circle (Palmer 1969; Rabinow and Sullivan 1987; C. Taylor 1985). But the hermeneutic understanding of reflective equilibrium fails for the same reason that the natural science model failed. Interpretations are not ordinarily considered better the more they change the text, yet a moral theory that succeeds in deeply transforming our considered moral judgments is surely the better for it.

This brings us to a third interpretation of the method of reflective equilibrium, which I will call the "moral force" interpretation. According to this view, the considered judgments of right and wrong are "readings" of the strength of moral force for or against an action or an institution. They are indicators of the persuasive force of moral arguments for or against the action or the institution. The moral theory we construct in (narrow) reflective equilibrium is simply a particularly coherent set of arguments which reproduces this set of readings as nearly as possible. Such an exercise, though, has no special interest by itself. Our real goal is not to reproduce the existing set of readings but to produce a theory with the maximum moral force. Our considered moral judgments tell us something about what we have *already* found persuasive. We should be able to construct a moral theory at least as good as that—hence the rationale for using narrow reflective equilibrium. But we can also hope to do better, to construct a different moral theory which is capable of a deeper transformation of our considered moral judgments.

According to the "moral force" view the relation between a moral theory and considered moral judgments in narrow reflective equilibrium is not (primarily) logical, as on the naturalistic view. It is also not an aesthetic relation of fittingness, as on some hermeneutic views. The relationship is *causal*. The considered judgments are the *effects* of the force of moral arguments contained in the moral theory. The move beyond the moral anthropology of narrow equilibrium reflects this, taking two basic forms. First, we now combine the construction of moral theories backed by the greatest force of moral argument with a more basic task: the study of what contributes to the force of moral argument. Second, to perform both of these tasks we must understand the nature of the other social forces that routinely interact with and distort the force of moral argument. First to understand and then to limit distortions is a crucial prerequisite for objectivity.

We must recognize the sources of distortion in our own judgments and in the judgments of others. The more such sources we recognize, and the better we understand how they operate, the more effectively we can diminish or control their effect. Thus, moral development can be seen as a series of stages characterized in large part by a greater and more precise recognition of how the distortions operate. In early childhood, we routinely fail to see how moral judgments are driven by our narrow interests, especially the interests in obtaining parental reward and avoiding punishment. As we grow, we learn to differentiate moral judgments from prudential judgments, and the distorting effect of self-interest on our moral judgments diminishes. If Kohlberg's understanding of moral development (Kohlberg 1969, 1979, and 1981) is roughly correct (at least as far as the morality of justice is concerned [see Gilligan 1982]), then the second step moves us from the conventional to the postconventional stage, controlling for the effect of the various social pressures on our judgment. When we do that, the force of convention loses some of its grip.

At each stage, we develop procedures to counter the effect of distorting forces. These are normally *mental* procedures, such as those demanding that we put ourselves in the other person's shoes. Many moral theories incorporate a more fully articulated and formalized version of these procedures (e.g., Harsanyi 1982; Rawls 1971; Ackerman 1980; also Fishkin 1984). But mental procedures, too, are notoriously subject to distortion. Articulating and formalizing them may not be much help. It has not prevented, for example, the controversies about what would be chosen in Rawls's original position. Nor is it clear how to decide among the various philosophical reconstructions of this mental procedure. A more reliable next step is the development of *real*, empirical, procedures that diminish the effect of distortions. In this light, the mental procedures we commonly use will appear as nothing more than crude approximations and pale substitutes for the real tests of objectivity. I know of at least two examples of work developing and applying such procedures (Sołtan 1987; Frohlich and Oppenheimer 1992). It seems to me that this is the most promising path for mapping out the more objective aspects of morality, thus providing a credible basis for institutional reform.

Conclusion

I have sketched in this paper three of the most important aspects of the microfoundations of institutional design. The neoclassical-economic and rational-choice models are the background for all three. We can build microfoundational models in these three areas, so that the utility-maximizing theories of rational choice can be derived as a special case. Much of the institutionalist tradition in the social sciences has been driven by hostile criticism of the behavioral foundations and methodology of neoclassical economics. This is not true in the version sketched here: the effort should be to incorporate, not reject, the more "economic" models. Perfection in decisionmaking, assumed in mainstream rational choice, is simply a special case of a model that allows imperfection. Autonomy in decisionmaking is similarly a special case of choice within a power field.

But the perspective on microfoundations I have sketched above is not all about limits and impediments. It recognizes also human moral aspirations, giving them a distinctive objectivist interpretation. Thus the behavioral microfoundations of a Madisonian political science, as I see it, include the empirical study of the moral force of ideals, using methods I have sketched briefly above (and, more elaborately, in Sołtan 1987).[8]

The constitutionalist tradition is centered on three concerns: power and the limitation of power; error avoidance and error corrections; and the moral foundation of institutions in objective natural law and natural right. All three issues can be understood more deeply and in more detail if we adopt the principal methodological commitments of mainstream social science. The resulting account of the "competence of an ideal citizen" can also contribute to a better understanding of the behavioral foundations of institutions.

REFERENCES

Ackerman, Bruce. 1980. *Social Justice and the Liberal State*. New Haven, Conn.: Yale University Press.

Aivazian, V. A., and J. L. Callen. 1981. "The Coase Theorem and the Empty Core." *Journal of Law and Economics* 24:175–81.

8. See also Frohlich and Oppenheimer 1992.

Arrow, Kenneth. 1963. *Social Choice and Individual Values*. New York: Wiley.

Axelrod, Robert. 1984. *The Evolution of Cooperation*. New York: Basic Books.

Chomsky, Noam. 1965. *Aspects of the Theory of Syntax*. Cambridge: MIT Press.

Coase, Ronald. 1960. "The Problem of Social Cost." *Journal of Law and Economics* 3:1–44.

Daniels, Norman. 1979. "Wide Reflective Equilibrium and Theory Acceptance in Ethics." *Journal of Philosophy* 76:256–82.

———. 1980a. "On Some Methods of Ethics and Linguistics." *Philosophical Studies* 37:21–36.

———. 1980b. "Reflective Equilibrium and Archimedean Points." *Canadian Journal of Philosophy* 10:83–103.

Durkheim, Emile. (1897) 1951. *Suicide*. Glencoe, Ill.: Free Press.

———. (1893) 1964. *The Division of Labor in Society*. New York: Free Press.

Dworkin, Ronald. 1985. *A Matter of Principle*. Cambridge: Harvard University Press.

———. 1986. *Law's Empire*. Cambridge: Harvard University Press.

Elkin, Stephen, and Karol Sołtan, eds. 1993. *A New Constitutionalism*. Chicago: University of Chicago Press.

Elster, Jon. 1976. "Some Conceptual Problems in Political Theory." In Brian Barry, ed., *Power and Political Theory*. London: Wiley.

Finnis, John. 1980. *Natural Law and Natural Rights*. Oxford: Clarendon Press.

Fishkin, James. 1984. *Beyond Subjective Morality: Ethical Reasoning and Political Philosophy*. New Haven, Conn.: Yale University Press.

Frohlich, Norman, and Joe Oppenheimer. 1992. *Choosing Justice: An Experimental Approach to Ethical Theory*. Berkeley and Los Angeles: University of California Press.

Gilligan, Carol. 1982. *In a Different Voice*. Cambridge: Harvard University Press.

Girard, Chris. 1993. "Age, Gender, and Suicide: A ×-National Analysis." *American Sociological Review* 58:553–74.

Habermas, Jürgen. 1979. *Communication and the Evolution of Society*. Boston: Beacon Press.

Harsanyi, John. 1982. "Morality and the Theory of Rational Behavior." In Amartya Sen and Bernard Williams, eds., *Utilitarianism and Beyond*. Cambridge: Cambridge University Press.

Hart, H.L.A. 1961. *The Concept of Law*. Oxford: Clarendon Press.

Heiner, Ronald. 1983. "The Origins of Predictable Behavior." *American Economic Review* 73:560–95.

Johnson, B. D. 1965. "Durkheim's One Cause of Suicide." *American Sociological Review* 30:875–86.

Johnson, James. 1991. "Rational Choice as a Reconstructive Theory." In Kristen Monroe, ed., *The Economic Approach to Politics*. New York: HarperCollins.

Kahneman, Daniel, and Amos Tversky. 1979. "Prospect Theory: An Analysis of Decision under Risk." *Econometrica* 47:263–91.

Kaminski, Bartlomiej. 1991. *The Collapse of State Socialism*. Princeton, N.J.: Princeton University Press.

Kellett, Anthony. 1982. *Combat Motivation: The Behavior of Soldiers in Battle.* Boston: Kluwer-Nijhoff.

Kohlberg, Lawrence. 1969. "Stage and Sequence: The Cognitive-Developmental Approach to Socialization." In David Goslin, ed., *Handbook of Socialization Theory and Research.* Chicago: Rand McNally.

———. 1979. "Justice as Reversibility." In Peter Laslett and James Fishkin, eds., *Philosophy, Politics and Society.* 5th ser. New Haven, Conn.: Yale University Press.

———. 1981. *The Philosophy of Moral Development.* San Francisco: Harper & Row.

Kolm, Serge-Christophe. 1985. "The Buddhist Theory of 'No Self.' " In Jon Elster, ed., *The Multiple Self.* Cambridge: Cambridge University Press.

Kuhn, Thomas. 1962. *The Structure of Scientific Revolutions.* Chicago: University of Chicago Press.

Lakatos, Imre. 1978. *The Methodology of Scientific Research Programs.* Vol. 1 of *Philosophical Papers.* Cambridge: Cambridge University Press.

Lester, David. 1989. "A Test of Durkheim's Theory of Suicide Using Data from Modern Nations." *International Journal of Comparative Sociology* 30:235–38.

Lindblom, Charles. 1976. *Politics and Markets.* New York: Basic Books.

Loomes, Graham, and Robert Sugden. 1982. "Regret Theory: An Alternative Theory of Rational Choice under Uncertainty." *Economic Journal* 92:805–24.

Mackie, J. L. 1977. *Ethics: Inventing Right and Wrong.* Harmondsworth: Penguin.

Mansfield, Harvey. 1990. "Social Science and the Constitution." In Allan Bloom, ed., *Confronting the Constitution.* Washington, D.C.: AEI Press.

Marx, Karl. (1845) 1977. "Theses on Feuerbach." In *Selected Writings.* Edited by David McLellan. Oxford: Oxford University Press.

Moore, Michael. 1982. "Moral Reality." *Wisconsin Law Review* 1982:1061–1167.

Mueller, Dennis. 1989. *Public Choice II.* Cambridge: Cambridge University Press.

Nagel, Thomas. 1986. *The View from Nowhere.* New York: Oxford University Press.

North, Douglass. 1981. *Structure and Change in Economic History.* New York: W. W. Norton.

———. 1990. *Institutions, Institutional Change and Economic Performance.* Cambridge: Cambridge University Press.

Nowak, Leszek. 1977. *Wstep do idealizacyjnej teorii nauki* [Introduction to the Idealizational Theory of Science]. Warsaw: PWN.

Oye, Kenneth, ed. 1986. *Cooperation under Anarchy.* Princeton, N.J.: Princeton University Press.

Palmer, Richard. 1969. *Hermeneutics.* Evanston, Ill.: Northwestern University Press.

Parsons, Talcott. 1971. *The System of Modern Societies.* Englewood Cliffs, N.J.: Prentice-Hall.

Rabinow, Paul, and William Sullivan. 1987. *Interpretive Social Science: A Second Look.* Berkeley and Los Angeles: University of California Press.

Rawls, John. 1971. *A Theory of Justice*. Cambridge: Harvard University Press.

Sen, Amartya. 1970. *Collective Choice and Social Welfare*. San Francisco: Holden-Day.

Simon, Herbert. 1979. "Rational Decision Making in Business Organizations." *American Economic Review* 69:493–513.

———. 1982. *Models of Bounded Rationality*. Vol. 2. Cambridge: MIT Press.

Smith, Rogers. 1988. "Political Jurisprudence, the 'New Institutionalism,' and the Future of Public Law." *American Political Science Review* 82:89–108.

Sołtan, Karol Edward. 1987. *Causal Theory of Justice*. Berkeley and Los Angeles: University of California Press.

———. 1992. "A Marriage of Gandhi and Madison." *The Newsletter of PEGS* 2:1–4.

Taylor, Charles. 1985. *Philosophy and the Human Sciences*. Cambridge: Cambridge University Press.

Taylor, Michael. 1987. *The Possibility of Cooperation*. Cambridge: Cambridge University Press.

Walzer, Michael. 1984. "Liberalism and the Art of Separation." *Political Theory* 12:315–30.

———. 1985. *Interpretation and Social Criticism*. Cambridge: Harvard University Press.

Williamson, Oliver. 1975. *Markets and Hierarchies: Analysis and Anti-Trust Implications*. New York: Free Press.

———. 1985. *The Economic Institutions of Capitalism*. New York: Free Press.

PART TWO

Conceptions of the Good Society

The chapters in this section can be divided into two groups, representing two styles of thought about the good society. The chapters by Charles Anderson and Stephen Elkin each identify a set of features of the mentality that the good society requires, as they see it. For Anderson (Chapter 5) this is the instinct of workmanship; for Elkin, in an essay more narrowly focused on politics (Chapter 6), it is a set of deliberative virtues. The first-order institutional requirements of a good society, then, are those that make these virtues effective, or at least do not get in the way. The second-order institutional requirements are those that help develop the relevant virtues. Anderson talks of schools and universities, Elkin of local democracy.

In a good society we need people who care about the quality of their institutions (and of other things as well, Anderson stresses) and people who are capable of deliberating about the quality of those institutions. They must know at least enough to be able to elect representatives capable of deliberative lawmaking, not just manipulation and bargaining (as Elkin stresses). But exactly what is the *content* of such skills and knowledge? The Anderson and Elkin chapters do not address this question at any length.

To get a better sense of what is needed, we must turn to the chapters by Gar Alperovitz and Philip Green. These two essays (Chapters 7 and 8) have a similar structure, quite different from the Anderson and Elkin chapters. Green posits a goal for the good society (democratic political equality), identifies impediments (chiefly gender and class inequality), and considers various strategies for diminishing the force of those impediments. He works, as he puts it, constrained by the limits of *historical imagination* (and is thus limited to various versions of democratic capitalism) but impelled by demands of *normative imagination*.

Each one of us is likely to sketch a different picture of a good society—in large part because our normative imaginations will work differently, giving us varied conceptions of values and ideals, but also because we will identify differently the relative strength of these two forces (the limits of historical imagination and the demands of its normative counterpart). Among the authors in this section, the limits of historical imagination are most serious for Anderson: he starts by identifying existing good societies (Costa Rica, Wisconsin, Denmark). Elkin and Green are intermediate, both searching for better forms of capitalist democracy or commercial republic. Alperovitz is willing to stretch the historical imagination the most. His essay is a search for a Third Way, neither capitalist nor socialist. Alperovitz considers various alternative institutional strategies, some of them substantial departures from the status quo, but all potentially better instruments, he argues, in the service of the traditional political values of the Enlightenment tradition: equality, liberty, and democracy.

CHAPTER FIVE

How to Make a Good Society

CHARLES W. ANDERSON

WHAT MUST WE KNOW in order to design institutions for the good society? The question is marvelously presumptuous. Not only are we to design utopia, we are to reduce the making of utopia to a technique, to a standardized procedure that anyone, anywhere (assuming, I suppose, the right cultural and environmental conditions), could use to make one. The whole idea could be dismissed out of hand. It is outrageously unrealistic, and I am a resolute realist. Yet the exercise is intellectually irresistible. So what would it take to make a workable good society? Let us start there. I will first present my image of the political economy of the good society. Then I will try to extract the essential principles of the good society from this image—and thus sketch the rudiments of its public philosophy. Finally, I will try to describe the method by which one would create a reliable template for producing good societies.

Exemplars of the Good Society

What is a good society anyway? Today's utopias seem to be presented as formal models. The good society adopts these principles of justice or those rules of neutral discourse, or it exhibits this kind of civic virtue or has this method of aggregating preferences. Utopia is an axiomatic system. Nobody actually lives there. However, I cannot think of the "good society" as an abstract proposition. I need a concrete referent.

I think I know what a good society is. I have lived in three of them: Costa Rica, Denmark, and Wisconsin. (I am sure there are many other exemplars, stretched across the globe, perhaps on every continent. But these are the ones I know—and I know two of them intimately, at the level of the soul.)

These good societies are very different. The first is Hispanic, and its standard of living is only about one-eighth that of the other two. The second is an ancient Nordic kingdom and a modern welfare state. The third is an average American Midwestern state. All are roughly the same size and population: small polities, each on the periphery of major power centers.

I shall argue that what makes these societies good is a certain state of mind and a common commitment—that quality which it is today fashionable to call "civic virtue." I think, however, that the distinguishing feature of this "virtue" is something a bit different from the qualities commonly applauded in contemporary liberal, democratic, and republican theory. It is a quality of thought more nearly political-economic than purely political. It is not quite the "public-spiritedness" celebrated by the civic republicans (though each has plenty of that). It is not precisely the instinct for neutrality and tolerance applauded by the liberals. I think it looks more like what Thorstein Veblen (1914) called "the instinct for workmanship."

To cite such matter-of-fact examples may seem a disappointing answer to the question of utopia. Is this really what all the majestic imagery and profound speculation, the deepest yearnings of our heritage of political thought come down to? I think so. I think that the daily life of the people of Costa Rica, Denmark, and Wisconsin better captures the civic ideal of the ages than do our mistily romanticized portraits of Periclean Athens, the New England town meetings, or the Swiss mountain cantons that so inspired Rousseau. To be sure, if one *suggested* to the people of Costa Rica, Denmark, or Wisconsin that they lived in ideal polities, they would respond with crude sarcasm (and that, too, would be part of their virtue). But looked at coolly and realistically, in the hard light of day, through all the long efforts of free people to govern themselves decently, this is probably about as good as it gets. The answer to our quest, then, is close at hand. We can study it at leisure and in detail. If we could *universalize* the essential traits of these polities, we would pretty well have it made.

The Political Character of the Good Society

What are the distinguishing qualities of these three polities? What is it that makes them good?

In the first place, they seem to exemplify the kind of public life that is so much commended in contemporary political theory. They are the practitioners of a robust, but unexaggerated, version of liberal democracy.

Though these practitioners do not make much of it (for they are not given to ideological ostentation), there is in such societies a general respect among persons. There is a general sense of responsibility for the fate of fellow citizens. There is also a defiant willingness to stand up for personal rights. Each is law-abiding, sometimes punctiliously so, but none could be accused of excessive deference to authority. Each is a community of individualists.

There are class distinctions in these societies, but they are of the porous kind and fundamentally democratic. The better-off are conspicuously under-ostentatious, at least by comparative standards. A lack of obsequiousness in any form is one of the more evident, and appealing, traits of each of these peoples. None deals easily with minorities in their midst. But those who would call them "racist" have not penetrated very far into their hearts.

In all three societies, there is a vital interest in the "public thing." Political talk runs constant and runs deep., It is what you hear in the cantinas of the Meseta Central, the country taverns of Boscobel and Brodhead, the cafés of Aarhus and Odense. However, these are not "participatory' or "strong" democracies. This is not at all what Pateman (1970), Barber (1984) or, in his more idealistic modes, Dahl (1979) would seem to have in mind. These people would not be enamored of attending endless meetings devoted to "undistorted communication," where each puts forward "authentic subjective feelings" about the nature of the "public good." That would take too many evenings, and it wouldn't get you anywhere. Talking politics either has to be good sport, or it has to be practical and purposeful.

There is, as I say, respect for authority. Still, it pays to keep a wary eye on public officials. One runs for office (generally) out of disgust, to "clean up the mess" and gets things running again. There is little glory—or money—in it. All three states are conspicuously lacking in corruption. The lurid details usually concern a lobbyist feeding a legislator. (A Costa Rican president was once convicted of appropriating to his own use a lamp borrowed from an agricultural experiment station. In Wisconsin, to make personal calls on state telephones can bring humiliation and disgrace.)

These are proud societies, more than a little irritating in their smug self-assurance about the righteousness of their ways. Their tolerance (and they are tolerant) is not the tolerance of the skeptic, who thinks all opinions count the same. It is, rather, the tolerance of those who understand that not as much can be expected of the others. These are people who know they have it good and are determined to keep it

that way. They are acutely conservative. They are given to long conti-
nuities in belief and practice. They are not restless experimenters or
innovators. They are also, by some lights, boring, self-satisfied, paro-
chial, and pompous; indeed, these may well be among the *essential*
traits of the good society.

The good society is, in short, a working liberal democracy. These
are reasonable approximations of the great ideal of a free, open, and
well-ordered society. These are societies in which democracy is understood to imply intelligent deliberation about public affairs—where democracy is more than interest-group bargaining, more than collusion
in bigotry or among free riders.

To be sure, my good societies will not appeal to everyone. They
reflect a predilection for what some will call "bourgeois morality." Industrial democrats will prefer Mondragon, true conservatives Haps-
burg Vienna, and socialist romantics 1960 Havana or 1969 Haight-
Ashbury. So be it. Still, if we are looking for an image of the good
society that will appeal to "the common sense of humankind" as it is
constituted today, and that will reflect our most *persistent* political ideals, I think my exemplars can fairly be said to have it all over the evident alternatives.

The Political Economy of the Good Society

So far I have discussed only the *politics* of my good societies. I have
not yet considered their *political economies*. To be sure, all three are what
might be called "centrist market economies." They are committed to
free enterprise but also to progressive regulatory, welfare, and environmental policy. None is conspicuously undergoverned according to
the current fashion. These are not libertarian utopias. But none of this
is, for me, the heart of the matter.

What does strike me as a distinctive quality of these three societies
is that things work right. Public services are reliable. Maintenance is
good. Things happen on time. (Granted there are differences here.
Costa Rica is, after all, a Third World nation and cannot afford the
level of precision in performance of Denmark or Wisconsin. Nonetheless, in comparison with other nations of its income level and cultural
heritage, the quality of education, mass transit, environmental protection, medical care, of performance generally, both in the public and
the private sector, is conspicuous.)

I want to dwell on this propensity for "good practice," for what
Veblen called "the instinct of workmanship" in my good societies. I
think it is the key to the question of what makes them good.

Just as political theorists now argue that there is more to liberal-democratic politics than procedural rules and arrangements, that good politics requires certain dispositions and attitudes widely spread out among citizens, so I would argue as a corollary that the good political economy requires more than competitive market institutions which give incentives to high production, that it implies an instinct for good practice, for quality performance in every endeavor. I think this is truly the distinguishing trait of these societies. Each of my good societies, it should be noted, is only moderately wealthy in comparative terms. What makes them *successful* as political economies has nothing to do with affluence, or with leading the international-league rankings for economic growth, productivity, or gross national product. By the standard utilitarian measures of economic success, these societies are modest also-rans. Where they stand out is in the craftsmanship of their products, the quality of their services, the skill of their workers, and the general level of well-being of their people.

I would go so far as to suggest that this ethic of good practice is really the *source* of the "civic virtue" of these polities. I think their political character is derived from their political-economic ethic rather than the other way around. *Scrupulousness* in concern for individual rights, for the universalization of basic public services, for due process of law, and for protection of health, safety, and the environment is perhaps simply an extension of scrupulousness in dairying, the manufacture of machine tools, the maintenance of automobiles, and the management of resort hotels.

I have identified a trait of the good society that is curiously neglected in our discussions of liberal-democratic politics and political economy. The reason for this, I think, is clear. An ethic of good practice requires that we talk publicly about particular goods, about performance. And pure liberalism requires neutrality among ideas of the good. Quality is not taken to be a public concern. It is in the eye of the individual, as consumer.

Let us not say that we must then choose between an ethic of good practice and liberalism. That sort of dogmatics is ruining both political and political-economic theory. Our good societies manage to have it both ways. Let us ask, rather, how we can modify liberal doctrine to account for this vital consideration.

A Touch of Aristotle

The first premise of liberalism, it is often said, is that the state should be neutral among human purposes. Rooted in Cartesian skepticism, classic liberalism holds that the individual is committed to no notion of truth or social purpose unless it is demonstrated irrefutably.

Failing that, each individual becomes an equal judge of the worth of beliefs and potential human endeavors.

The problem of political design, then, is to make sure that individual preferences count equally in establishing public ends. This is not as easy as it looks. In fact, it is something of a conjurer's trick. The object, as Rousseau ([1762] 1978, 37) put it, is that "each while joining himself with others should yet remain as free as before." This sounds a bit like the problem of squaring the circle.

In fact, it is not clear that truly neutral democracy is possible at all. If it is, its conditions are extremely demanding and are rarely found in practice. True equality of voice and vote is an extremely strenuous test of political legitimacy. Political theorists keep discovering obstacle after obstacle, ever new paradoxes of true democracy. Democratic theory is a thicket of catch-22's. We have become aware of all the enigmas related to intensity of preferences, agenda setting, and circular majorities. Now we are discovering all the problems that come with trying to specify what a truly neutral or undistorted discourse would look like.

To be sure, it is a good thing that we have finally become interested in the process of political deliberation. Democratic theory was too long concerned with the mere summing up of preferences, with a mindless, mechanical vision of democracy. It is heartening that we are now taking seriously the idea that democracy is also a process of reasoning together. However, our early doctrines of democratic deliberation seem crude and awkward. We are just beginning to notice the pitfalls that lie in wait for those who would describe the requirements of such a process. This is particularly true for those who seek pure impartiality.

The current position, usually derived from Jürgen Habermas (1971 and 1973), is that democratic deliberation must be unconstrained and unprefigured. There should be no privileged positions in the public debate. Communication should be undistorted. Each individual should have the same opportunities to put forward claims and statements, to express doubt and solidarity, to criticize and revise the positions of others. There should be no prior assumptions about the potential worth of any statement.

Now I honestly have no idea of what pure, undistorted political discourse would look like. It is not clear to me that people *can* or *should* deliberate without preconception—unless they are totally baffled, lost on an ice flow without a clue as to how they got there or where they were going. We are always deliberating about *something*. We have an object in mind. Deliberation is inherently purposive. We reason together to come to conclusions about what we should do and how we should do it. Politics is just another form of practical reason.

This means that deliberation *will* be prefigured. There will be preferred positions, tests of pertinence, appropriate method, good reasons—all determined by the logic of the purpose at hand. To be sure, it is often well worthwhile to step back from the whole affair and get a fresh perspective: "What are we trying to do here anyway?" However, the object of trying to achieve such "authentic self-consciousness," as they say in the trade, is inherently practical. This is simply part of the *method* of self-correction of practical political reason. The object of going back to first assumptions, of reexamining the question in all its details, is not to create undistorted discourse. The point precisely is to prefigure discourse on new foundations: to set up *new* assumptions and new rules of inquiry that will distinguish the pertinent from the beside-the-point, the suggestive from the foolish.

The basic problem with the proponents of the ideals of neutral, undistorted deliberation is that they take politics to be essentially *constitutive* in character. It is as though we were always going back to the original position, always reexamining anew our conception of "the public good." The problem, again, is our lingering commitment to Cartesian skepticism. We are supposed to doubt everything and keep on doubting, to start all over again on every occasion of political discourse.

Of course, as Charles Sanders Peirce (1935a) long ago pointed out, we do not think that way, either individually or collectively. We do not begin by "doubting everything." We begin "where we are"—with expectations, beliefs, and habits. It is only when these beliefs become problematic—puzzling, perplexing—that we are led to inquiry. And the object of inquiry is "the fixation of belief," the reestablishment of settled opinion or workable practice.

So we need a touch of Aristotle—an idea of *telos,* of what John Dewey called "the end in view"—if we are to develop a theory of political deliberation that is appropriate to the political economy of the good society. The rules of undistorted communication or neutral discourse, as currently discussed in democratic theory, are not only inadequate but misleading. Of course one must never "close the door to further inquiry" (Peirce 1935b, 167). But the point of that is to secure the self-corrective method of science and practical reason. The aim is not perpetual neutrality.

There is a second feature of the liberal ideal of neutrality that does not fit well with the ethic of good practice, which I think is essential to the political economy of the good society. In classic liberal thought, social arrangements, to be legitimate, must be shown to arise out of the free choices of individuals, equally considered. Contract and marketlike arrangements, in every sphere of life, are the basic building blocks of the social order, the basis of all associations and organizations. In the most traditional versions of liberalism, this settles the question of public purpose. The sole function of the state, apart from defense, is to secure the conditions of contractual probity. If government maintains the rights essential to free contract, the total social order that emerges will reflect the interests of individuals better than any conscious plan. Adam Smith provides the answer to Rousseau's question of how individuals can join with others and "yet remain as free as before."

The difficulty of this approach for a political economy that would feature the idea of good practice is clear. In classic liberal theory, the purposes of an association are taken to be the business only of those who are parties to it. The *performance* of an association (barring externalities) is of concern only to those who have a contractual relationship with it. The practices of organizations are a strictly private matter. The quality of performance is not up for public discussion and possible control. Market choice will be the arbiter of performance, and performance means nothing more than responsiveness to consumer demand.

The difficulty is that we do not believe any of this is so. We do not believe that voluntary associations have absolute license to define their own ends and assess their own performance. We do not assume that a family, or a church, or a science, is anything that the parties to a contract decide to call by that name. We believe that we are perfectly able, and entitled as a matter of political judgment, to decide what a corporation, or a union, or a school, *is* and what it is *expected to do*.

When we think of it, we find that it is quite natural for those of us who live in good, exemplary, liberal-democratic societies to deliberate publicly on the performance and the practice of our industries, our medical system, our educational and cultural institutions, just as we deliberate on the performance of the state itself. And if that deliberation is to be rational, we do have to begin with a rather high level of agreement on the "essential" aims of these "natural" associations. Thus must Aristotle be reconciled to liberalism if we are to have a sensible political economy for the good society.

Pragmatic Liberalism

A short while ago I wrote a book named *Pragmatic Liberalism* (1990). The idea was to combine liberalism's concern for nonarbitrariness and impartial principle with pragmatism's interest in purpose and performance. Thus I could generate at once a political theory, an ideal of rightful order, and a political economy, a vision of how the world's work is properly done.

The basic theme is that political deliberation does not pertain to the activities of the state alone. Every human enterprise has a political aspect. Participation in any purposive undertaking is a public responsibility, and its performance is a matter of public concern. To be sure, every liberal has an interest in the autonomy of the critical institutions of the society. But this does not mean that the character and quality of their product is a matter of public indifference or that their internal life is a strictly private affair.

Practical reason is largely a matter of the criticism of prevailing ideas of practice against standards of inherent point and purpose. One invokes questions of the ends sought as a way of provoking inquiry that will lead to the perfection of technique. In *Pragmatic Liberalism* I suggest that fundamental liberal principles represent qualities that we would see realized in diverse performances as much as they represent ends in themselves. They provide a ground for our critique.

Thus efficiency—which here means "fittedness to purpose," following John Dewey—is a remarkably apt test of how well a performance serves the overall liberal scheme of things. The aim of liberalism is to create a rational order within which individuals can lay plans and projects with a fair sense of being able to calculate their chances for success. It is for this reason that rule of law is so important to liberals and why they are so hostile to tyranny, to arbitrary and capricious authority. But if *reliability* and *nonarbitrariness* are tests of good law, so are they tests of social performance. It is our ability to *count on* the performance of law, of scientific principles, of airline schedules, supermarkets, motel chains, and surgical procedures that makes the free life possible.

Liberal principles become meaningful only in relation to an idea of purpose. Sheer economy, a concern only with maximizing production and profit, yields a tawdry liberalism when it is taken as a focal conception of purpose. But linked to efficiency, to the performance of a valued social function, economy becomes a counsel of frugality, that any practice can be improved by the elimination of waste.

Similarly, liberal justice is concerned with relevant distinction. The principle is saved from hopeless abstraction only by particularity of purpose. As a principle of compensation, liberal justice has much to do with differential reward for differential contribution to performance. As a principle of distribution, justice has much to do with the diffusion—or universalization—of specified forms of practice, such as schooling, medical care, transportation, energy. Does it take much imagination to see how these questions can give specificity and depth to a political deliberation that goes far beyond concerns for aggregating preferences, responding to demand, and maximizing utility?

My basic point in all of this is that political deliberation in the good society is centrally concerned about performance. Bad societies either are *indifferent* to performance or think that if people "mind their own business" performance will take care of itself. People in the good society are not buttinskys, but neither are they willing to let shoddiness and carelessness pass without comment on the theory that "if I leave you alone, you'll leave me alone." (Universities afford good examples of polities that operate on this principle of mutual irresponsibility.)

Thus, political discourse in the good society is not just gossip about the maneuvers and misfeasances of the powerful and the power-seeking. It is not just a matter of feuds and enmities. It is fundamentally concerned—critically and constructively—with how well things are done.

To consider the performance of enterprise as part of the "public thing" is of course to raise tricky questions about the relation of the state to economy and society. All of my good societies are liberal to the core, with a strong presumption in favor of limited government and with a free, open, and pluralistic approach to social organization. However, all three also have long activist traditions of progressive government. In none is the relation to the state and the enterprise seen as fundamentally adversarial. Rather, it is thought that the state often has a positive role to play in *enhancing* the performance of enterprise through regulation that makes best practice the norm: through incentives to innovation, inquiry, and experiment; through the universalization of practices essential to the public good and the good life. To be sure, the question of the appropriate extent of state involvement in purposive activity is a focal theme of public debate. Partisan politics turns on these issues, a perpetual confrontation of proponents of "a little more" or "a little less" along lines now well rehearsed. On the whole, our good societies tend to leave the question of the precise line between the public and private realms ambiguous. None of these societies has ever actually tried to put into practice the rigid free market or the rigid socialist doctrine, those twin impairments to intelligent political-economic deliberation and policy in this century, those twin bookends which serve only to hold up the varieties of meaningful discussion on the relations of the public and private realms.

The important point in this context, however, is that the performance of enterprise is taken to be one of the most pertinent subjects of political discussion in my good societies. The rules and expectations of discourse reinforce it. In these lands, the greatest attention and respect in discourse goes not to those who have achieved "authentic subjectivity," nor to those who can deconstruct and demystify, nor to those who speak mainly of first principles and comprehensive ideologies. Rather, it goes to those for whom the quality of the schools, the condition of the roads, the exuberance of the arts, the erosion of the fields, the competitive potential of the machine-tool industry, the sprawl of the cities, the quality of the air, or the maintenance of the bandstand in the village park really matters.

Design Principles for the Good Society

Now it is time to go behind the scenes, to move from the showroom to the machine shop. Now we must discuss how a good society might be constructed. Again, the metaphor is preposterous. Societymaking is not a bit like manufacture. But again, the heuristic might reveal something about how to tighten the rigging of ships of state already at sea. Furthermore, we *normally* think this way. It is part of our cultural heritage of political ideas. So let us ask again. What are the principles of political design? How does one go about fashioning the institutions of a good society? As far as I can tell, there are three general approaches to political architectonics.

The first is what I shall call "mechanical liberalism." This is the classic Enlightenment conception of political design, and it is so familiar that we seldom recognize how fantastic it is in its imagery of state building. Here the political order actually is visualized as a machine, and political science is portrayed as an engineering discipline. The object is to contrive mechanisms that will channel the efforts of self-interested people to do the public good, automatically and predictably. One need not reform humankind or instill civic virtue. You can take people pretty much as you find them so long as you tune up the apparatus just right. This is the object, of course, of free-market economics and the checks and balances of the U.S. Constitution. The metaphors are manifestly Newtonian. The object is to bring diverse forces into equilibrium and thus achieve a dynamic, stable order. The idea of political design is our direct legacy from the seventeenth and eighteenth centuries, still very much alive and influential. A large part of contemporary discussion—ranging from public-choice theory (and efforts to remove the paradoxes of majority voting) to "choice" in the schools—is fundamentally a matter of tinkering with the machinery, trying to perfect it, to get it to operate a little more automatically and neutrally.

The second great approach to the design of institutions for the good society is fundamentally conservative. The object is to try to preserve and protect solidarities deemed essential to an intricate, familiar, and rightful order. Political science is a matter of understanding, and preserving, the prescriptive constitution. Here, root metaphors are organic and biological rather than mechanical and physical. Constitutive political action is more like medicine than it is like engineering or architecture. The style of analysis tends more toward prophetic lament than toward ingenious contrivance. The good society, then, is a stable relationship of interdependent traditional normative orders: patterns of authority and deference, organic communities, families exhibiting specifically defined moral qualities, religious observances that instill a sense of reverence for the collectivity. The problem of political design is to sustain the institutions of the good society in the face of chronic tendencies toward decadence and disintegration.

The third approach is to stipulate neither institutions nor solidarities but, rather, the rules of discourse, a logic of inquiry. Here the good society is pictured metaphorically neither as mechanism nor organism, but as something resembling an ideal scientific society, what Peirce called a "community of inquiry."

I have already suggested that the existence of such rules of discourse, widespread expectations of the proper temper of the public debate, is the crucial element in the success of the good society. It is a way of speaking that binds a culture together. And to be sure, this "language game" promotes some values and deprecates others. The disciplines of deliberation specify the "good reasons" of the public forum. They tell us what will be taken seriously and what will be regarded as foolishness or frivolity.

It has been intellectually fashionable, ever since Plato, to disparage conventional opinion. All good liberals, with J. S. Mill, fear the deadening effect of conformity to orthodox belief. Postmodernists, with Michel Foucault and Jacques Derrida, assume that all systems of discourse are instruments of domination, intended to "normalize" humanity to the purposes of the powerful. Intellectual anarchy is in the air these days. One should be quick to spot the contingency, and the constraining force, of any method. One should applaud the maxim "Anything goes." Discourse should be undistorted and unconstrained. But all of this applies only if the dominant conventions of discourse are in fact debilitating. They might also be empowering and ennobling. They might be the very source of what is good about the good society.

My thesis throughout has been that my good societies are good because they are communities of inquiry and sound practice, with widely shared conventions of practical reason that fuse with commitments to a liberal-democratic order to form a political philosophy that is both political and political-economic in character, and that makes a way of life out of the finest political ideals of our civilization. Granted, my good societies represent all three of the principles of political design I have cited. They have formal political arrangements and market-based economies of the standard, mechanical, Enlightenment kind. They also venerate traditional institutions and regard them as essential to the persistence of their way of life. But I still think that what sets them apart is a certain way of talking about public and practical affairs. Many other societies have Enlightenment constitutions and deep commitments to tradition. El Salvador does. So do Lebanon and Louisiana. Yet such societies lack the qualities distinctive of my good societies. What else can account for the differences?

I have said that the good society rests, fundamentally, on an idea of method, on habits of thought. I shall also argue that these ways of thinking can be contrived, intentionally developed in a nation. Granted, the attitudes toward practical reason, toward taking pains, taking care, thinking things through, must have roots that tap deep into culture and history; and they must be reinforced by institutions like the family, the community, and the informal networks of life. In our good societies, these attitudes are pervasive. One runs into them everywhere. The edifying examples on which to build the conduct of one's own life are all around.

Nonetheless, these are all school-made societies. Each is distinguished for its faith in education, its investment in education. And each deems education to be centrally important, precisely as an instrument for developing the attitudes, skills, and habits of mind that a citizen should have.

The schools are but an instrument. They can teach whatever doctrines and skills a people may feel they need. And this means that the rules of discourse, the way of thinking, of a society can be an intentional act, a product of political deliberation. We can decide, within limits, on the constitutive frame of thought that will regulate and define our own affairs.

This thought also tells us something about the appropriate function of the university in the good society. For the central task of the university, through all the ages, has been to think through the rules of discourse, the best methods for the use of the powers of mind. It is the task of the university to set the standards of truth seeking for a society, to establish the criteria that will distinguish sound judgment and good sense from fantasy, illusion, and foolishness. It is also the task of the university to recommend a public philosophy. It is the work of the university to set the presumptions of the public debate (as in liberal society it is assumed that people are free to act on their own responsibility unless there is good reason to constrain them). It is the task of the university to set general standards that distinguish right from wrong, "problems" from "states of affairs," good practice from bad. The church, to be sure, plays a preeminent moral role in two of our three good societies. But it is the institutions of rational inquiry, exemplified by the university, that deliberate, stipulate, and underwrite the rules of good practice that distinguish these societies, that commend a secular ethic to the body politic for its deliberation and refinement and, finally, for propagation through the many institutions of practical inquiry and action, exemplified by the schools. All of this, the more one thinks of it, is a humbling responsibility.

Yet the upshot is that discourse in the good society is not neutral or impartial. It is intentionally distorted and dominated. It is consciously and deliberately manipulated, by premeditation, as a fundamental act of policy. These are societies that have decided to propagate the ideals of the Enlightenment, to endorse them, to declare other ways of thinking to be spurious or suspect. (Small wonder rebellion against the dominant way of life often takes the form of an affirmation of Christian fundamentalism.) These are societies that endorse the Enlightenment ideal of absolute freedom of thought, conscience, and expression. By this, however, they do not mean that all diverse points of view are deemed equally worthy. Rather, they mean that one is entitled to believe, and profess, all sorts of foolishness, so long as it has no chance of actually defining the way in which practical affairs will be conducted. (People, including the occasional Secretary of the Interior, may believe as they wish in the Second Coming, but we still base environmental policies on the longer-run expectations of the earth sciences.)

Conclusion

The ideal of political reason that I have identified as a constituent principle of the good society is an intricate and subtle habit of mind, as intricate and subtle as the dispositions of liberal democracy itself. It is purposive thinking, in Aristotle's sense, concerned with that mystical process whereby we conjure up ideas of excellence and criticize extant performance in the light of ideals. As Charles Sanders Peirce taught, it is like scientific reason—demanding resolute commitment to specific theory and technique, yet always maintaining a fallibilist sense that one might be fundamentally mistaken, that prevailing technique must always be open to reexamination and correction. Practical reason implies faith in one's own powers of analysis and judgment. But it also means that reliable knowledge is a common affair, that the test of the worth of a statement is intersubjectivity. Practical reason implies conviction, but not so much as to impair wariness and caution; doubt, but not so much as to inhibit action; trust that never overrides the commandment that one think things through for oneself; intellectual resourcefulness and self-reliance that never verges on solipsism, that always admits the shared nature of inquiry. Articulate all the other intricate facets of this habit of thought, integrate it with the suggestively similar commitments of liberal democracy, and you will have the political-economic philosophy of the good society.

REFERENCES

Anderson, Charles W. 1990. *Pragmatic Liberalism*. Chicago: University of Chicago Press.

Barber, Benjamin. 1984. *Strong Democracy*. Berkeley and Los Angeles: University of California Press.

Dahl, Robert A. 1979. "Procedural Democracy." In Peter Laslett and James Fishkin, eds., *Philosophy, Politics, and Society*. 5th ser. New Haven, Conn.: Yale University Press.

Habermas, Jürgen. 1971. *Knowledge and Human Interests*. Boston: Beacon Press.

———. 1973. *Theory and Practice*. Boston: Beacon Press.

Pateman, Carole. 1970. *Participation and Democratic Theory*. New York: Cambridge University Press.

Peirce, Charles Sanders. 1935a. "The Fixation of Belief." In *Collected Papers of Charles Sanders Peirce*. Vol. 5. Edited by Charles Hartshorne and Paul Weiss. Cambridge: Harvard University Press.

———. 1935b. "The Scientific Attitude and Fallibilism." In *Collected Papers of Charles Sanders Peirce*. Vol. 1. Edited by Charles Hartshorne and Paul Weiss. Cambridge: Harvard University Press.

Rousseau, Jean-Jacques. (1762) 1978. *On the Social Contract*. Edited by Roger and Judith Masters. New York: St. Martin's Press.

Veblen, Thorstein. 1914. *The Instinct for Workmanship*. New York: Macmillan.

CHAPTER SIX

The Constitution of a Good Society: The Case of the Commercial Republic

STEPHEN L. ELKIN

A practical man is a man who practices the errors of his ancestors.
BENJAMIN DISRAELI

POLITICAL ACTORS WHO ARE unwilling to accept major failures in their political economies must engage in good-society thinking. They must face the question of whether to pursue reform of the existing political economy within which they act or to attempt to bring a new one into being. In either case, they must consider the essential features of the regime under consideration and how to create and maintain it.[1]

The task of good-society thinking is to set out what might be called the theory of the political-economic constitution of desirable regimes.[2] Good-society thinking is an exercise in constitutional judgment. Theories of political constitution specify the particular institutions that compose a regime—those that give it its characteristic manner of working—and how they are to be related to one another. These institutions define how the people who carry on their life within the regime are to relate to one another—as they go about coping with the difficult-to-predict possibilities and problems that will arise, and the conflicts at-

A number of colleagues have helped me develop the arguments in this paper. They include Ed Haefele, Jyl Josephson, Karol Sołtan, Jennifer Hochschild, Jenny Nedelsky, and Shelly Burtt.

1. In talking about a "regime" here, as opposed to the more common term "political economy," I mean to distinguish that which *is*—the political economy—from the political-economic whole that is desired because it is just or good—the regime. Aristotle says that a regime is "the regulation of offices in a city, with respect to the way in which they are distributed, what is sovereign . . . , and what the end of each community is" (*Politics* 1289a).

2. For the sake of brevity, I will refer to such a theory as a "theory of political constitution." But there is also a substantive reason for doing so. Political regimes are composed not just of governmental institutions but of all institutions—governmental as well as economic—that shape the overall way of life of a people. To talk about the political constitution of a regime is to talk about all its constitutive institutions.

tendant on their common fate. A political constitution is composed of the modes of association a people will employ as they go about attempting to confront collective problems, cope with the conflicts that will accompany such efforts, and deal with the continuing temptation to use political institutions for political domination.[3]

In thus helping to define the terms under which people have access to one another, the political constitution of the regime helps shape the habits of mind and mores of a people. It shapes their overall way of life. "Constitution" in the sense employed here refers to the "shape," "composition," or "establishment" of a people in their political association.[4] The constitution of a regime, then, does not just set out offices and powers, the framework of government. It is more generally an "ordering" whereby the organization (order) of something gives it its constitution. A constitution thus forms a polity, enabling it to act by giving it form. A theory of political constitution defines the constitutive institutions through which a regime acts.

There are two kinds of theories of political constitution. One kind, which might be called generic theory, has as its concern the general features of the type of regime under consideration. The second kind focuses on particular attempts to create and maintain a given type of regime. This kind must modify the generic theory to take account of the history, present situation, and overall character of the people who are to operate the regime.

My principal concern here is with the generic theory of one desirable political regime—the commercial republic—although I will make some concluding comments about American efforts to realize one. I will not argue the value of such a commercial republican regime, although I am prepared to take as serious evidence of its value that it is deemed by thoughtful Americans, among others, to be a worthy object of their aspirations.[5] I also take seriously as evidence the fact that the world at the moment does not offer much in the way of successful alternative regimes. A commercial republican regime may not be the best possible regime, but that is another matter.

A commercial republican regime is a republic in the sense that the opinions of the governed will be regularly consulted and will constrain the action of the governors. Additionally, and crucially, while republican government may involve the active exercise of political authority, it must also be limited with respect to means and purposes. Republican

3. This and the succeeding paragraph is freely drawn from my "Constitutionalism's Successor" (Elkin and Soltan 1993).

4. Maddox 1982, 806–7; Cicero 1938.

5. See Elkin 1987.

government also requires limits on the exercise of private power, which is as much a threat to the ability of individuals to conduct their own lives as public power: as Madison teaches, private, factional power is a danger to individual liberty. Moreover, without limits on private power, government responsive to the opinions of the governed is effectively impossible: public authority will be used for private purposes. The regime is commercial in the sense that republican government is to be combined with an enterprise-based market system. Economic life, that is to say, will have a significant role in some form for private ownership of productive assets.

The Public Interest and Deliberation

An essential feature of the political constitution of a commercial republic is deliberative lawmaking. James Madison, one of the earliest and greatest theorists of the commercial republic, suggests why.

To begin with, Madison is clear that republican lawmaking is to include, as against deliberation, some amount of aggregation of interests: he speaks of the "aggregate interests of the community," suggesting that law in a republic should reflect in part a summation of the preferences or expressed interests of the various groups that compose the society.[6] It could hardly be otherwise in the complex heterogeneous society that any commercial republic is likely to be. Even more important, we can add, lawmaking organized around bargaining will likely lead to increases in aggregate well-being, as representatives trade off votes for items their constituents care little about for votes on matters about which they care deeply. Moreover, bargaining has the additional advantage of allowing those who are most knowledgeable, because they are most interested, to shape the legislative outcome. Bargaining may then help solve the problem of how to weight the varying intensities of citizen preferences and how to encourage the application of expert judgment where, given the complexity of modern legislation, it is likely to be in limited supply.[7]

We can plausibly say that if this were all there were to lawmaking

6. *The Federalist* no. 10 (Madison, Hamilton, and Jay 1961).

7. For different versions of the specifics of such political processes and their benefits, see the following: Banfield 1961; Haefele 1973; Lindblom 1965; and Dahl 1961. Additionally, a commercial republic will require citizens who are skilled in the judging and serving of their own interests, not least because they will need to compete in the marketplace and create the private cooperative schemes that typically will be a feature of a limited-government regime. Republican citizens will also need to be assertive and self-reliant if they are to judge their lawmakers. A politics that has room for bargaining will at the least not undercut these self-regarding virtues, and it may encourage them.

in the commercial republic, there would be little difficulty in creating the necessary institutions. For it is reasonable to suppose that, by its very nature, a commercial republic will produce legislators skilled in being attentive to the particular interests of their constituents and in the arts of trading and bargaining. For a commercial people, it will be natural to see politics as an extension of economics.

Madison explains why something more is required. He comments that

> no man is allowed to be a judge in his own cause, because his interest would certainly bias his judgment, and, not improbably, corrupt his integrity. With equal, nay with greater reason, a body of men are unfit to be both judges and parties at the same time; yet what are many of the most important acts of legislation, but so many judicial determinations, not indeed concerning the rights of single persons, but concerning the rights of large bodies of citizens?[8]

William Leggett, a passionate commentator on American politics in the Jacksonian period, makes a similar point: "Nothing could be more self-evident than the demoralizing influences of special legislation. It degrades politics into a mere scramble for rewards obtained by violation of the equal rights of the people; it perverts the holy sentiment of patriotism; it induces a feverish avidity for sudden wealth, it fosters a spirit of wild and dishonest speculation."[9] To paraphrase John Taylor of Caroline, no interest should be able to cook others in the mode most delicious to its appetite.[10]

Just as one party to a legal dispute should not be the judge of the dispute, because he or she will be biased, so in the legislative case, says Madison, the parties to a struggle over how public benefactions are to be distributed, or over what rules are to be applied for guiding public behavior, cannot justly settle these disputes among themselves or through legislators who will speak for them. They, or those who speak for them, he notes, will be inclined to settle the matter at the expense of those who are not present or represented—namely, the rest of the citizenry.

Following Madison's line of thought, we might say that citizens must rely on the legislature to speak for them as a whole in these matters. At its best, the legislature can move beyond the particular interests being promoted and invoke the principles the citizens would invoke if they had the time, resources, and skills. A legislature that is

---

8. *The Federalist* no. 10 (Madison, Hamilton, and Jay 1961).
9. Leggett, June 3, 1837, as quoted in Blau 1954.
10. Taylor 1814, 51.

composed of interest-driven representatives and that merely weighs the claims of these same interests would have a tenuous claim on the citizenry's allegiance. Its lawmaking would be, after all, merely a sorting out of things to suit the tastes of those involved. It is only when lawmaking aims at more—at stopping those who just wish to say "I want" and forcing them to offer reasons—that the citizenry as a whole might plausibly acquiesce in their requests. This is especially so when any given law is likely to be a source of significant cost to various groups of citizens. Their willingness to count law as legitimate depends, at least in part, on their belief that there are good reasons for its content, that the law in not merely the imposition of some people's preferences on others.[11]

Madison, then, goes beyond a simple assertion that republican lawmaking cannot be the mere settling of conflicts by representatives who speak only for those interests that can make themselves heard. In a more positive vein, he says that the essential task of lawmaking in a fully realized commercial republic (which he hoped America would become) was to "refine and enlarge public views" passing the peoples' "temporary or partial considerations" through the machinery of lawmaking.[12] Lawmakers—if they are properly chosen and if lawmaking itself is properly designed—would be in a position to "discern the true interest of their country and . . . [would] be least likely to sacrifice it to temporary and partial considerations."[13] In short, lawmaking would be the culmination of an effort to understand what "the comprehensive interests of the country" might be.[14] Lawmakers would render what Madison (and Hamilton) referred to as "the deliberate sense of the community."[15] These lawmakers would discern, in Madison's phrase, "the permanent and aggregate interests of the community."[16]

Madison sums up his view when he says: "The aim of every political constitution is or ought to be to first obtain for rulers men who possess most wisdom to discern, and most virtue to pursue the common good of the society; and in the next place, to take the most effectual precautions for keeping them virtuous whilst they continue to

11. To anticipate a possible objection, I am supposing here that no legislature is capable of taking account of all preferences in the manner of some Herculean utilitarian calculator, or at least not in a manner that would claim our allegiance. In short, it must choose among interests and preferences, and to do so it must employ principles and invoke reasons—at least if those subject to the law are likely to count it as legitimate.

12. *The Federalist* no. 11. For several views of Madison that parallel the one presented here, see Wills 1981; Sunstein 1988; and Muir 1982.

13. *The Federalist* no. 10 (Madison, Hamilton, and Jay 1961).

14. *The Federalist* no. 51 (Madison, Hamilton, and Jay 1961).

15. *The Federalist* nos. 63 and 71 (Madison, Hamilton, and Jay 1961).

16. *The Federalist* no. 10 (Madison, Hamilton, and Jay 1961).

hold the public trust."[17] If Madison is correct, lawmaking must in significant part be deliberative. For how else can these permanent interests be given a meaning concrete enough to inform lawmaking except through argument and discussion. But this whole line of argument would be more compelling if we could say something concrete about the permanent interests of a political community that wishes to be a commercial republic. We would then be more certain that lawmakers have something to argue about, that they are not being asked to do something that is impossible because it is impossibly vague.

We can start by noting a central feature of republican regimes— that they are regimes of limited powers and purposes, and that they must also be concerned with limits on the exercise of private power. We can be reasonably certain that the ability to define such limits—to set down compelling accounts of the limits and to revise them in light of changing circumstances and continuing inquiry—cannot be taken for granted. The kinds of institutions that will be able to do so must not only be created but maintained, their foundations made secure.

Otherwise said, if we desire a regime in which public and private power is limited, we must also desire a regime whose institutions are capable of defining those limits in compelling fashion: to desire the ends is to desire the means. This is a permanent interest of the community in the sense that for there to be a regime capable of limiting public and private power, there must be institutions of a specific kind.

To determine what those institutions are and how they are to work would require extensive discussion of the competence of courts and legislatures and of the character of practical and legal reasoning. But if it is accepted that not all the work of defining limits on the exercise of public and private power can be done by courts—a point I will make in a moment—then some of the work must be done by the legislature. This, in turn, will mean that the legislature must be capable of reasoning about the appropriate content of limits, and this leads us to a question: What will enable the legislature to so act? Part of the answer is likely to be that the citizenry must have certain abilities or virtues.[18] And this means that an essential component of the permanent interest of a republican regime is to secure those qualities of the citizenry that will enable a legislature to play its role in defining the limits on the exercise of public and private power.

A parallel argument has been made by both Samuel Huntington and Bernard Crick. Huntington comments that "the capacity to create political institutions is the capacity to create public interests," and "the

---

17. *The Federalist* no. 57 (Madison, Hamilton, and Jay 1961).
18. See the discussion on republican citizenship in the next section.

public interest is the interest of public institutions."[19] Crick says that the public interest is simply a way of "describing the common interest in preserving the means of making public decisions politically."[20] Stated most generally, a major component of the permanent interests of a political community whose citizens want a republican regime is to secure the foundations of those institutions that give the regime its essential character.

The essential character of a commercial republican regime is not exhausted by a concern for limiting the exercise of public and private power. Nor, then, are its permanent interests. It is, after all, a commercial republic. At a minimum, this means that republican lawmaking should aim to promote material prosperity through an organization of wealth production that has a significant role for private ownership of productive assets and for markets. On balance, lawmaking should support and encourage private ownership of productive assets; among other things, this means taking account of the fact that if there is to be significant material prosperity, controllers of productive assets must have considerable discretion in how they deploy those assets. Without such discretion, they are unlikely to invest at a level that will promote significant material prosperity: without the possibility of pursuing sizable economic rewards, controllers of productive assets will consume them, send them abroad, save, or engage in some combination of the three.[21]

Not only will controllers of productive assets need discretion, they will also require stability in the rules that govern economic life. A central purpose of a commercial republic is widespread prosperity; without stable expectations among asset-holders on the content of economic rules, this is unlikely to be achieved. Whatever else those with capital need, they need some sense of what the near-term future will bring. This is as true of those who are thinking about investing in new plants and equipment as it is of those who are thinking of improving their skills through education. If they cannot form reasonable expectations about the near future, they cannot plan. And if they are even modestly rational, they will not entertain even relatively small costs for such uncertain future gains.

Stability of rules, however, cannot mean simply strengthening the rules that happen to exist at present. Those who run businesses are upholders of profits, not of competition, and they will naturally enough argue for the sanctity of the existing rules under which they

19. Huntington 1968, 25.
20. Crick 1972, 177.
21. Lindblom 1977, chap. 13; Elkin 1987, chap. 7.

have fattened their pocketbooks. Those businessmen who seek to innovate and those who have yet to appear on the scene may thus face considerable obstacles.[22] Republican lawmaking, while it must certainly aim at promoting economic prosperity in the present, must also, if it is to promote long-term prosperity, enact laws that keep paths open for new businesses and new techniques. Republican lawmaking must not sacrifice a vibrant competition to a desire to increase the comfort of present-day major asset-holders, under the supposition that those who are now significant contributors to national prosperity will remain so. Instead, law should aim at facilitating the commercial activity of all who have the means and desire to participate.

There is at least one other component of the commercial dimension of a commercial-republican political community's permanent interests. A well-functioning commercial republic is composed of a citizenry whose able-bodied members are all capable of securing at least modest levels of economic welfare through remunerative work. This extends the thought behind Publius's (Hamilton and Madison's) argument that a commercial society is necessary for republican government: the fruits of economic growth should be available to more than a few, and economic production should not be in the service of creating an oligarchy with the status and material comforts of an aristocracy.[23]

In the most fundamental sense, the law of commerce in a republican regime is not law for the express purpose of promoting the fortunes of businessmen—at least not the fortunes of present businessmen to the exclusion of those to come, and not the fortunes of businessmen present or future to the exclusion of others who can help create widespread prosperity. More generally, law cannot be used as a means of creating a society built around inherited economic privilege if that law is to be commercial republican law. For commercial republican law is in the service of republican government and, in this sense, is political law and not economic law.

These various institution-building and commercial interests are permanent interests of the political community, either because they concern the defining purposes of the regime—widespread prosperity and a significant role for private ownership of productive assets—or because they are needed to make the regime work in ways necessary for a republican regime to survive.[24] They are valuable, then, quite

---

22. Stigler 1975.

23. See the discussion in Elkin 1987, chap. 6.

24. Widespread material prosperity and a nontrivial role for private ownership of productive assets are permanent interests of the community for both reasons.

apart from whether their value is widely recognized by the citizenry. They are in the interests of republican citizens insofar as those citizens want a republican regime—even as they may be unable to say just what that entails by way of lawmaking.

Republican lawmaking must not only concern itself with the permanent and aggregate interests of the community: it must also define the substance of the limits on public and private power.[25] It must not be concerned only with the ability of institutions to define these limits, but also with the substance of the limits themselves. Giving meaning to these limits is also a defining characteristic of a republican regime.

Taken together, the permanent interests of the community and a concern for limits on public and private power may be said to compose the *public interest* of a commercial republican regime. If a citizenry aspires to a commercial republican way of life, a regime that realizes that aspiration must be in the citizenry's interest. It is in their interest as members of a political community: it is their common or public interest. These interests, however, are public interests not because they are actively held and articulated by the citizenry, but because they are intrinsic to the workable commercial republican regime to which they aspire.[26]

In broadest terms, the public interest of a republican regime consists of securing and expanding the capabilities of those political institutions that speak for the people to do the following: (1) reason about and set down the appropriate limits on the exercise of public and private power; (2) promote material prosperity through an organization of economic life that both has a significant role for private ownership of productive assets and provides widespread remunerative work. The public interest may then point either to conserving and strengthening existing institutions or to a need to reform them drastically. It is thus neither inherently conservative nor radical.

The emphasis in this definition of the public interest is on creating and maintaining institutions that give the regime its characteristic manner of working—institutions that enable it to pursue its essential

25. For now, I will not say anything more than I already have about the aggregate interest of the community. A comprehensive theory of political constitution, though, would have to say more not only about the meaning of the aggregate interests of the community but also about how those aggregate interests are to be related to its permanent interests and to the limits on the exercise of public and private power. The theory would also need to address how the central institutions of the regime are to be structured so that they can deal with the connections between these three concerns of republican lawmaking.

26. Lawmaking that undercuts the public interest, then, is arbitrary at best, tyrannical at worst.

tasks of defining the limits on public and private power and promoting widespread material prosperity through an enterprise-based market system. The definition also makes it clear that the task is, in part, a reflexive one. The institutions that are to reason about the concrete meaning of limits need to attend to their own ability to do so. Lawmaking in the public interest is also essentially constitutive, securing the foundations of the institutions that give the regime its essential character.

It is crucial to see that the public interest of a commercial republican regime is not exhausted by the concern to limit the exercise of power. Once we recognize that an effort must be made to secure and expand the ability of institutions to reason about these matters and to promote material prosperity, the way is open for the active exercise of governmental power. The problem for lawmaking in the public interest is to tie the active exercise of governmental power to a conception of limits that is not simply an arbitrary imposition on what the people and those who speak for them may do. The concept of the public interest that I have sketched out defines the basic concerns of such an active, limited government—and, indeed, it is difficult to see how else, except through such a conception of the public interest, the ideas of active and limited government can be combined. Republican governments can be active in the pursuit of that which will secure and expand their ability both to consider the appropriate limits on public and private power and to promote widespread material prosperity through an economy that has a significant component of private ownership. Effective government, then, is government that makes progress in securing the foundations of institutions able to so reason.

Evidently there is no one right answer to the content of the public interest in a commercial republic—not over time and not at any given moment. Indeed, if there were one correct answer, then a theory of political constitution would need to address only one question: Who is likely to know the true content of the public interest? Then power could be given to these republican philosopher kings. However, the features of the public interest that I have identified are broadly defined and can thus be interpreted and brought together in different ways. Among other things, particular circumstances will affect how this is to be best accomplished. The weight to give to the components of the public interest cannot be thought about in the abstract.

The public interest is capacious. A narrowly conceived one could hardly serve in any complex and heterogeneous society. But "capacious" does not mean "empty." The public interest is broad enough to invite discussion and clear enough to indicate what kind of arguments are appropriate in defining its concrete meaning. Thus, it is plain that arguments for the passage of a law that simply assert that it will be in the interests of major constituencies are not arguments in the public interest, nor are arguments that all those affected by the law should receive something like equal benefits.[27]

While there is, therefore, no right answer to the appropriate content of the public interest, there are wrong answers. The public interest points to the kind of reasons that are to count in lawmaking. It is not, then, an empty honorific to invoke whenever we wish to argue for the use of public authority for reasons that are not in themselves likely to be convincing.

There is nothing particularly strange about a commercial republic—or, for that matter, any good regime—having a public interest. Madison was not a victim of intellectual slovenliness, as some midcentury sophisticates of American political science assumed when they encountered his work or that of anyone who supposed there was any such thing as a commercial republic with a public interest. Surely, they implied, Madison could not really have meant what he said. But all we need remember is that political regimes rise and fall, that effort can plausibly be expended to encourage the first and forestall the second, and that institutions capable of reasoning about the limits of public and private power and promoting material prosperity are desirable. If all this is conceded, then we are well on our way to understanding the public interest of the commercial republic.

Deliberative Ways of Lawmaking

There is no presumption in this discussion that the public interest is free of internal conflicts. There will, for example, likely be conflicts between the discretion that asset-controllers need and the economic foundations of republican citizenship. Nor is there any presumption that there are no difficulties in giving concrete meaning to the public interest, or that the institutions that will need to give it content will find it politically easy to do so. These are real difficulties, and designing institutions to meet them is a principal task of the theory of political constitution of a commercial republic.

I have now, however, said enough about the contours of the public interest to begin a discussion of the *design* of these republican institutions. If the central task of republican lawmaking is to give concrete meaning in particular cases to the set of components that constitute the public interest, then those who engage in lawmaking must be capa-

---

27. Such arguments are appropriate, however, for lawmaking concerned with the *aggregate* interests of the community.

ble of practical reasoning. They must be capable of arguing about how these components are to be brought to bear in particular choices. They must, in short, be able to deliberate.

One possibility for the design of institutions capable of deliberation is a simple division of labor between a high court and a legislature, the former dealing with the definition of limits on the exercise of public and private power and the latter with the permanent interests of the regime. I have implied that such an arrangement is unworkable and unattractive, but it will help to clarify the whole question of institutional design if the reasons are made explicit.

First, if it is accepted that the legislature must play a role in defining the limits of public and private power,[28] it follows that the character of the citizenry that chooses the members of the legislature must be a crucial concern of lawmaking in the public interest. Now a high court plausibly can have much to say about, for example, the prerogatives and responsibilities of citizenship. But that court is unlikely either to be interested in or compelling in its remarks about, say, the question of whether republican citizenship requires a certain distribution of wealth or employment. On the broad relation between citizenship and the organization of productive life, a high court can have no privileged view, while a legislature in principle can have an informed opinion. In the decisions concerning how to secure the foundations of the constitutive institutions of the regime, both legislature and court must play a role.

Second, in regard to promoting widespread economic prosperity through an enterprise-based market system, a high court will have important things to say because the question of property rights will inevitably arise; but there should be little doubt that a legislature must also have a significant role. Once again, the ability of the legislature to reason—this time about the appropriate arrangements of economic life—is at issue. Obviously again, political questions are at stake: once more, these have to do with the qualities necessary in the citizenry as well as how to restrain organized business from subverting legislative efforts to define the best market arrangements for promoting general

28. See the argument to this effect below. To avoid confusion, it is important to see that there are two different questions under consideration: (1) which institutions are to give definition to the limits on public and private power, and thus what is involved in securing the foundations of such institutions, and (2) which institutions are actually to work to secure those foundations. It will help here to notice that the matter is partly a reflexive one: for example, the legislature is to play a role in defining limits, and the same legislature must secure its own ability to do so. There is nothing mysterious about this. The legislature is concerned both with defining limits and securing the permanent interests of the regime.

prosperity. In short, both legislature and court will need to be concerned with how best to serve the economic dimension of the community's permanent interests.[29]

Third, in giving content to the limits of public and private power, a high court can draw on a long and sophisticated tradition of what those limits ought to be. But, again, a high court can have no privileged view of the problem. Although the matter is exceedingly complex, consider that on the question of limits to public power, some of the rights that are adduced—those that we might call "primary political rights," such as freedom of speech and assembly, are best understood as the conclusions of political thought and observation concerning the requirements of popular government.[30] There is little specifically legal about the matter. In much the same way, consider that freedom of religion almost certainly grew out of similar political reflection on the need to keep religion off the political agenda of popular regimes.[31] As for property rights, since the question of their appropriate definition is deeply bound up with questions of economic efficiency, political justice, and the character of good political regimes, it is difficult to see just how one could sustain a case that legal reasoning should here have a privileged status. As regards limits on private power, consider that the issue of the political prerogatives of business corporations—Are they to be treated as fictive persons?—can be settled by a court engaging in what is usually thought of as *legal* argument only if the whole question of the *political* power of business is largely ignored.

Fourth, and perhaps simplest of all, because the various dimensions of the public interest are intertwined, there cannot be any straightforward division of labor between court and legislature. It is hard to imagine how any careful discussion of the ability of the legislature to consider the way to promote widespread economic prosperity will not become entangled with the question of limits on the political power of business. Similarly, discussion of what kind of citizenry would be needed to enable a legislature to consider limits on public and private power will become entangled in questions of the prerogatives of private property.

Thus, in the effort to give concrete meaning to the public interest

29. Again, it will help to bear in mind that there are two questions here: (1) which institutions are to decide on how to interpret the permanent interests of the regime—how to promote widespread economic prosperity through an enterprise-based market system—and (2) which institutions are to secure the ability to do so.

30. See Dahl 1985, 21–31; Sunstein 1988.

31. See Judith Shklar, "The Liberalism of Fear" (Rosenblum 1989).

of a commercial republic, consideration of the full range of its components must be undertaken by both legislature and court.

I want now to concentrate on the legislature as a deliberative body, since we know more about courts in this regard. It is relatively clear what deliberation entails in a high court: after all, such a court is likely to be designed so that its judges conduct their business through an exchange of highly crafted arguments. As for what enables courts to so deliberate, the answer is in effect the history of the development of the idea and practice of an independent judiciary.[32]

What does it mean for a legislature to engage in deliberative ways of lawmaking?[33] We can follow Madison's suggestion that what is crucial is a disposition to think about public matters in terms of how they might affect one's country as a whole, instead of solely in terms of one's own interest or the interest of some particular group in the society. As Arthur Maass says, legislators must have "breadth of view."[34] The key, then, is the question "What is the public interest here?" rather than simply "What is my or our group's interest?" Lawmakers must try to answer the implicit question posed by any piece of legislation—Is it in the public interest?—by *discussing* it. That is to say, they will argue, adduce evidence, point to comparable cases, etc.,[35] and general ideas about "what constitutes good public policy" will be "important in determining the results of the process."[36] As William Galston says, lawmakers must possess "deliberative excellence."[37]

Agreement, of course, may not result from such efforts at deliberation. Bargains will then have to be struck and trades arranged. This can be an extension of the deliberative process so long as the compromised items are versions of the public interest. That is the crucial point. It is not desirable to have lawmakers attempting unaided heroic

32. For a small sample of the very large number of treatments of this matter, see McIlwain 1947; Corwin 1955; and Berman 1983. Since both high court and legislature—not to mention the executive and the bureaucracy—will need to be involved in giving concrete meaning to the public interest, a theory of political constitution will need, as I have said, an account of the relations between institutions involved in lawmaking.

33. I have here expanded my discussion in "The Good Society and the Commercial Republic" (Redner 1993).

34. Maass 1983, chap. 1.

35. See the discussion by Karol Sołtan where he characterizes the process described here as one in which resources are "attached" to alternatives, not to actors. In short, collective decisionmaking will be shaped not by the resources that the parties to the choice can bring to bear but by the various kinds of "reasonableness" displayed by the alternatives. See Sołtan, "Generic Constitutionalism" (Elkin and Sołtan 1993).

36. Kelman 1987, 208.

37. Galston 1988, 1284.

feats of discernment with respect to the content of the true public interest, as if lawmaking in the public interest were an exercise in logically deducing conclusions from first principles. It is not likely that anyone will succeed in convincingly pulling off such a feat, even if attempting it were desirable. If this were the only alternative to simple trading of votes, then vote trading is all we would have and it would be preferable.

By contrast, in deliberative ways of lawmaking, the question—What is in the public interest?—is not an abstract one with the answer waiting to be discovered. Instead, lawmakers will start from what they believe are the policy views and interests of their constituents as modified by their own views on the matter. They have, after all, run for election, and in the process will undoubtedly have articulated some policy preferences to which substantial numbers of voters will have given their assent. The crucial point is how they go about arguing for and making sense of their initial positions.

Lawmakers, in fact, must *understand* these to be their *initial* positions. These are *partial* viewpoints that will be subject to expansion and revision, especially as lawmakers, alone and in common, try to reconcile their positions with the broad principles of the public interest as I have set them out.[38] Such policy positions, then, are not to be counters in a trading game, but partial, tentative answers to the question, What is in the public interest?

Lawmakers who stand in relation to each other as deliberators will then have a disposition to reach beyond that to which they are already committed, to revise these initial positions in light of argument and evidence. They do this because, among other reasons, they believe that law and policy involve a search for the concrete meaning of the public interest. They may start with self and group interest—indeed, I have said that they should and undoubtedly will—but that is not where they stop. For them there is no simple juxtaposition of private and public interest, as if the latter were wholly distinct from the former. Their commitment to the public interest is not a pledge to remain unacquainted with private interest but, rather, a promise to engage in a deliberative process that transforms such interests.

Deliberative lawmakers will offer *reasons* for their positions. But lawmaking is not to be some counterpart to a debating society where great speeches are delivered by modern-day Pericles. Because widespread agreement on important legislative measures is not likely to emerge quickly or easily, but must be built up from diverse starting

---

38. In saying this, I do not mean to imply that I have exhausted all discussion of the components of the public interest.

points, for such lawmakers the premium will be less on oratory and more on drawing out and reconciling various policy positions. Similarly, there will also be a premium on forming a group of people who work together over time to give patient attention to some problem and who will then be able to implement the "train of measures"[39] that is necessary to give concrete meaning to the public interest.

What is wanted, then, is a kind of "principled inclusivity" on the part of lawmakers, a disposition to attend to diverse views and to make an effort to reconcile them. The effort is one of trying to forge new principles out of the conflicts between old ones, of adjusting principles to facts—in short, it is what people do when they reason together. In this sense, little more is being asked of lawmakers than what ordinary citizens are capable of at their best.

Now it is not necessary or possible for the legislature to act as a deliberative body all the time. Not all legislation raises the question of the public interest. Some at least is concerned with the aggregate interests of the community. But it would be a grave mistake to believe that it is unheard of for lawmaking to be deliberative—a fantasy of the political theorist as utopian republican. Legislatures widely counted as "good" by both observers and participants act in the ways described here at least some of the time.[40] The problem, then, is not that something impossible is being called for. It is instead one of getting something good to happen with greater regularity. Put in the most modest way, the problem is to see that simple vote trading—or, what is worse, constant efforts to extract votes by the exercise of power—is not the dominant form of lawmaking.

It may be a sign of the times that anyone would feel compelled to offer such an elaborate description of deliberative ways of lawmaking. Many will simply assume that this is the way it is supposed to be—and sometimes is.[41] Their assumption probably stems from an intuition of what lawmaking would look like if it were not concerned with serving the public interest. Even in the most benign version of such lawmaking, where legislators are concerned only with reelection, the temptation to plunder the public treasury in order to spread the booty among

39. *The Federalist* no. 63 (Madison, Hamilton, and Jay 1961).

40. For some evidence, see Muir 1982.

41. Perhaps we think that such deliberative modes of association are difficult or impossible to make work because we have been taught by our social science to expect people typically to act in narrowly self-interested ways. But we take this teaching seriously, if we do, partly because we have in our heads rather high-flown abstract visions of what a deliberative mode of association would look like. If instead we picture patient attention to facts and the exercise of reasoning, the prospect does not look so daunting, at least if the people and circumstances are right.

constituents would be difficult to resist.[42] To this would likely be added the kind of behavior that past majority leader of the U.S. Senate says is already widespread: when it comes time to vote, lawmakers remark to one another, "Watch out for this one, guys; this could really be made into an effective 30-second [television] spot."[43]

Promoting Deliberation

While a republican legislature must be designed to accommodate particular interests—it is after all a representative institution—it must be capable of deliberation about the content of the law. It cannot be just the home of particular interests, of skilled bargainers working to aggregate the particular interests of the community.[44]

Will lawmakers as a matter of course have the disposition to act in deliberative ways? Perhaps. But most lawmakers inclined to deliberate will not be possessed by civic virtue.[45] Some indeed may display "a disinterested attachment to the public good, exclusive and independent of all private and public attachments."[46] For the most part, though, this is neither desirable nor possible—especially because in a commercial republic there cannot and ought not be so sharp a line between public and private interest. Yet it *is* possible for them to show that modicum of attachment to the public interest that is characteristic of all decent people in not utterly wretched regimes. For these lawmakers, however, such attachment to the public interest will be insufficient to generate a consistent and ample disposition to engage in delibera-

---

42. See William Muir's comments (1982, 183), where he is considering David Mayhew's argument in *Congress: The Electoral Connection.*

43. George J. Mitchell, as quoted in the *New York Times,* March 19, 1990.

44. It is no small question just how deliberation and aggregation are to be combined in the legislature. This is surely one of the questions that a comprehensive theory of political constitution must answer. I have already said that lawmakers will bargain and trade when the warrant of reason runs out, and that deliberation and bargaining cannot be wholly distinct processes, at least if both take account of particular interests. I will add only that in a well-functioning commercial republic there will be less aggregation of interests through lawmaking than is sometimes supposed. Much can and will need to be done outside of political institutions, however, not least through markets.

45. It is worth remarking here that even those inclined to doubt that there is anything for lawmakers to deliberate about or that such a thing is possible—i.e., those who insist that the fundamental legislative act is one of interest aggregation—end up by saying that officials in republican regimes must have meaningful attachments to *some* standards of behavior, to something other than advancing their own interests or those of their constituents, narrowly understood. It appears to be difficult to give an account of republican government without making room for the idea of the public interest. In quite different veins, see Buchanan 1986 and Dahl 1961, chaps. 27–28.

46. Carter Braxton, Williamsburg, Va., 1776, as quoted in Wood 1969, 96.

tive ways of lawmaking. They are not, after all, likely to be Solons. To the contrary, they will be ordinary people who will act in deliberative ways, if at all, for the same reason that most people do—because it will be personally rewarding to do so. They will be self-interested.

But their self-interest is unlikely to be narrowly construed and will probably include a desire to be held in esteem by their colleagues for showing great knowledge of public matters and a concern for the public interest. In addition, lawmakers will likely be motivated by fear of being revealed by their legislative adversaries as ignorant and in the pocket of special interests. They will also find satisfaction in the prospect for political advancement that a reputation for being devoted to the public interest and knowledgeable about public affairs will bring.

The motives just outlined might be harnessed by the legislature: it can be a school for learning the arts of deliberative lawmaking.[47] Much can be done in this way.[48] But it is doubtful that alone the legislature-as-school can engender the necessary habits and dispositions. Moreover, the legislature must have the right pupils to begin with; otherwise it will fail in its teaching. Indeed, it cannot be the proper sort of school without the right teachers—and who are they but legislative leaders who are willing to organize a legislature that encourages deliberation? A legislature largely composed of abject mediocrities cannot by some hidden hand turn itself miraculously into a lawmaking body of great distinction. John Stuart Mill tartly said in this regard that "a school of legislative capacity is worthless, and a school for evil, instead of good, if through want . . . of the presence within itself of a higher order of character, the action of the body is allowed, as it so often is, to degenerate into an equally unscrupulous and stupid pursuit of self-interest of its members."[49]

Additional, and crucial, incentives for deliberative ways of lawmaking must come, then, from the citizenry—and they must reward through reelection those who evidence a disposition to deliberate. Some students of republican government have argued that legislative lawmakers "should not reflect those who choose them"[50]—implying that the lawmakers will somehow be a cut above those who elect them. But this leaves unanswered how citizens are able to rise above their

---

47. "In a good legislature, most members acquire what James Madison called the three competencies of democratic leadership: patriotism, love of justice, and wisdom" (Muir 1982; see also Malbin 1987).

48. See the remarkable account of the California State Legislature in Muir 1982.

49. In Mill 1991, 417.

50. Walter Berns, "Does the Constitution Secure These Rights" (Goldwin and Schambra 1980, 67). See also the comments by Wilmore Kendall, quoted in Wills 1981.

inadequacies in judging those who are to represent them. However unsettling the thought, the citizens of a commercial republic must be in their own way as capable as its lawmakers. They must have those qualities of judgment that allow them to say who among the prospective lawmakers understand lawmaking to be, in significant part, a deliberative process and who will have either the skills necessary to make it so or the inclination to learn those skills.[51] It is in the combination of the legislature as school and the capacity for judgment by the citizenry that the hope for lawmaking in the commercial republic lies.

Not surprisingly, then, the commercial republic, being a republic, stands or falls on the qualities of its citizens. No amount of mechanical contrivance can make up for a citizenry that cannot judge the qualities of its lawmakers. Madison put it this way:

> But I go on this great republican principle, that the people will have the virtue and intelligence to select men of virtue and wisdom. Is there no virtue among us? If there be not, we are in a wretched situation. No theoretical checks, nor form of government, can render us secure. To suppose any form of government will secure liberty or happiness without any virtue in the people, is a chimerical idea. If there be sufficient virtue and intelligence in the community, it will be exercised in the selection of these men, so that we do not depend on their virtue, or put confidence in our rulers, but in the people who are to choose them.[52]

Elsewhere Madison simply comments that

> in bestowing the eulogies due to the partitions and internal checks of power, it ought not the less to be remembered, that they are neither the sole nor the chief paladium of constitutional liberty. The people, who are the authors of this blessing, must also be its guardians.[53]

How will the citizens learn to make the necessary distinctions? The political constitution of the commercial republic must make provision for their education as well. Some assumptions first need to be made about these citizens. Even to get started on the project of fostering

51. Jefferson said simply that it was the task of the citizenry to engage in the "free election and separation of the *aristoi* from the *pseudoaristoi*" (Thomas Jefferson to John Adams, as quoted in Mason 1965, 385).

52. James Madison, June 20, 1788, as quoted by Ann Stuart Diamond, "Decent Even Though Democratic" (Goldwin and Schambra 1980, 38). For a modern statement, see Galston 1988.

53. James Madison, "Government of the United States," in *The Papers of James Madison*, ed. Hutchinson and Rutland et al., as quoted in Lance Banning, "Some Second Thoughts on Virtue and the Course of Revolutionary Thinking" (Ball and Pocock 1988, 208).

certain qualities of citizen judgment, we must assume that a significant number of citizens have some inclination to judge political life in terms of interests and concerns larger than their own and those of their immediate circle. They may be only weakly inclined, but the disposition cannot be absent. They may also have only the weakest idea about how to go about such judging and about what its content should be, but there must be something to build on. Political life can only reinforce or diminish what is already present, not create dispositions out of nothing. What is wanted, then, is a mode of association among citizens that, by giving expression to such public-regarding sentiments, reinforces them and, by allowing them exercise, permits the citizenry's powers of judgment to be refined. What mode of association is this, and where is it to be found or constructed?

The citizens of a republican regime must have the experience of deliberating and struggling over the content of the public interest if they are to judge the inclinations and capacities of their lawmakers. If they are to develop the capability to distinguish deliberative-minded lawmakers devoted to the public interest from cynical hacks, they must themselves have some experience of trying to answer the question, "What is the public interest in this case?" Since, in the nature of the case, this will be a complicated matter to judge, and since the incentive to dissemble, for present as well as aspiring lawmakers, will be great, an inexperienced citizenry will be easily misled and will make the gravest mistakes. As V. S. Naipaul says, "When men cannot observe they don't have ideas: they have obsessions."[54] If we substitute "participate in deliberative processes" for "observe," the possibility for mischief and worse becomes apparent.

Experience in deliberation is the teacher of citizen judgment. But where is the experience to come from, and how are the necessary skills to be honed? The answer, long posited by republican theorists, is *local government*.[55] A crucial component of the theory of the political constitution of the commercial republic, then, must be its design for local government.

Local political institutions must accommodate the following features in their design. First and foremost, local political institutions must place citizens in relation to each other as deliberators, as persons who think that a crucial feature in decisions about public choice is the giving of reasons.[56] Where possible, the making of public choices should elicit arguments about what is beneficial to the members of the com-

---

54. Quoted in Shattuck 1989, 5.
55. For example: Mill (1861) 1974, 181; Tocqueville (1835) 1945, bk. 1.
56. Here I draw freely on Elkin 1987, chap. 8.

munity; it should not just reflect the summation of wants and interests. It follows that local political institutions must be open and participative in their operations, for each citizen must be a prospective deliberator. In a word, local political institutions must be heavily legislative in form.

Second, it is one thing to say that institutions must emphasize deliberation and the giving of reasons. It is another to get them to actually work that way. Institutions, after all, are not bits of machinery but are forms of human interaction, and so we must consider what kinds of motives can be at work to allow them to function in the desired ways. In the context of a commercial republic, we must look to the harnessing of powerful private motives, as against some abstract concern for the public good. For ordinary citizens, political argument about the public interest must concern such things as neighborhood matters, schools, the land-use patterns of their localities, and public safety.

The collective choice literature, however, teaches that purposes or goals by themselves are unlikely to be sufficient motivation, even if they have some direct connection to self-interest.[57] This means that additional motives are necessary to get republican citizens involved in giving content to the public interest—and, once again, these motives must be private-regarding. As an example, citizens can be drawn to reason giving and deliberation out of a concern for enjoying the esteem of others. Concern for the esteem of others, as Tocqueville pointed out, is a powerful motive in all popular regimes.[58]

Regard for the esteem of others and a connection to vital day-to-day interests are motives that can, in principle, be harnessed in the context of local political life. Indeed, this is probably the only context where such private-regarding motives can be systematically employed in ways that will lead commercial republican citizens to engage in a deliberative politics.

There is no doubt that relying on the structure of local politics to foster public-spiritedness has its difficulties. Not the least of these is that the political constitution will rest on a set of political experiences that is several steps removed from a consideration of the public interest of the republic as a whole. The principal experience of deliberation for most citizens will be one concerning the content of the local public interest. Still, there seems to be no way around relying heavily on local political life if a commercial republic requires that a significant number of its citizens have the direct experience of a politics oriented to the public interest. Nor is this just a case of there being nothing else to rely on. At its best, local political life can do valuable work: it can develop a

57. The classic exposition is Olson 1977.
58. See the discussion of Tocqueville in Diggins 1984.

sense of what it is like to struggle with questions like those that national lawmakers must face—and thus what kinds of evasions are likely, what ploys are used to cover up laziness and abject self-interest, and what sort of clues identify who is really inclined toward deliberative law-making.

Third, a deliberative mode of association must rest on a foundation of mutual respect among citizens. Unless citizens regard each other as equals, they are unlikely to deliberate, whatever the formal rules of the institution might require. Mutual respect is the minimum form equality must take, and it can be roughly understood as respect for persons as against abilities or attainments. Mutual respect is especially important if the natural inequality of reasoning ability—and reasoning is the center of deliberation—is not to subvert the education of judgment that is to flow from participation.

The principal sources of mutual respect lie outside local politics. Local political life can have some effect on it, however, if only by preventing material inequality from being added to unequal reasoning ability. If these two forms of inequality are conjoined, then the sense of equality that underlies mutual respect probably cannot be achieved.[59] Material equality may also have the positive effect of enhancing mutual respect, as visible signs of equality may bolster what is essentially a moral assessment. Thus, the design of local political institutions must also attend to the problem of material equality. At a minimum, local political life must be so designed that its outcomes do not exacerbate any existing material inequalities. More ambitiously, local political life must, if possible, actively promote equality.

How much material equality is necessary to sustain mutual respect? Perhaps a modest amount will suffice—more than, say, characterizes the United States but less than any strong egalitarian standard would call for. The prospects for a deliberative local politics turn very much on how stringent a standard must be met, for anything like strong material equality will be difficult or impossible to achieve within the minimum requirement of a commercial republic—that is, within some form of the private ownership of productive assets.[60]

59. There is an additional question here. Can mutual respect flourish in the context of private control of productive assets—that is to say, where there is a division between owners and workers? Even if such a system could be arranged so that it generated high levels of material equality, would the divisions created by ownership itself create insurmountable barriers?

60. There are, of course, various possible ways to organize the private control of productive assets. We are not bound to the present ways of doing things, if for no other reason than because we have not always organized private control in the present fashion. Still, there remains the question of how much material equality can be generated from any version of such a system. One path along which this discussion has proceeded is the design of self-generating systems of equality. See, for example, Meade 1965 and Dahl 1985.

How much mutual respect is needed? If a commercial republic needs very substantial displays of mutual respect among the citizens of its localities, then the chances for success are small. If, on the other hand, mutual respect can be built upon modest displays—of the kind readily to be found among decent people who are encouraged to act in mutually respectful ways by, for example, some measure of material equality—then the prospects are brighter.

In addition to the design of local government, at least four other features of the political constitution of a commercial republic are relevant to the fostering of public-spiritedness.

1. In fostering public-spiritedness through local political life or through other means, a republican constitution must not rely on a tutelary approach. Since government must be limited, learning must be, for the most part, indirect—reinforcing through the experience of political life what is learned in the home, school, neighborhood, and church.

   To say that republican government is limited government, however, is not the same as saying that it must not "intervene" in the private sphere. For the fostering of public-spiritedness is a legitimate concern of republican government—unless we suppose that friends of such government can be indifferent to whether public-spiritedness is present in sufficient degree, or that public-spiritedness will always be sufficiently present without any sustained governmental attention to its sources. But while fostering public-spiritedness is an appropriate exercise of public authority in a republican regime, some ways of doing so are not: for example, through governmentally imposed penalties for insufficient display or through spying on citizens to determine whether they actually are public-spirited.

2. A principal source of public-spiritedness in a commercial republic is likely to be civil society—that which is public but not of the state. Without a vital civil society, it seems unlikely that citizens can learn the distinction between public and private interest. If the only way that citizens can try to give concrete meaning to public interests is through participation in government, then the prospects for a successful republican regime are poor. Fortunately, various kinds of civic associations can both provide an opportunity to understand the value of transforming the private interest into public interest and show the means by which this can be done.

3. Any account of how republican citizenship is to be fostered

must consider the powerful effects of modern mass media. If the messages of the media undercut the virtues of republican citizenship, a republican regime will be difficult to sustain.

4. Any account of republican citizenship must take into consideration the following two features of modern societies: (a) their inhabitants are mobile, changing residence and workplace with a frequency which suggests that the required hold on them of local institutions will not be easy to achieve; (b) their inhabitants are heterogeneous, by gender, region, race, ethnicity, and sexual orientation, and thus republican citizenship must have room for what has been called the "politics of difference."

A final point to make about republican citizenship is that a public-spirited citizenry is simultaneously one of the foundation of a deliberative-minded legislature and one of the principal objects of its concern. It is both cause and effect. As I have said, lawmaking in the public interest must be reflexive: the legislature is trying to lift itself up by its own bootstraps. It must attempt to secure those conditions that will prompt it to take seriously the need to focus on those same conditions. Is such a thing possible? That it is difficult few will deny. To think it uncommon, however, is a mistake. Some circles are virtuous, a series of reciprocal, mutually reinforcing interactions. But what gets the circle started in the first place? That such virtuous circles do in fact start, we know from our own experience: we have a desire to see some result; we make an effort to secure conditions that will improve the chances of it occurring; those conditions give us increased confidence and incentive and so on, until what we wish for is more or less realized. This is no more than a hint of how a public-spirited citizenry can come about, but it does suggest that one starting point for the process might be simply a widespread sense that such a citizenry is needed. Perhaps public-spiritedness can be without such a prior sense, but it is not clear how.

The Commercial Republic in America

At the heart of the political constitution of the commercial republic are the following relationship: how lawmakers shall stand in relation to each other; how lawmakers shall stand in relation to citizens; and how citizens shall stand in relation to each other. Lawmaking must be deliberative both in a high court and in the legislature; citizens must be able to judge whether prospective lawmakers are disposed to struggle and debate the concrete meaning of the public interest; and citizens need the experience of deliberative lawmaking if they are to be able to judge lawmakers.[61]

With these features of the constitution of the commercial republic in mind, several characteristics of the actual workings of the American political constitution come into view. Accepting that the United States can be understood as a sustained effort to realize a fully developed commercial republic, two ways in which we have fallen short stand out. First of all, we have relied far too heavily on the Supreme Court to carry the deliberative burden of the regime, and concomitantly we have allowed the Congress to be the home of particular interests. The result is that the public interest of the regime has been given a truncated definition: namely, the one largely offered by the courts. In particular, short shrift has been given to those aspects of the public interest that are more obviously political: (1) limits on the exercise of private power; (2) promoting a widespread ability to secure at least modest levels of material well-being through remunerative work; and (3) securing the foundations of institutions able to give concrete meaning to the public interest. Our other great shortcoming is that we have given little sustained attention to fostering the qualities necessary for a republican citizenry. We have given almost no serious thought to how public-spiritedness might be promoted, particularly to how the mutual respect in which it is rooted can be strengthened.

Friends of the American commercial republic must seek to repair such deficiencies. They must somehow continue the work that the founders of the republic started—repairing what has declined, completing what has been left incomplete, and revising what was improperly designed at the beginning. They must do *in medias res* what Madison and his colleagues did during the founding period. In the broadest sense, the great question is whether the people, acting through the organs of self-reflection that they themselves have created (or at least have consented to), can secure and strengthen the foundations of a commercial republican regime. This is a journey—a democratic journey—that has about it the quality of a self-levitating act. Being so precarious an exercise, there is no guarantee of success.

Thus, one of the questions such a journey will encounter is this: Given the significant degree of private control of productive assets that

---

61. Each of these relations in turn has its foundation in other features of the political constitution of the regime. This complexity in the features of a republican constitution raises the question of whether the central constitutive relations and their foundations are mutually compatible. We are, after all, concerned with a workable as well as attractive constitution. As such, its various elements must be, if not mutually supportive, at least not so deeply at odds that no sizable collection of people could act simultaneously in the ways required.

characterizes the U.S. economy, can the necessary changes in the qualities of the citizenry be set in motion, especially as these changes will require attention to the distribution of income and work? This may be called *the political question*.

There is also *the economic question*. Is there in fact any version of an enterprise-based market system that will generate something like the levels of material equality necessary for mutual respect? It is unlikely that a redistributive politics can do the whole job.

Perhaps most perplexing of all, there is what might be called *the constitutive question*. Can we as a people and those who speak for us come to the sort of political understanding necessary to secure the essential features of a commercial-republican political constitution? In political life generally, there is enormous pressure to focus on the here and now. The fruits of a well-functioning political constitution are diffuse and well in the future. They are all too easy to discount and all too difficult to explain to people who are rightly concerned with the problems that lie immediately before them.

Just as the citizenry must move beyond narrow self-interest in its choice of lawmakers, so must it act in those moments when it attempts to act constitutionally as *We The People*. This is where our mettle as a people is shown. Our mettle is not determined by some genetic endowment or even by an inherited culture, if by that is meant a set of ideas dancing around in our heads. Whether we as a people have the ability to think and act constitutively depends, as I have said, on the institutions through which we can act. These institutions must act reflexively—acting through what we have in order to get closer to where we wish to go. They are, in short, institutions for learning as much as for doing; and, of course, there is no easy separation between the two. Whether we can more fully realize an American commercial republic depends very much on our institutional inheritance: what the founders of this republic bequeathed to us as well as what succeeding generations have put into place. Thus, we can reform ourselves—but not just as we please, for there is no "we" apart from the existing institutions that form us as a people.

REFERENCES

Aristotle. 1932. *Politics*. Translated by H. Rackham. Cambridge: Harvard University Press.

Ball, Terrence, and J. G. Pocock, eds. 1988. *Conceptual Change and the Constitution*. Lawrence: University Press of Kansas.

Banfield, Edward C. 1961. *Political Influence*. Glencoe, Ill.: Free Press.

Berman, Harold J. 1983. *Law and Revolution*. Cambridge: Harvard University Press.

Blau, Joseph, ed. 1954. *Social Theories of Jacksonian Democracy*. New York: Liberal Arts Press.

Buchanan, James. 1986. "Then and Now, 1961–1986: From Delusion to Dystopia." Paper delivered to the Institute for Humane Studies, November 13.

Cicero, Marcus Tullius. 1938. *De Re Publica, De Legibus*. Translated by Clinton Walker Keyes. Loeb Classical Library. Cambridge: Harvard University Press.

Corwin, Edward S. 1955. *The "Higher Law" Background of American Constitutional Law*. Ithaca, N.Y.: Cornell University Press.

Crick, Bernard. 1972. *In Defense of Politics*. Chicago: University of Chicago Press.

Dahl, Robert. 1961. *Who Governs? Democracy and Power in an American City*. New Haven, Conn.: Yale University Press.

———. 1985. *A Preface to Economic Democracy*. Berkeley and Los Angeles: University of California Press.

Diggins, John Patrick. 1984. *The Lost Soul of American Politics: Virtue, Self-Interest, and the Foundations of Liberalism*. New York: Basic Books.

Elkin, Stephen. 1987. *City and Regime in the American Republic*. Chicago: University of Chicago Press.

Elkin, Stephen, and Karol Edward Sołtan, eds. 1993. *A New Constitutionalism*. Chicago: University of Chicago Press.

Galston, William. 1988. "Liberal Virtues." *American Political Science Review* 82(4): 1284.

Goldwin, Robert, and William Schambra, eds. 1980. *How Democratic Is the Constitution*. Washington, D.C.: American Enterprise Institute for Public Policy Research.

Haefele, Edwin. 1973. *Representative Government and Environmental Management*. Baltimore: Johns Hopkins University Press.

Huntington, Samuel P. 1968. *Political Order in Changing Societies*. New Haven, Conn.: Yale University Press.

Kelman, Steven. 1987. *Making Public Policy: A Hopeful View of American Government*. New York: Basic Books.

Lindblom, Charles E. 1965. *The Intelligence of Democracy: Decision Making through Mutual Adjustment*. New York: Free Press.

———. 1977. *Politics and Markets: The World's Political Economic Systems*. New York: Basic Books.

Maass, Arthur. 1983. *Congress and the Common Good*. New York: Basic Books.

McIlwain, Charles Howard. 1947. *Constitutionalism: Ancient and Modern*. Ithaca, N.Y.: Cornell University Press.

Maddox, Graham. 1982. "A Note on the Meaning of Constitution." *American Political Science Review* 76(4): 806–7.

Madison, James, Alexander Hamilton, and John Jay. 1961. *The Federalist*. Middletown, Conn.: Wesleyan University Press.

Malbin, Michael. 1987. "Factions and Incentives in Congress." *The Public Interest* (Winter): 86, 91–108.

Mason, Alpheus T. 1965. *Free Government in the Making: Readings in American Political Thought.* 3d ed. New York: Oxford University Press.

Mayhew, David. 1975. *Congress: The Electoral Connection.* New Haven, Conn.: Yale University Press.

Meade, James. 1965. *Efficiency, Equality, and the Ownership of Property.* Cambridge: Harvard University Press.

Mill, John Stuart. (1859) 1974. *On Liberty.* Baltimore: Penguin.

———. 1991. *On Liberty and Other Essays.* Edited by John Gray. Oxford: Oxford University Press.

Muir, William. 1982. *Legislature: California's School for Politics.* Chicago: University of Chicago Press.

Olson, Mancur. 1977. *The Logic of Collective Action: Public Goods and the Theory of Groups.* Cambridge: Harvard University Press.

Redner, Harry, ed. 1993. *An Heretical Heir of the Enlightenment: Public Policy and Science in the Work of Charles E. Lindblom.* Boulder, Colo.: Westview.

Shattuck, Roger. 1989. "The Reddening of America." *New York Review of Books* (March 30): 5.

Shklar, Judith. 1989. "The Liberalism of Fear." In Rosenblum, Nancy, ed., *Liberalism and the Moral Life.* Cambridge: Harvard University Press.

Stigler, George. 1975. *The Citizen and the State: Essays on Regulation.* Chicago: University of Chicago Press.

Sunstein, Cass. 1988. "Beyond the Republican Revival." *Yale Law Journal* 97(8): 1539–90.

Taylor, John. 1814. *An Inquiry into the Principles and Policy of the Government of the United States.* Fredericksburg, Va.: Green & Cady.

Tocqueville, Alexis de. (1835) 1945. *Democracy in America.* New York: Vintage.

Wills, Gary. 1981. *Explaining America: The Federalist.* Garden City, N.Y.: Doubleday.

Wood, Gordon. 1969. *The Creation of the American Republic, 1776–1787.* Chapel Hill: University of North Carolina Press.

CHAPTER SEVEN

Speculative Theory and Regime Alternatives: Beyond Socialism and Capitalism

GAR ALPEROVITZ

FOR MOST OF THE twentieth century the progressive "vision" of the future in many parts of the world revolved around socialist theory: namely, that equality and democracy could best be achieved by a "system" in which ownership of society's wealth ("the means of production") is vested in a structure beholden to, and controlled by, society. This "system theory" has now collapsed. However, the crisis of mainstream liberalism (or social democracy) leads to a closely related problem. What happens if socialism's "distant cousin"—the welfare state—also loses its capacity to achieve the fundamental value goals its core theory affirms? A less commonly recognized question concerns the implications when the fundamental basis of the conservative theory of liberty falters. All three issues, I believe, point to a shared regime problem: the disintegration of traditional articulations of the relationship between values and systems.

It is instructive to discuss the last issue first. Against the socialist idea, thoughtful conservatives (as opposed to demagogues and self-serving right-wing politicians) have for more than a century argued that vesting both economic and political power in one institutional structure must inevitably lead to the destruction of individual rights, of democracy, and of the human spirit. They have applied a similar structural critique to the expansive welfare state.

Friedrich Hayek, whose book *The Road to Serfdom* became a conservative bible, pushed the argument well beyond narrow economic ideas. Thus: "The most important change which extensive government control produces is a psychological change, an alteration in the character of the people." Hayek cited Tocqueville approvingly: "The will of man is not shattered but softened, bent and guided; men are seldom forced by it to act, but they are constantly restrained from acting. Such a power does not destroy, but it prevents existence; it does not tyrannize, but it compresses, enervates, extinguishes, and stupefies a people, till each nation is reduced to be nothing better than a flock of timid and industrial animals, of which government is the shepherd." (Hayek [1944] 1972, xi, xiii).

Most progressives rejected the general conservative argument because it was commonly oblivious to the moral and political importance of equality, and because it often served to mask a base form of conservatism willing to use any argument to justify private-enterprise exploitation. Many urged that vesting the ownership of the means of production in private hands inevitably produced great inequalities of income and wealth, powerful private interests which lead to the subversion of democracy, the desecration of the environment, and an equally disastrous spiritual result—the worship of money, materialism, greed.

Most progressives threw the important conservative baby out with the dishonest bathwater for these reasons. Only a very few argued the importance of listening to the main point of the critique and of engaging genuine conservatives in a serious dialogue about theory. The era of Cold War polarization also provided numerous "reasons" that permitted many to avoid reflecting deeply upon the conservative structural argument and upon similar themes in anarchist and libertarian antistatist thought.

It is undeniable that the socialist system in the Soviet Union and Eastern Europe was severely handicapped by the devastation of World Wars I and II—and because it was introduced into essentially underdeveloped societies which had only a minimal historical experience with democracy. Further, the Cold War generated an environment that gave priority to "national security," military expenditures, rigorous "internal security" measures, and a Soviet imperial occupation. However, the fatal underlying structural flaw can hardly be denied, and it has now demonstrated its tremendous importance as millions in the East have undertaken a sweeping rush away from the disaster they knew directly to a seeming solution they know only vaguely: "democratic capitalism."

In practice, however, the experience of capitalism in the formerly communist areas has also been radically different from its promises—as unemployment, social dislocation, ecological horror, and profound disillusionment have set in (sometimes even leading to the election of old communists as seemingly the least disastrous of the available alternatives!) If—as many in the West know so well—democratic capitalism also contradicts important values, what possible alternative can be conceived and affirmed for the future?

Authentic conservatives are aware of another profound difficulty at the very heart of their preferred option. The conservative argument against statist socialism held not only that the concentration of economic and political power in the institution of the state was dangerous, but that there had to be alternative structural sources of independent support for the individual—else, liberty could never be sustained over time.

The essential notion involves a balance of forces: At the same time that they contended against a strong state, most conservatives argued the importance of small-scale, entrepreneurial enterprise. In this "system" the underlying structural basis for the principle of "liberty" cannot be compromised: a free political culture requires that society rest upon the foundation of a citizenry sustained by economic independence. "It is widely believed," observes conservative economist Milton Friedman, "that politics and economics are separate and largely unconnected; that individual freedom is a political problem and material welfare an economic problem; and that any kind of political arrangements can be combined with any kind of economic arrangements. . . . [S]uch a view is a delusion. . . . [T]here is an intimate connection between economics and politics . . . [and] only certain combinations of political and economic arrangements are possible" (Friedman 1962, 7–8).

Thomas Jefferson urged a broadly similar theory of the requirements of a meaningful political-economic "system." In his 1781 *Notes on the State of Virginia,* Jefferson wrote: "Dependence begets subservience and venality, suffocates the germ of virtue, and prepares fit tools for the designs of ambition" (Jefferson [1781] cited in Macpherson 1977, 18). His hope for a new "system" in early nineteenth-century America also had a very specific structural foundation: "everyone may have land to labor for himself, if he chooses; or, preferring the exercise of any other industry, may exact for it such compensation as not only to afford a comfortable subsistence, but wherewith to provide for a cessation from labor in old age. . . . [S]uch men may safely and advantageously reserve to themselves a wholesome control over their public affairs, and a degree of freedom" (letter to John Adams, 1813, quoted in Macpherson 1977, 18).

For all its other difficulties, pre-twentieth-century American society did in fact rest upon a footing of millions and millions of *individual* entrepreneurs. These were mostly farmers or, more accurately, farmer-businessmen (an entrepreneurial breed very different from the farmer-peasants of many other societies). A majority of the society, including spouses and children, actually had the experience of individually risking capital and being directly responsible for their own economic enterprises.

By the late twentieth century, however, only a very small fraction of Americans, no more than 15 or 16 percent, can in any reasonable sense be called "individual entrepreneurs." The United States has become a society of employees, most of whom work for large or medium-size bureaucracies, private or public. "As the consolidation of economic power progresses," the traditionalist conservative Russell Kirk admonished in 1957, "the realm of personal freedom will diminish, whether the masters of the economy are state servants or the servants of private corporations" (Nash [1976] 1979, 161).

From this essential perspective, the difference between a "system" dominated by General Motors and Exxon and one based upon the individual landholding farmer and small businessman of an earlier day in American history may very well be as important—in the actual life experience of the average person—as the difference between a system based upon large private bureaucracies in the United States and public bureaucracies in the "socialist" nations. Moreover, irrespective of the hopes of conservatives and (give or take an election) largely irrespective of who has been in power—including Herbert Hoover and Ronald Reagan—the state has generally grown in size and power. The government, which accounted for less than 8 percent of the GNP at the turn of the twentieth century, has grown to roughly 34–35 percent of GNP in recent years (U.S. Bureau of the Census 1975; Council of Economic Advisers 1995). Although marginal changes may occur, there are no signs the scale of government will be fundamentally diminished.

The dangers of statism in socialism are now clear to all. However, the truth is that serious conservatives, like serious progressives, must confront a direct contradiction of both basic structural elements of their cherished theory of liberty in the experience of the West.

Is there any meaningful way forward that promises to honor equality, liberty, and democracy—to say nothing of ecological rationality and even, perhaps, community? Might it be possible to begin to define a viable Third Way, a structural option other than traditional socialism and traditional capitalism?

What is needed is not a set of rhetorical goals, but a serious discussion of the outlines of an alternative "system" of institutions and relationships which might one day nurture, rather than erode, core values in an ongoing fashion. Space restrictions permit only an introductory set of "notes" and "elements" that might contribute to a dialogue aimed ultimately at fashioning such a vision. Let us begin with equality.

Democracy obviously requires a reasonable degree of equality if it is to be a meaningful expression of the idea not only of "one person, one vote," but of "each and all" having an equal capacity to influence the governing decisions that determine the fate and shape of the society in which they live. By this test, the underlying condition of "democracy" in the United States is clearly weak . . . and fading.

Money and television, as innumerable studies show, tend increasingly to dominate elections. Even more fundamental is that when there are vast differences in earnings, wealth, education, free time, and personal security, those with low incomes are systematically disadvantaged: they do not have the wherewithal to influence politics, their education does not provide them with as many skills, they have less free time, and often—fearful of losing their jobs—they must be silent rather than speak their minds.

Any reporter in any American city can easily find abundant examples of citizens who express profound disillusionment with the actual operation of democracy. These people need no instruction in the limits of what some call "electionism"—a process in which mudslinging, distorted advertising, and a lack of significant issues make a mockery of the idea of "democratic decisionmaking" with respect to important public matters.

The traditional American progressive or liberal answer to inequality has been that "reform" (or "activism" or "political demands" or "organizing") can correct such imbalances and move society toward greater equality. In a sense, politics is seen as somewhat independent from—and capable of correcting—the essential functioning and structural basis of the economic "system." This idea, in fact, is at the very core of social-democratic or liberal "system theory."

The statistical record, however, confirms that there are deep linkages between the structure of the economic system and the kind of "politics" it generates or permits. There is little evidence, for instance, that what we commonly understand as "reform," "activism," "political demands," or "organizing" has been able to move the American system toward greater economic equality in the twentieth century.

In fact, the only times when there have been brief improvements in the relative distribution of income have been during major crises: World War I, the Great Depression, and World War II. But these brief shifts, indisputably, were associated with fundamental, system-shaking explosions. Clearly they are not evidence that politics on its own in "normal" times has the capacity to alter the underlying trend. Buoyed again by the special circumstances of the postwar boom, the Korean War, the Cold War, and the Vietnam War, the relative distribution of income in the United States improved briefly and held reasonably constant for two decades. However, the painful deterioration that has been in process now for a number of years since the boom ended continues a much older and deeper trend of growing inequality.

To be sure, the situation would undoubtedly be worse without progressive political activity. Yet it is one thing to say that such politics may have prevented or slowed down a trend toward even more regressive patterns of inequality—and quite another to say, as the traditional theory argues, that it has the capacity to move society toward greater equality.

Today, roughly 52 million people in the top fifth of U.S. society receive approximately 48 percent of all household income (including interest, rent, and dividends). Just about the same number of human beings in the bottom fifth make do on 3.6 percent of that income (DeParle 1994). Still lower, at the very bottom of the system, there is extreme poverty—concentrated overwhelmingly among women, children, and minorities in general. In 1992, for instance, 14.5 percent of American society lived in "poverty" by official definitions: *36.9 million people*. In that year 46.3 percent of all black children (including 50.7 percent of those under age six) were living in poverty (U.S. Bureau of the Census 1994).

But clearly this understates the full impact of inequality. If you receive $1,000 in one year and I receive $50,000, and a few years later you have $2,000 and I have $100,000, the ratio between our incomes has not changed. Economists will tell you, correctly, that the "relative distribution" of income has not been altered. But, self-evidently, in the real world the gap between us has exploded from $49,000 to $98,000—and the "real world inequality" between persons has increased dramatically.

This, in fact, is precisely what has been happening in the United States. One recent study concludes that the real-world gap between those at the top and those at bottom of the American income pyramid has more than doubled since the end of World War II. The income gap between families in the bottom 20 percent and families in the top 5 percent, for instance, exploded from $31,000 in 1947 to more than $68,000 in 1987 (in 1985 dollars) (Winnick 1989, 68–69, 105). One Congressional study calculates that the gap (measured in 1993 dollars) between a family of four at the eightieth percentile of income and a family of four at the first percentile grew by more than $98,000 just in the brief period from 1977 to 1989 (U.S. House 1992). More recent U.S. Census data indicate that the real-life gap between a family at the fifth percentile and one at the eightieth percentile of income distribution increased from $74,623 to $89,549 between 1980 and 1992 (in 1992 dollars) (U.S. Bureau of the Census 1994).

It may be that in some special cases "social-democratic politics" can achieve sufficient momentum so that the underlying structural tendencies of capitalism can be countered by a politics sufficiently powerful to alter significantly the trends and patterns of real inequality between people. The evidence from countries like Sweden is mixed; but even if it were not, this possibility would clearly be an exception to the general rule, especially as that rule has been experienced in twenti-eth-century America.

The fact is the essential "system theory" as it relates to the affirmed value of equality has lost all serious operational meaning.

For those who reject the traditional conservative, socialist, and liberal (social-democratic) alternatives, another commonly discussed "struc-tural possibility"—the basis of still another system theory—is "worker ownership" of the "means of production." By this arrangement it is hoped that the dangers of statism, on the one hand, and private capi-talist ownership and exploitation, on the other, can be avoided. There are many important advantages to worker-ownership schemes, espe-cially those which offer some effective participation. However, they are clearly no panacea.

First of all, there is very little evidence that worker-owned firms significantly alter society's *overall* distribution of income. Within the local or the national community, for instance, privileged workers in rich industries do not easily share their advantage with the community as a whole or with workers in other industries, the elderly, the poor, or women and children outside their own families. Second, worker-owned firms tend to develop their own "interests." Worker-owned steel mills, for example, generally seek similar kinds of subsidies (and trade protection) as privately owned mills. Nor, for that matter, do worker-owners have any great interest in expensive pollution controls which may benefit the larger community but which cost their own firm money.

Some worker-owned firms or worker co-ops have more-equitable internal pay scales, all teach that structural alternatives different from either major "system" are at least possible, and many provide experi-ence with meaningful participation in general and with economic mat-ters in particular which may be important to the future development of still other forms. Any open vision of the future would be wise to include a rich variety of small-scale co-ops, worker-owned firms, neighborhood corporations, and the like.

The structural principle of worker ownership, however, does not provide a fundamental answer to the problems entailed in a serious and comprehensive vision. Nor does it suggest a "system" of institu-tions which might undergird such a vision in ways that could nurture such fundamental values as liberty and equality.

Another structural formulation worth reviewing involves the no-tion of "community" and institutions that give the community as a whole power through specific forms related to everyday life. The idea of community is inclusive: in principle, it extends beyond "the work-ers" in a firm (or even as a class) to embrace everyone. The philosopher Martin Buber argued the necessity of creating institutions (locally, where people live) which would embody the idea that the community as a whole should own and benefit from wealth. Traditional conservatives have stressed the parallel idea that strong structures of local community are required to support individual liberty—that community and liberty are mutually reinforcing values.

"Society is naturally composed not of disparate individuals," Buber held, "but of associative units and associations between them." What is required is a particular form and structure which nurtures cooperative democratic activity through direct experience. For "an organic commonwealth—and only such commonwealths can join together to form a shapely and articulated race of men—will never build itself up out of individuals but only out of small and ever smaller communities: a nation is a community to the degree that it is a community of communities" (Buber 1950, 14, 136).

A community must be sufficiently small and local so that those who are affected can participate in decisions. And, in general, the social principle of involvement, of participation, of subsuming strictly economic goals to larger social goals, must be given priority. The fundamental question "How do we wish to live together?" is more important than more limited questions such as "How do we compete?" "How do we become number one?" or "How do we increase the national product?"

A number of modern ecological thinkers have also urged the importance of building new structural relationships upon the principle of community. Thus, Herman E. Daly and John B. Cobb, Jr., in their book on the economics of a sustainable future (1989), urge rebuilding local-community economic institutions. The ecologist Murray Bookchin has put forward a local community concept he terms "libertarian municipalism":

A gap, ideological as well as practical, is opening up between the nation-state, which is becoming more anonymous, bureaucratic, and remote, and the municipality, which is the one domain outside of personal life that the individual must deal with on a very direct basis. . . . Like it or not, the city is still the most immediate environment which we encounter and with which we are obliged to deal, beyond the sphere of family and friends, in order to satisfy our needs as social beings. (Bookchin 1990)

A related question is how to provide structural means to alter the dynamic which commonly develops when private interests move into the political arena to secure special benefits. The notion of the community as a whole, locally, owning substantial wealth-producing firms, at least in principle attempts to negate this feature of capitalism. It also counterposes local community structures against statist socialist forms.

Community-based institutional experiments—from land trusts to joint community-worker-owned firms—have multiplied as national social and economic difficulties have increased over the past several years. Many are important as suggestive and preliminary prototypes. Simply by way of illustration, a recent U.S. survey by Dawn Nakano found the following: close to ten thousand worker-owned firms; more than forty-seven thousand co-ops; numerous municipalities which have "communitized" capital ownership (including community-owned cable systems, hotels, fertilizer-manufacturing companies, towing services, real-estate development efforts, and thousands of city-owned electric utilities); many forms of neighborhood ownership dating back to the original community-development corporations of the mid-1960s; and "eco-city" projects which combine innovative environmental technologies, democratic planning, and alternative living arrangements (Nakano 1994).

"Liberty"—defined as a further requirement of a comprehensive vision—is rarely assessed in systemic or structural terms in modern discussions. However, if the individual must have an independent "place to stand," and if the small-entrepreneurial basis of liberty can never be retrieved, what then?

The vast majority of liberals and conservatives have simply avoided this issue: conservatives especially have mostly looked away even as the institutional basis at the heart of their "system theory" has largely disappeared. Only a very few have had the courage to acknowledge with Henry C. Simons, founder of the Chicago School of Economics, that the corporate-dominated economy is not the same as a truly competitive free-enterprise system. In 1948 Simons noted that "the corporation is simply running away with our economic (and political) system," and he warned that "the cause of economic liberalism and political democracy faces distinctly unfavorable odds" (Simons 1948, 58, 56).

Nor, avoiding the gaping hole in their theory, have many confronted the possibility that without some secure new footings for liberty the present system can all too easily be shaken by the scapegoating of minorities, unpopular political groups, or nonconformists in general. That a new institutional *theory* is needed if liberty is to have meaning has rarely been acknowledged.

One of the few even to have stated the problem is Peter Drucker, who points out that in Western society "the overwhelming majority of the people in the labor force are employees of 'organizations' . . . and the 'means of production' is therefore the job." Accordingly, he affirms that jobs should (and in many ways have already) become a form of property; the *right* to a job should therefore be accepted as fundamental. In the modern era, he argues, such an approach "is compatible with limited government, personal freedom" (Drucker 1980).

If "the job" is to provide the foundation for "liberty," however, obviously the job must be made secure. Some liberals and socialists have proposed (mainly on equity grounds, since few have confronted this aspect of the institutional problem of liberty) that there be a legal right to a job. But to be meaningful—to be truly a *right,* not merely a hope—this would require certain guarantees. In the mid-1970s the initial drafts of the Humphrey–Hawkins full-employment legislation contained provisions allowing an individual to obtain a court order for a government-guaranteed job if no other possibility were available.

Another solution involves the direct provision of a substantial share of income to individuals as a matter of right. The aim here is not simply "to help the poor," nor to "assist the aged," nor to support any idea other than the most fundamental one that if liberty and democracy are to have meaning, then ultimately individuals must have real economic security. Simply put, there must be a "structural basis" for liberty.

In his book *The State* the British political theorist Bill Jordan argues that in order

> to reconcile political authority with individual autonomy the state needs to take certain steps to ensure a basis of equality and freedom amongst its citizens. . . . The new principle is that the state should pay to each citizen, simply by virtue of his or her citizenship, an income sufficient for subsistence. This should be unconditional, and paid equally to all, employed and unemployed, men and women, married and single. . . . This state-guaranteed subsistence income (sometimes referred to as the social dividend or social wage) would give every citizen the *basis* for equal autonomy. (Jordan 1985, 12)

Again, to be quite clear, the issue we are considering here is not simply one of "social justice." Rather, it is how to ensure that the conditions necessary for democratic participation and liberty are met in societies which are long past the era of the individual yeoman farmer and small entrepreneur.

Only a few decades ago, the idea that individuals should receive direct funding from the government—as for instance, in the Social Security program—was regarded as illusory. One of the most interesting modern political innovations is the Earned-Income Tax Credit, a system which puts cash directly into the hands of ordinary citizens who work but receive inadequate pay. The concept is very different from welfare payments, which increase the dependency of a class of poor people on the state (as well as the state's coercive power over the person's life). It points to a much more powerful possibility—allocating to each individual a part of the wealth created by the community in order to provide sufficient independence and security to make liberty meaningful.

The notion that there must be an alternative guarantee for some degree of economic security is also a core element in the very long-term system vision proposed by such diverse theorists as Paul and Percival Goodman, on the one hand, and Jacques Maritain, on the other. In their book *Communitas,* the Goodmans suggested a dual vision based on the distinction between production of necessities and production of luxury goods. Part of each day would be devoted to "necessary work" important to the entire community, and income would be assured; the other part would be free for the individual to work in whatever way— and at whatever intensity—he or she desired (Goodman and Goodman [1947] 1960).

If at least part of the solution to the system problem lies, on the one hand, in building local structures which embody the principle of community and, on the other hand, in providing direct individual economic security so that there can be individual independence—and, hence, substantive liberty—then obviously there must be a way to ensure that these things happen. This requires some form of planning.

Neither progressives nor conservatives are fond of the idea of planning. In practice, planning has often been bureaucratic and inefficient, perpetuating "top–down" elite management. However, if stable structures of community are a goal, it is all but impossible to ensure that goal unless there is an overall capacity to deal with growing problems of local economic instability. Nor can we ensure individual economic security without a similar capacity. The crucial issues are whether planning can be made accountable, whether it can be made reasonably efficient (compared not with an absolute ideal, but with the inefficiencies of real-world capitalism and real-world socialism), and whether other "elements" of a long-term solution can confine planning to a supportive rather than an excessively controlling role.

A full-blown account of how planning might become an effective feature in an alternative system is beyond the scope of this essay. Even to begin such an account, however, we need a more balanced appraisal of the pluses and minuses of planned versus market systems than most discussions convey. For instance, it is difficult to reconcile conventional criticisms of "planning" and "nationalized industries" with the successes of the Soviet space program—both on its own terms and in comparison with the American record. To choose an example on the other side of the ledger, the disastrous productivity experience of private U.S. steel companies during the 1970s and early 1980s must be included in any fair assessment.

Again, for all their difficulties, the United States and the other major Western nations stand on the threshold of a new postindustrial century—a period when social, individual, and ecological goals could at least in theory take greater precedence over all-out efforts to achieve ever-greater production and consumption.

It is also important to understand that a vision which accords importance to ideals of both community and liberty does not require a totalist form of planning—and should not urge such planning. What is required is sufficient predictability to give stability to local community structures and to allow the long-term buildup of a genuine culture of liberty and community.

In any community of, say, a hundred thousand people, there are now roughly forty-five thousand full-time workers. Children, the elderly, young people in school, people at home taking care of children and the elderly, patients in hospitals, and so on make up the rest. If, say, fifteen thousand jobs can be assured, then "multiplier effects" might well be able to give substantial stability to perhaps twice as many more—especially if combined with community-building "import substitution" programs. Planning to stabilize a certain percentage of jobs could then allow paychecks to "recirculate" as people pay for groceries, houses, teachers, doctors, etc.—and as these people in turn pay for (and give work to) still others.

Some form of planning is also needed if the notion of a guaranteed *right* of employment for each person is to be meaningful: there is no other way to ensure that real jobs exist when they are needed. (One possible form of planning—long urged here and abroad—involves establishing an inventory of future blueprints for the construction of needed school, road, bridge, rail, water, and other projects to be taken down "off the shelf" in time of need.)

Similarly, if ecological goals are important, there must be a systematic way to ensure that there are new jobs—to take one example—for coal miners thrown out of work as provisions are implemented to curb "acid rain." The same is true with respect to conversion from military production. Put another way, the realization of individual equity, a secure basis for individual liberty, ecological balance, movement toward a peace-oriented economy, and the ability to maintain community stability requires in each instance meaningful and coordinated planning.

A further feature of planning for community and liberty involves yet another possible element of a longer-term system solution. Businessmen and conservatives commonly argue that a society's wealth should belong to those who take risks and invest capital; labor organizers and progressives commonly argue that those who work should receive the fruits of their labor. A more fundamental understanding of wealth creation, both economic and moral, involves a somewhat different emphasis.

Compare the living standards of most African countries with those of the United States. Entrepreneurs invest both in Africa and the United States; and workers work, often very long and hard hours, in both societies. However, income levels are radically different in the two settings. Such enormous differences in "the wealth of nations" are related not primarily to individual effort but to an extended history of *community investment*—many generations of schooling, the historical construction of highways and waterways, the steady evolution of overall skill levels, and the slow development of a productive culture.

Still more fundamental, of course, is the even longer and larger community investment which produced centuries of science—from before Newton to after Einstein—and the development of technologies and inventions and education in their use among hundreds of thousands of scientists and engineers, on the one hand, and millions of skilled working people on the other. When a young computer inventor produces an innovation which makes him a billionaire, he commonly thinks he "deserves" all that he has received. His "invention," however, is literally inconceivable without generations—indeed centuries—of previously accumulated knowledge, skills, and wealth. He has picked the ripe fruit of a tree which grows in the rich earth of investment by the human community. Often, too, he has benefited from specific public investments, such as U.S. wartime investment in computer technology.

Rarely do we explicitly recognize this *community inheritance*. An alternative theory might make it a central feature of a new "system," both morally and politically. Building on inheritance laws, on the one hand, and public-land precedents, on the other, we might conceivably evolve our thinking so that major wealth (not necessarily small businesses, homes, etc.) would regularly be returned to the community that made the creation of such wealth possible.

A tiny group of Americans today owns a huge share of the national wealth. Recent data collected by the Federal Reserve Board show that the top 10 percent of U.S. households owns more than twice as much of the nation's net worth as the remaining 90 percent taken together. The top 1 percent alone owns just under two-fifths of that wealth (Wolff 1994, 47). The moral case for such wealth being passed on through inheritance to those who do not even *claim* to have earned it is exceedingly weak. Tightening inheritance laws is one obvious element of a new approach.

Over time, within local communities, major buildings and major land ownership (again, not individual family homes) might pass slowly to the local community as a whole—a shift that could also yield revenues and help in the development of new "community-building" land use and location strategies. A more creative use of eminent domain might also play a role in a comprehensive strategy. At the same time, a new approach might wisely allow true individual entrepreneurs to pass on a significant share of what they *personally* earn in their lifetime.

A public trust to establish community ownership of major wealth—at the national, state, regional, and local level—could also produce a positive income stream for public use. Part of this income might be allocated by the community as a whole to offset taxes and to provide needed services; part might be used to provide security for individuals in the interest of a new structural basis for liberty and democratic participation. Public-trust control of substantial economic wealth could also help in the implementation of planning for more stable communities.

I have already cited the precedent of the Earned-Income Tax Credit. Also noteworthy in this connection is the current Alaskan practice whereby an acknowledged communitywide interest in oil royalties has built up a large "permanent fund" which at present yields a direct cash payment of almost $1,000 to each resident. In addition to funding this dividend payout, the oil royalties are also a major source of revenue for the state government.

A related question has to do with the provision of adequate free time to make possible a higher level of democratic participation and allow more room for individual self-development and fulfillment.

Even with all its economic problems, the United States is so wealthy today that if its gross national product were divided equally among all its citizens, each family of four would receive more than $100,000. Allowing for only moderate growth, a conservative projection of actual twentieth-century trends suggests that this figure could well reach $200,000 or even $400,000 and, by the end of the next century, substantially more (all in today's dollars; higher if inflation is assumed). Indeed, a linear projection of twentieth-century trends would eventually yield over $500,000 for every four people (U.S. Bureau of the Census 1975; Council of Economic Advisers 1995). This implies no change in the conventional forty-hour workweek. (The numbers would be much larger if, say, Japanese trends were projected.)

An alternative possibility would be to maintain incomes at the "average" $100,000 level (with adjustments for family size etc.) and over time slowly reduce what might be called the "necessary" workweek to twenty hours, then to ten hours, or even lower. (Another logical option would be to work longer hours and allocate a share of production to the Third World.) Of course, with any of the options, recycling and ecologically oriented planning would be necessary to reduce environmental costs.

The most interesting choice from the point of view of democratic participation involves reducing the workweek in order to create greater amounts of free time in order to facilitate greater involvement in community decisionmaking. If democratic participation and personal liberty are defined as necessary requirements of a new system, then time for participation must be fairly divided. Today some people work an eighty-hour week, and some are unemployed and without income—an inevitable result of the haphazard functioning of the market. Planning is needed to ensure not only that greater amounts of free time are available, but that a reasonable degree of equality of free time is assured for each individual.

More "free time" does not necessarily mean more time spent not doing productive work. If a portion of "necessary work" is required to meet overall economic objectives, individuals would of course be free to spend the remaining time in a variety of self-directed ways. A dual conception of future economic life—one in which a portion of work is defined as necessary for overall community goals, and another portion is defined as "free"—is a commonsense (if all too little discussed) approach. Such an economic conception mirrors a dual moral outlook which gives equal weight to "community" and to "individual independence," liberty and fulfillment.

Also implicit in such structural conceptions is what might be called a "community-building cycle" of relationships. In contrast to the all-too-common cycle in which economic inequality limits democratic participation, which in turn weakens a politics of reform that might hope to achieve positive movement toward greater equality, a community-building cycle would aim at managing the "community's inheritance" so as to target economic activity to sustain community, on the one hand, and individual liberty on the other. Not only is the kind of planning required here premised upon nontotalist objectives, but its specific goals are to produce greater individual security and more free time—which in turn are conditions needed to sustain liberty and real participation and, thus, to ensure that planning itself can be made increasingly democratic and accountable.

An implicit aim of the potential systemic elements sketched thus far is at least the partial development of a structural basis for a more egalitarian culture. Questions of "equality" are not independent of the culture that might emerge from different institutional relationships—especially if these relationships remove significant wealth from private to community control (and allocate the proceeds democratically), establish democratic management of local economic institutions, move toward increasing amounts of free time, attempt to build more stable local communities, and strive to nurture a range of cooperative practices. Such structural and procedural underpinnings might also help establish the preconditions of a less materialist culture and in addition, might facilitate community-based planning systems to implement more rational ecological decisions.

A final element in a possible alternative system has been little discussed, either by theoreticians or citizens: the United States now spans a continent. It includes roughly 260 million people. Does anyone really believe that "participatory democracy" can be meaningful in a nation which comprises such huge sweeps of geography and such large numbers of people? (By way of comparison, the state of Oregon is bigger than the former West Germany.)

The visceral disgust many Americans now direct at "Washington" suggests that it is all but impossible to make such an overextended federal government responsive. The attack on "big government," I believe, is not simply an attack on absolute size; it is also a reminder that it is extraordinarily difficult to achieve accountability over huge distances involving very large populations.

In towns and cities, and even in small states, far more people know each other than is possible on a larger scale; it is also much easier to learn directly, and with some confidence, the reputation of people who are not known personally. Organizing efforts by grass-roots groups—which depend heavily upon individual contacts and person-to-person relationships—are also easier in smaller-scale units. In large geographic "systems" involving large numbers of people, what counts is the mass media—which means, as the saying goes, that money talks. Indeed, the disproportionate advantages that the rich enjoy in a highly unequal society are multiplied when large numbers and large areas are involved.

There is a further consideration, one which James Madison, the architect of the U.S. Constitution, understood very well. Long before Karl Marx, Madison argued that the "principal political division" in society was between those who owned the means of production and those who did not. As a representative of the propertied class, Madison worried that the "majority" would overwhelm the people he believed should guide the new republic. His checks-and-balances system was one method of slowing down the majority, but equally important (if less discussed) was his argument that large geographic scale gave the wealthy elites special advantages: the opposition could be divided and conquered.

Madison also recognized that large scale—and the power it gave elites to break the people up into contending groups—could be dangerous. Writing to his friend Thomas Jefferson in 1787, when the nation was little more than a strip of colonies on the very edge of the ocean, Madison pointed out that if the nation grew too large ("too extensive"), then "a defensive concert may be rendered too difficult against the oppression of those entrusted with the administration" (Madison 1867, 353). This, he predicted, was a recipe for tyranny.

We do not like to confront this argument head on. It implies that if we wish to take the idea of a democracy seriously, we must ultimately come to terms with the need for smaller-scale units. This implies regionalism, an idea urged by several important conservative theorists before World War II. Similarly, the radical historian William Appleman Williams argued that a large nation like the United States would be wise to consider the possibility of one day restructuring in terms of its regional units—so that, say, ten or twelve groups of states might be brought together as the geographic elements of a longer-term vision (Williams 1964). The "United States" would then constitute a confederation of these units. There would be much greater decentralization of authority, and at the same time the regional units would have to work together in matters of defense, foreign policy, ecological balance, and so on.

The fundamental question is whether at a certain point largeness of scale inevitably runs counter to democratic values. If so, there is little choice but to take the need for smaller units seriously in any thoughtful "system theory." Meaningful planning, administration, and stewardship over a substantial share of the "community inheritance" might also logically take place at the regional, subnational level. Regional units, too, would be the logical locus for any larger-scale public enterprise.

As the federal government deadlock grows, a number of U.S. states are taking on increasingly important and independent economic management functions (and even establishing new public enterprises, like state-owned railroads). Some, like California and Texas, are regions unto themselves, larger than many European nations. It is possible that this trend—born of frustration and failure—one day might also have positive implications for a new system.

REFERENCES

Bookchin, Murray. 1990. *Remaking Society*. Boston: South End Press.

Buber, Martin. 1950. *Paths in Utopia*. New York: Macmillan.

Council of Economic Advisers. 1995. *Economic Report of the President, 1995*. Washington, D.C.: GPO.

Daly, Herman E., and John B. Cobb, Jr. 1989. *For the Common Good*. Boston: Beacon Press.

DeParle, Jason. 1994. "Census Sees Falling Income and More Poor." *New York Times* (October 7).

Drucker, Peter. 1980. "The Job as Property Right." *Wall Street Journal* (March 4).

Friedman, Milton. 1962. *Capitalism and Freedom*. Chicago: University of Chicago Press.

Goodman, Paul, and Percival Goodman. (1947) 1960. *Communitas*. New York: Random House.

Hayek, Friedrich. (1944) 1972. *The Road to Serfdom*. Chicago: University of Chicago Press.

Jefferson, Thomas. (1781) 1954. *Notes on the State of Virginia*. Chapel Hill: University of North Carolina Press.

Jordan, Bill. 1985. *The State*. New York: Basil Blackwell.

Macpherson, C. B. 1977. *The Life and Times of Liberal Democracy*. New York: Oxford University Press.

Madison, James. 1867. *Letters and Other Writings of James Madison*. Philadelphia: Lippincott.

Maritain, Jacques. 1985. "A Society without Money." *Review of Social Economy* 43(1).

Nakano, Dawn. 1994. *Community Economic Development: Findings of a Survey of the Field*. Washington, D.C.: National Center for Economic Alternatives.

Nash, George H. (1976) 1979. *The Conservative Intellectual Movement in America*. New York: Basic Books.

Simons, Henry C. 1948. *Economic Policy for a Free Society*. Chicago: University of Chicago Press.

U.S. Bureau of the Census. 1975. *Historical Statistics of the United States: From Colonial Times to 1970*. Washington, D.C.: GPO.

———. 1994. *Statistical Abstract of the United States, 1994*. Washington, D.C.: GPO.

U.S. House. Ways and Means Committee. 1992. *1992 Green Book*. Washington, D.C.: GPO.

Williams, William Appleman. 1964. *The Great Evasion*. Chicago: Quadrangle Books.

Winnick, Andrew J. 1989. *Toward Two Societies: The Changing Distribution of Income and Wealth in the U.S. since 1960*. New York: Praeger.

Wolff, Edward. 1994. *Trends in Household Wealth in the United States: 1962–1983 and 1983–1989*. New York: C. V. Starr Center for Applied Economics, New York University.

CHAPTER EIGHT

The Political Institutions of the Good Society

PHILIP GREEN

IT IS POSSIBLE, in some fairly clear sense to know, or think we know, what is "the good," or the good life. It is certainly not possible in that same clear sense to know what is the good society, let alone what are its political institutions. The inescapable burden of history is much too great: indeed, the traditions of dead generations weigh like a nightmare on the brains of the living. It may be that the good society is and can be only as self-sufficient as Plato thought, as simple as Rousseau imagined; that its political institutions must be as transparent as Marx claimed, or as cooperative and deauthorized as in the fancies of Kropotkin, Morris, Bellamy. None of these revisioned worlds, however, is thinkable in any meaningful way for us. Here and now, the good society and just political institutions can only be some historically conceivable variant, however distant, of society and political institutions at this time, in this place. The owl of Minerva does take flight only at dusk.

At the same time, the political institutions we want to discuss can hardly be immediately practical, for then they would not be political institutions of the *good* society, but only of the immediately realizable society: a far different matter. Constrained as we are by the limits of the historical imagination, on the one hand, and impelled by the demands of the normative imagination, on the other, our most obvious recourse is to assume that to discuss the "political institutions of the good society" is to discuss *democracy*—but to push that discussion as far ahead of our own partially democratic practices as it can reasonably go. That is to say, in any perspective from which democratic institutions are also good institutions, to describe those institutions will be to describe both what is familiar and what is somewhat less than familiar.

This much having been said, it is instructive to ask why democracy is the appropriate subject of discourse. Suppose, for example, we were to begin by accepting Marx's claim, in his critique of Hegel's *Philosophy of Right*, that all governments are ultimately either democracies or monarchies, and that monarchy in any of its guises is only a deformation of the "real" form of government: democracy. It is a deformation in that the singular will of the monarch fraudulently impersonates the collective will of the people. That may be, but why is the singular will of the benevolent despot not the kind of will that should govern the good society?

In answering this question, we begin to see the outline of a good society's political institutions, insofar as we can envisage them. The failure of benevolent despotism, put simply, is that it cannot be theorized or even described; it can only be invoked with pious hopes.[1] Although the behavior of the benevolent despot may by some happy chance actually be benevolent, the institutions of benevolent despotism are identical with the institutions of despotism *tout court*. Democratic institutions, *per contra*, are not inherently despotic. Or rather, democracy may degenerate into a form of despotism, but it is uniquely possible to describe democratic institutions that are not themselves in any way despotic. These are the necessary, even if not sufficient, institutions of a good society: for whatever else marks a good society, the absence of despotism is its sine qua non. Otherwise, it is only a good society for some; an oppressive society for others, who are used as means to the potentially ulterior ends of the despot (or despotic ruling class or majority). From this historical juncture, at which self-evidently partial moral claims clash endlessly with each other in the name of multiple sources of self-proclaimed absolute moral authority, no singular conception of "the good" is believable unless it is believable to every reasonable person hearing it. No one, no matter how elevated to power, can be benevolent from the standpoint of those who are defined, morally or politically, as Other.

A good society, then, must at least potentially be a good society for all who are addressed in its name (whatever fates may befall individual persons). This condition is what tells us that a good society must be democratic. Only democracy—manifested as institutions of compromise, negotiation, fair competition, and equal right—suggests the promise that, as a regular matter, the chance to be the subject rather than merely the object of political authority is open equally to every element within the social order. More precisely, the democratic princi-

---

1. Consider the sheer irrationality of Hegel's climactic description of the monarch in paragraph 275 of *The Philosophy of Right*, in the midst of the amazingly rationalized description of every other aspect of the political order (Hegel 1952).

ple (i.e., the principle of political equality) is that expounded by J. S. Mill: "Everybody to count for one, nobody to count for more than one."[2] Any person who counts for "more than one" subjects others to his will, and for those others the goodness of a good society is contingent on arbitrary benevolence. Any persons who count for "less than one" are subjected to the will of others, and for those persons the goodness of a good society is again contingent on the arbitrary benevolence of others.[3]

However, to say that democratic political equality, and thus any good society, demands the equal counting of persons is only to begin a discussion. What does it mean "to count"? To be counted? To count for more or for less than one? To answer these questions is ultimately to describe, in broad outline, just political institutions. The questions, though, are not easy to answer. Thus, mere legal possession of the right to vote in no way guarantees political equality. Neither representative democracy (the form of government which such a right produces) nor majority rule (the decisional procedure which actuates it) by itself ensures that citizens shall have an equal say. On the contrary, representative government and majority rule together can easily institutionalize political *in*equality. Representative government quickly devolves into rule by a stratum of ambitious, typically male, careerists in a kind of elective and bureaucratic oligarchy—for which democratically elected legislatures and parliaments are, as Max Weber, Lenin, and C. Wright Mills suggested in their different ways, and as a stream of disillusioned U.S. ex-senators and representatives attest, "the best possible shell."[4] If we think of the act of voting as the political labor that the mass of citizens engage in, then the relationship of voter to representative (and to those millions of officials whom representatives ap-

2. This formulation, which Mill himself calls not the "democratic principle" but "the explanatory principle of Utilitarianism," appears in chapter 5 of his essay on that subject (Mill 1991). Some version of filial piety must have led Mill to attribute it, as he does there, to his godfather Jeremy Bentham: for such wording can be found nowhere in Bentham's writings and, as far as one can tell, is uniquely Mill's.

3. The sole exception to the rule of representation (that is to say, children) is the exception that illustrates the rule. At what point a human being stops being necessarily an intellectually dependent child and becomes potentially an intellectually independent adult is a matter for endless debate (though a debate conducted perhaps not as seriously as it ought to be). Yet no one disagrees with the general proposition that, for some length of time, "children" ought not have equal rights to exercise political power; and the reason for this is that *children,* as opposed to minorities or women or workers etc., will in the normal course of events stop being children and become adults.

4. See Bob Jessop's (1980, 59) discussion of Lenin on parliamentary democracy. Weber's cynicism about democracy turns up throughout his work on bureaucracy and political economy (e.g., Gerth and Mills 1946, chap. 8), and it was essentially borrowed by Mills in his discussion of executive ascendancy (Mills 1957).

point) all too obviously mimics the relationship of factory worker to factory owner, to which Marx gave the familiar designation "alienated labor." The moment in which we install our representatives in office is the moment in which they have passed out of our control.[5] As for majority rule, it all too easily becomes majority despotism; minorities, rather than being a random collection of citizens who lost the last vote but who might win the next one, become permanent outriders of the body politic.

"Democracy," furthermore, only describes politics. But this must be the politics of some kind of society, built around some kind of social division of labor. To revert to where we began: at the present moment it is, unfortunately, not possible to see past what is, in its broad outlines, a *capitalist* division of labor; that is to say, a materially productive division of labor, oriented to capital accumulation and competition for scarce resources in national and international marketplaces.[6] Such a social order inscribes not merely political differentiation but, more crucially, social differentation as well, and therefore seems to forestall any possible discussion of the good society before it is even under way. The accumulative economy, as we know it, is built on divisions of class and gender that inherently subvert democratic citizenship *and* render the idea of self-fulfillment (or the pursuit of happiness, which is historically its accompaniment and morally its necessary component) as hopelessly chimerical for some as it is at least imaginably attainable for others. By the time the formal counting of votes takes place, many have already been counted out, and others have been counted in without having to win any votes at all.[7] In what follows, then, I take up the various obstacles to being counted equally, and I attempt to imagine how they might be overcome.

5. For a more extended version of this argument, see Green 1985.

6. Richard Miller, starting from a philosophical framework of moral pluralism, offers a similar analysis in which he concludes that the discussion of social justice must, reluctantly but necessarily, be placed within the framework of capitalist economic relations (Miller 1992).

7. The world capitalist economy is also, and perhaps most crucially of all, built fundamentally around a racial division of labor. However, that is not necessarily true of national economies, as such diverse examples as South Korea and Iceland attest. Thus, for the purposes of this volume, I assume that "the good society" refers, as all classical political theorists would have assumed, to a national economy to some extent insulated from, and in great degree nonexploitative of, the international market for labor and natural resources. From this standpoint it is pointless at the present moment in time to be thinking about the United States when postulating the outlines of a "good society," even though some version of the United States is precisely what an American such as myself, engaged in this exercise, will always seem to be describing. On this point, see Stuart Hampshire's discussion (1993) of John Rawls.

I

Is civic equality possible? Can we engage with gender and class inequality in any significant way at all? To begin with the former, we know that differences of strength, size, and biological function have always been convertible into male domination and social stratification by gender. Does this not suggest a "natural" inequality?

Luckily, we do not need to answer that question, for it is, as Rousseau put it, fit only to be discussed by slaves in the presence of their masters. What we who live within extremely complex and artificial Leviathans want to know, after all, is not whether inequality in general is inherent in a nature we have long since brutally discarded, but rather how our particular inequalities came about. Here, the record is clear. The historical development of capitalism and the capitalist corporation has generated something new and unique, and quite outside nature: a bifurcated system of generalized male independence, on the one hand (however attenuated for many specific males), and female dependence on the other. To the extent that democratic politics is, uniquely, the aggregate of voluntary acts of individual will, the sexual division of labor in this political economy, even a drastically reformed version of it, necessarily renders large numbers of women as objects rather than as potential authors of social policy (see, e.g., Pateman 1989, 71–89).

The key to this social and ultimately political division of labor by gender has been the historically specific ability of productive capital to debarrass itself of all legal and social responsibility for the reproduction of its labor force—a responsibility which, given a prior history of thousands of years of sexual hierarchy, "naturally" but by no means naturally, then falls (or is placed) on women. Under capitalism, however, and again not at all naturally, only labor exchanged against capital, or providing services paid for by the circulation of capital, is remunerated. Therefore, women's reproductive labor, which consists of not only what we usually call childrearing and childcare but also (and primarily) the provision of family medical care and education or training, is unpaid labor. Yet since reproductive labor has real costs, someone, somehow, must pay for it. Often men do so out of their wages, but often they either cannot or will not.

Thus, unless they have marketable skills of the kind reserved for men through most of the history of capitalism, unsupported mothers must either enter the work force while *also* doing (unpaid) reproductive labor or become dependents of a welfare state that in most cases was created for exactly the purpose of keeping them dependent. The two alternatives are in any event not really alternatives, for the kind of wage work women can undertake while also being primary childcare providers will often be insufficient, and the welfare state will again have to provide them with auxiliary support. Moreover, this particular kind of wage labor, which can only be done episodically or as a secondary role in the division of labor, becomes known as "women's work," and women become known as the people who do that kind of work. So now the sexual division of labor appears not only between the workplace and the home, but within the workplace itself. In the light of this division, managers of productive capital come quite rationally to treat *all* women as present or potential mothers, and thus as second-class workers, regardless of what the intentions of individual women might be and regardless of what the potential capabilities of many of those mothers might be.

It follows that political institutions, which can be staffed only by people with relevant skills and expectations developed in the primary labor market, themselves come to replicate the sexual hierarchy of the productive corporation. Like the corporation, the state becomes a male institution with some female hangers-on (much like the contemporary genre of action movie in which, as a bow to feminism, the male hero has a tough female sidekick). Consequently, much state policy—especially welfare-state policy—comes to consist of men making rules to coerce the behavior of dependent or semidependent women. Gender becomes politics; and organized democratic politics, whatever other inequalities it resolves, becomes the preserve of independent men and of that handful of women capable of acting like independent men. It remains opaque to all others; and the needs and interests of all others, on the whole, are opaque to it. No matter what theories of representation tell us, such a politics cannot be representative.[8]

The first requirement of a democratic society in which everyone counts equally, therefore, is to break the hold of gender on the state—the state that perhaps ought to wither away but that will not do so as long as we live even remotely the way we do now. We could attempt to describe in great detail the institutions that would do this, but the attempt would amount to a pointless exercise in academic rationalism. Rather, we need to grasp the general principle at stake. Thinking about the institutions of a good society starts with a general agreement to treat childbearing and childrearing as voluntary labor, for the good society can hardly countenance involuntary servitude: again, that

---

8. See Catherine MacKinnon's analysis (MacKinnon 1989). It is instructive that in *Who Governs?* (1962) Robert Dahl, who later praised MacKinnon's work, did not even notice that women are the most economically and politically excluded population in New Haven. If he were redoing that work today, though, after years of feminist political theorizing, he certainly would make that a central point. The political invisibility of women can never be overestimated.

could only be true of a society that is good for some but not for all. Reproductive rights are thus intrinsic to the notion of the good society. Beyond that, however, the larger principle is that parenting ought to be treated in its broadest outlines as productive, and thus remunerative, labor, perhaps the most productive labor of all. It would obviously be easier in every way, and possibly less humanly debilitating as well, if direct parenting was shared rather than being the monopoly of women. But, in either case, the fundamental institutions are institutions that provide public support of childcare, institutions that undo the privatization of reproductive labor. Clearly this entails the availability of more-extensive family health and childcare services, and of better income-maintenance programs, than now exist in the United States. Otherwise, not only is a good society unimaginable, but we can scarcely conceive of civilized society.

More broadly, though, treating women as ends rather than means requires elimination of the double bind in which corporate capitalism places young women: in the first place, they are pressed to be "good mothers," to have and spend as much time as possible with their children; in the second place, in every social milieu they encounter thereafter, including the political, they are savagely penalized for having accepted that responsibility.[9] Contrarily, the principle of appropriate remuneration for reproductive labor is that if women (or men) with children choose to do paid labor or education or political activism rather than remain in the home, these environments, and the careers therein, as well as the social order in general, should be as hospitable and rewarding to them as to men (and of course women) who have taken on no such responsibility. Conversely, if women (or men) choose to remain in the home with their children, then that should be treated as their free choice in a labor market which rewards that choice equally with the choice to engage in "productive careers," rather than treating such a choice as sponging, parasitism, or "dependency." In either case, the division of labor in a good society has to provide opportunities for the appropriation of leisure time, and for the pursuit of self-fulfillment, that are equal for all regardless of gender. For that is the self-justification not only of socialism or utopian liberalism but of traditional capitalism as well. In particular, the political *mis*representation of women (and the virtual *non*representation of children) can be overcome only when the political and social division of labor meets the complementary conditions that (1) political or, generally, public ca-

---

9. The English single mother who was jailed in 1994 for leaving her two-year-old alone at home while she went out seeking work could tell us something about just how draconian that penalty can be.

reers are equally open to women and (2) the coercion of women into a narrow kind of labor-market behavior, a prejudicial version of the family, and a limited vision of what constitutes their life goals is no longer the root of public policy.

In sum, that is, the inhabitants of capitalist societies value *both* individual self-fulfillment *and* a (what is generally thought of as female) commitment to the nurturance of others. Only the first, however, is rewarded with more than pleasant words. In a good society, in contrast, men and women would be free to choose among alternative socially acceptable values because they truly did *prefer* the value they chose, not because of punitive threats or the promise of special privileges. Of course, to support childrearing as the public good that it really is would probably mean a major extension of public space, as the line between "private" and "public" came to be redrawn, as well as a broadening of our understanding of what goes on in workplaces or any places away from "home." It would also clearly mean a drastic change in our expectations about what kind of labor-market behavior constitutes a "career" and a significant shift of resources away from the production of other goods and services for privatized consumption. All in all, then, gender equality requires a considerable diminution in what we consider an appropriate return to owners of capital; and we have not yet even mentioned those inequalities of class which are separable from gender. But surely it is self-contradictory to imagine a good society built on the exploitation of one kind of socially valuable labor by those who do not have to engage in that labor.

II

It is perhaps possible to imagine a degendered state without descending into millenarian utopianism, although I doubt it. What sound like changes in civil society would force drastic revision in all our ways of living together, including the way in which we govern ourselves. Beyond this, however, it is not possible to imagine that *any* state charged with the responsibility of securing the conditions of economic growth and capital accumulation might be a *classless* state. That would be not just an unlikelihood but, again, a contradiction in terms. As commentators from Marx to Calvin Coolidge have agreed, the business of a capitalist society is business; the business of an accumulative society is accumulation. It does not matter who staffs the capitalist state: male, female; rich, poor; black, white; socialist, libertarian. Their business is encouraging and protecting business, and that is what they must do. State business may be and usually is conducted by an elite of planners, professionals, representatives, and experts drawn from the educated rather than the capitalist class: "The ruling class," in Fred Block's phrase, "does not rule" (Block 1977; see also Green 1985). Whoever rules, though, can never ignore the interests and expressed needs of the economic ruling class for long. In the long world-capitalist recession since the oil price break of the 1970s, for example, every reformist or laborist political party in the West has turned against its own constituencies, be they middle-class professionals or the organized working class, as the pressures of international competition have grown too strong to resist.

Thus, for millions of people, women and men alike, the very structure of capitalism ineluctably generates a crisis of human sufficiency and, literally, survival. From the standpoint of business and capital accumulation, the imperatives of competition and growth are unquestionable. They include maintaining a flexible labor market, achieving efficient and internationally competitive levels of wages and (un)employment, and forcing the pace of technological progress by substituting machinery for human labor wherever possible. These conditions of competition and *corporate* survival may require—in today's capitalist world, certainly, do require—that wages and benefits, even contractually obligated benefits, be slashed; that labor be sloughed off; that jobs be deskilled; that cooperative workers' organizations be smashed; that public services paid for in part from the earnings of capital be abolished. In sum, beyond the question of who controls the state, the condition for the continued prosperity of some of a society's inhabitants, nowadays even the majority, is a substantial increase in misery for the minority.

At this point, a vulgar utilitarian (certainly not Mill) might wish to argue that capitalism, in serving the majority, thus secures the greatest good of the greater number. However, no one wishing to discuss the concept of the "good society" can make any such argument. Let us imagine, for example, that a hundred of us are cast away together on a deserted island, that this island contains enough appropriate resources to guarantee a comfortable existence for all into the indefinite future, but that the price of developing these resources is labor so arduous and painful that the doing of it wipes out the promised comfort. Suppose, then, that our choices were reduced to the following. First, we could all lead a life of sufficiency but physical misery. Alternatively, eighty of us could, by enslaving the twenty others and inventing more efficient but still arduous technologies of production for the slaves to work on, realize the promise of comfort for ourselves, the majority, through the misery and pain of the minority. It is clear from this not entirely fanciful scenario that "the greatest good of the greater number" cannot be divorced from either distributive or political considerations—except on assumptions about goodness, happiness, and equality that are exogenous to utilitarianism itself, and therefore indefensible within its frame of reference.

Thus, before we can even begin to think further about whatever skeleton of a good society may be hidden within the corporeal body of capitalist civilization, we must first come to grips with the question of fundamental human need. In an accumulative society that we wish to claim is something more than merely materially beneficial to the majority, the central task of the state (which is necessarily a class and most likely a gendered as well as a democratic state) is to maintain the ground rules and support that further accumulation. Almost as central, however, is its responsibility, which no other institution can undertake, to compensate as much as is possible for the inevitable human destructiveness of productive efficiency and global competition.

The capitalist economy is built upon the free-market exchange of land, of capital, of commodities and, above all, of human labor power. Since all of these circulate and exchange by being expressed as money values, the various markets by their very nature do not respond directly to human need, or desire, but rather to monetary need or desire. The rule of the market is not "one person, one vote," but "one dollar, one vote": a human being does not earn a shelter by being willing to expend labor power to build it (in which case the entirety of the owning and executive classes would be homeless) but by being able to buy it. Nor is the outcome of the "one dollar, one vote" rule random. On a completely unregulated free market, wealth and economic power pyramid themselves; so does economic and all forms of social deprivation. Money, for example, may buy medical care and a secure foothold in the labor market, but lack of it "buys" such goods as tuberculosis, black lung, alcoholism, a hospital bed at best and a doorway at worst, and a future without hope for one's children.

The citizens of a good society would not allow anyone to be thrown away like so much waste material who is willing, in the same way as themselves, to make an effort to work, or to learn, or to take care of others, but who is for whatever reason unable to engage in any of these activities or to be remunerated for engaging in them. However, in the absence of countervailing forces, the outcome of the "free market" is cyclical mass unemployment, an insecure and often desperate reserve army of labor, a brutally unequal opportunity structure for men as well as for women, and the other familiar means of demobilizing and disciplining labor in a capitalist economy. On any day, perusal of the financial pages of a daily newspaper in the capitalist world will verify Marx's comment that generals become famous by recruiting armies, captains of industry by discharging them. It would be better not to cheer the latter along that road to fame, but rather to offer a different road in the first place.

Thus, precisely because of its service to capital accumulation and economic rationality, the state must also maintain or oversee institutions that, within the limitations of available resources and cultural understandings of the good life, resist the market's centrifugal force and ensure the chance for every member of society to meet fundamental individual and social needs. This means, above all, that on behalf of labor the state must counteract the operations of the free market, which produces many of the most wretched forms of unfreedom. In the first instance, employment, or access to the means of doing useful and remunerated social labor—the most fundamental human need of all—ought to be provided to those for whom the market does not provide it. We could say that the state, or the community, or the public, or however we denote the institutions that stand between people and the abyss of market freedom, ought to be the "employer of last resort."

This formulation, however, misses a crucial point about the good society, for many of the things that only the state is likely to undertake to a satisfactory degree are not last things, but first things: the conservation of an unpolluted environment for future generations; the maintenance of infrastructure; the basic provision of universal education, public health services, childcare. All of these can be provided to some extent by the private corporation, with appropriate public assistance in the form of favorable tax treatment; but none of them can be guaranteed except by the state. So perhaps we should say instead that the public ought to be the employer of *first* resort. That is to say, one of the most fundamental institutions of the good society is not so much an institution as a widely shared belief that goods produced for individuals to consume in private are of less moment to individual happiness than useful services that we benefit from collectively.

At the same time, no matter how deeply such a belief may come someday to take root, so long as we pursue the good life of material things, the market will always exert and reexert its disruptive force. Thus, without distributive and regulative institutions as well, *the* good still cannot be pursued: only the particularistic goods of the strong, the wealthy, and the successful can be pursued. Again, I have no wish to draw institutional blueprints, except to say that the redistributive taxation system of the social insurance state is not necessarily the only, perhaps not even the best, way of redressing labor market brutalities.

It might well be preferable to create a system of social cost accounting, which charges corporations for the spillover effects of their operations but rewards them for initiatives that absorb social costs. Such initiatives would include workplace programs for preventing industrial disease and accident and for continually upgrading workers' skills (human capital), worksharing arrangements instead of layoffs, provision of childcare facilities, and conversion to environmentally sound techniques of operation. Certainly redistributive taxation is politically the least satisfactory mode of regulation in the accumulative society, for it maximizes the ill feeling of those who work hard (or who think they do) for their incomes. Even worse, it widens the gap between "public" and "private," so that while earners pay the premiums for the insurance state out of their "personal" incomes, no one in fact has any public responsibility for maintaining employment or for helping at-risk persons *before* they have fallen into the expensive and self-defeating medical, welfare, and penal systems provided by the modern state. In a competitive world, however, it cannot always be economically rational to pass on these costs to those enterprises which are politically too weak to be able to resist the state; therefore, corporatist arrangements cannot possibly substitute in every instance for the authoritative state.

III

The problem of the materialist market is much more, though, than its inability to provide everyone with a decent sufficiency or a modicum of security. Amid all the rediscovery of civil society, it has rarely been mentioned that it was not Leonid Brezhnev or Erich Honecker but Margaret Thatcher who said, "There is no such thing as society." The need for institutions that mediate between people and the coercive state is matched by the need for institutions between people and the dissolving market. Wherever, for example, we do encounter institutions for promoting the production of things that are without immediate material value (e.g., the various agencies for supporting the arts that have been so much a part of European life), they are remnants of an earlier, precapitalist tradition and are everywhere now dying as the global market tightens its grip. Otherwise, as the market colonizes every nook and cranny of society, independent sources of value and pleasure are reduced to a vulgar materialist rubble. Thatcher's England is a cautionary example of the unfettered market's unmistakably totalitarian impulse. We see television surrender its historic and unique pluralism to the uniformities of the competitive ratings game; theater groups which are internationally famous face the threat of closure; local planning bodies cede their protective authority to ruthless private developers; the ethos of budgetary competition starves the health service; the privatization of rail transport threatens the closing of stations and cutting off of entire communities from that transport;

and citizens who were encouraged to convert secure public-housing tenancies into "homeownership" face eviction by the thousands for falling behind in their mortgage payments.

The invisible hand of market competition may maximize material productivity, but it cannot ensure even the minimal provision of anything that is not a material good, consumable by those with the economic ability to consume it. This is especially true of the labor-intensive production of collectively consumed services. No matter how highly we value them, their providers can never compete with profit-making institutions on the free capital market; for capital will usually flow where the greatest profit, the most efficient sloughing off of human labor, is promised. Except by accident, or by the good luck of an essential humanity that remains not for sale, the free market cannot satisfy our collective need for what is fair, or beautiful, or thought provoking; nor our need to nurture, to be farsighted, to conserve, or to cooperate.

However, for reasons already adumbrated, the state has contemporaneously earned a reputation for being oppressive, alien, and resistant to all efforts at establishing real accountability. To be sure, the idea of a really free market is loved by few, distrusted and feared by most; but this is even more true of the modern state. In a self-destructive manner, the state becomes more bloated, more resistant, more despotic, precisely as it becomes the only (even if unsuccessful) locus of attempts to restrain and regulate the more subtle despotism of the market. Worse yet, to the extent that the market's ideologists have managed to establish the notion of an unbreachable divide between the "private" economic world and the "public" political world, the market incurs little odium for being out of reach of our democratic powers. The disillusionment and hostility unleashed by the spectacle of poverty and insecurity in the midst of plenty, of futility in the midst of opportunity, and of complete unresponsiveness in the midst of representative democracy comes to focus not on the fundamental underpinnings of a social order out of control, but on the governments which we have been taught ought uniquely to be "ours"—and which, so evidently, are not.

Thus for most citizens of the enterprise society, including both the educated middle class and much of the wage-labor class in their different ways, the demands of the capitalist state in a democracy manifest themselves as a crisis not so much of capitalism as of democratic representation and participation. Seen from below, as I suggested earlier, political institutions in Western capitalist societies seem to "belong" to independent white men and to exclude dependent women and marginalized minorities; from the middle, however, the opacity of those same institutions to ordinary citizens, of any kind, seems universal.

What would an accountable state, or public sector, look like in the good society? The beginning of an answer to that question, oddly enough, is the opposite of what American "common sense" seems to tell us about alienated citizens and the alien state. To be responsive, government must be strong, not weak. The democratic participatory impulse will die out if there is nothing to participate *about,* if no institutions can be counted on to deliver the goods for which people have mobilized. Beyond that initital generalization, as I have already suggested, the accountable state would manifest a different notion of the divide between "public" and "private," of what properly belongs in each sphere.

The social organization of our material lives is public regardless of who does the organizing. The way businesses deal with workers and their families, or with the environment we all live in, or with the communities in which they are physically located, is as public as the way the state deals with transportation policy, land use, or foreign nations. In the first place, then, citizens should not have to think of the state as an alien bureaucracy reluctantly called in to redress the unexpected harms of commercial enterprise. The public in one form or another is already in any commercial enterprise, for none of the harms that accompany its productive activities is the slightest bit unexpected. They ought not to be considered as (at best) the subject of compensatory tort claims after the social damage has already been done, but as the normal side effects of doing unregulated business, and as the abnormal side effects of doing properly regulated business in the good society.

Industrial accident and disease, to take one obvious example, are inherent in the authority of management to treat human labor as a variably valuable commodity—labor power—in order to increase profitability. In this and other similar respects, therefore, the private authority of management (more precisely, of ownership) stands in opposition to any serious attempt to realize a good society and would have to be abolished outright. What the conditions of labor ought to be would not be anyone's "prerogative," least of all management's. It would be the subject of uncoerced negotiation between parties, all of whom bear a public responsibility and thus political accountability for their actions.

The inevitable market power of those who own and control productive capital would be balanced by the legitimate public political power of those who possess only their membership in the body politic; in this respect, the right collectively to withhold labor without fear of being replaced or starved into submission is the most fundamental of all social rights. This means, of course, that in the good society many of what we now consider to be appropriate incentives to engage in entrepreneurial activity would disappear. But there is no natural mode of private enterprise, and no natural set of incentives for engaging in it. No matter how ownership is hedged around with public accountability, some persons will always find more pleasure in owning what others labor on than in laboring on what others own.

Redefining "public" and "private" is only half of a solution, however. To be publicly accountable means to be accountable to representatives of the public, but it is precisely the failures of conventionally defined representation that generate so much of our hostility to the state. The failure is twofold. First, even defining democracy as loosely and permissively as we usually do, there are few democracies in the world today: most so-called democratic states (those which Robert Dahl calls "polyarchies") are oligarchies tempered by occasional elections (Dahl 1989). Although distant parliaments and alien chief executives cannot be dispensed with so long as the nation-state exists, they, like the provision of basic needs (of which political representation is surely one) can at least be made accountable to persons rather than to money. And if we cannot prevent the state from making the furtherance of capital accumulation its primary business, we can prevent capital from being able to act as though it owns the state.

When political candidacies require vast amounts of money, they become purchasable; when expensive television time is the lifeblood of politics, then politics has become a branch of advertising. The primary quality of the good society's political institutions is that, unlike the way things are in our present-day institutions, the attention of those who staff them cannot be bought by us, nor can our attention be bought by them. At a minimum, this requires either abolishing all private financing of elections or making sure that during elections there is nothing (e.g., time and space sold by privately owned mass-media outlets) on which to spend private finance (see Green 1985, 256–68).

But there is a limit to how much the apparently indispensable world of pseudodemocracy can be reformed. The other main reason for the contemporary "democratic" state's loss of credibility is that "representation" does not seem to be a vital connection between people and leaders. It is pseudorepresentation, and we expect very little even from the best of those who practice it. Conceptually, it is as though practitioners and critics of contemporary pseudorepresentation have agreed to think of "representation" and "participation" as antonymous, when they should more properly be seen as aspects of one another. In the good society, representation would be a constant affair expressing a constant connection, not just a matter of elections, letter-writing campaigns, lobbying, and visits "home" from elected representatives to meet a few of their constituents.

Both government and the corporate sphere can be brought under citizen control only if deputies and spokespersons appear everywhere, legitimately intruding on bureaucrats and managers alike, demanding accountable behavior here and now, and accountably reporting back to the constituents who authorized them. The safety inspectorate for dangerous workplaces should be elected representatives of workers, not occasional visitors from the outer space of labor departments or ministries; the lending policies of banks should be overseen by community deputies as well as by self-perpetuating boards; land-use policies should be subject to the determination not merely of urban planners and the construction industry, but also of the people who use or hope to use the land, through their deputies; placement of traffic lights should be responsive to spokespersons for parents with children, ahead of traffic engineers who have never personally tried to lead a child across a busy intersection; the construction or siting of nuclear power plants, recombinant-DNA facilities, and the like should be subject to referenda after extensive debate within the affected communities, among representatives chosen from among all those whose interests are vitally affected. In what pass for democracies nowadays, PACs, political parties, and bureaucracies—in a symbiotic relationship with those whom they are supposed to regulate—tend to mobilize special interests. Thus voluntary organizations of concerned persons are more likely to mobilize the public interest. If they make it harder and more time-consuming for the bulldozers to run and the scientists to experiment, that may well be what democracy, properly conceived, requires.

Dominant elites have always assured their disenfranchised subjects that only "experts" can appropriately make decisions such as these, but that is merely their peculiar fantasy of domination: citizens of the good society need not take it seriously. The first quality of any expert, or any planner, is to know what are the needs of whatever community he or she is part of, and to represent those needs; the second quality is to be able to persuade the members of that community, in rational and uncensored public discussion, that a proposed course of action is indeed the best among possible courses of action. Outside the small town, of course, government by direct and universal general assembly is impossible. But what classical and neoclassical theorists from Aristotle to Hannah Arendt thought of as the kind of participation which denotes the communally active and self-fulfilling citizen is not at all beyond the bounds of the possible; rather, it has to be rethought.

It is not necessary to make laws in order to be a participant; nor is it necessary to possess exceptional education or great intelligence. As Mill and Dewey both argued, in their different ways, we learn how to participate by participating, and in no other way; those who are dominant learn only how to dominate (Mill 1946; Dewey 1927; Dewey 1966). Choosing representatives and instructing representatives; negotiating needs and capabilities with experts; arguing with and on behalf of neighbors: these are the primary activities of political participation and, consequently, of community and individual development, and they are not beyond the capacities of ordinary persons.[10] In the good society, such activities would be the building blocks of all political decisionmaking, and of political leadership as well. A leader in the good society would not be an adventurous man who finds an ego-fulfilling career in the arena of power, but an active and determined member of any community who, step by step, has been thrust up the ladder of representation by that community. In one respect Rousseau was absolutely right: the true vocation of those who govern a self-governing society is to be good and faithful servants.

After all this has been said, however, one thing more remains to be said about democratic government in a good society. The real history of democracy, as opposed to even the most open-ended of conceptual schemes and utopian blueprints, is the history of popular struggle. Every democratic institution has in the first instance been fought for and realized not by courts or legislatures or benevolent despots, but by masses of people taking direct action in the streets, in factories, even at funeral processions. No competitive party politics, no competition for leadership, nor any other version of what contemporary theorists have come to call the democratic process, would have achieved women's suffrage in Britain, or the Civil Rights Act of 1964, or the National Labor Relations Act of 1935 (or the upsurge in union activity after its passage), or freedom of speech for activists and organizers. Recent democratic theory has had it backwards: for mass action is the heart of democracy; electoral and legislative politics, though its necessary condition, are too often the hardening of its arteries. Without democracy in that most meaningful sense, the "democratic process" is lifeless.[11]

10. It is worth noting that during John Major's term as prime minister of Great Britain, the collapse of the Labour Party as an intellectual force has meant that all effective opposition to Tory policies of privatization, attacks on welfare, etc. have been carried on by voluntary organizations, almost all of them led by women with no previous history of political activism, no expert credentials, and closer ties to their "constituents" than any political party now achieves. In television debates these women regularly make fools of Government ministers.

11. For an elaboration of this argument, see Green 1990, 234ff. See also Carter 1973; Benewick and Smith 1972; Cockburn 1977; and Ackelsberg 1993.

All institutions ossify, and the best institutions ossify most completely. Beyond everything we can say about institutions, about democratic representation and democratic leadership, we must also say that direct action is integral to the good society. All agendas are originally set in the streets, and if we wait for them to be set lawfully and orderly they will never change, no matter how democratic, no matter how faithfully representative, we think we are. It is direct action that spontaneously expresses those needs, desires, and solidarities of neighborhood, community, or locality which are inevitably repressed by the formalization of popular activity as democratic law and order. Through obedience to others, we learn to be like others; through action in cooperation with others, we learn to be ourselves.

If, as as in the theory and practice of "the democratic process," we make elections into absolute trumps, into the uniquely legitimate method for ascertaining the will of that cast of characters known as "the people," then the formal electoral system becomes the enemy of any attempt to eliminate whatever injustices are intrinsic to it—and, inevitably, there will be injustices in any set of formalized practices. The civic culture of the good society would be one which, in addition to generally multiplying avenues for participation and representation, did not value formally democratic procedures to the exclusion of demands for equal rights, access to useful and remunerative labor, or community preservation. Rather, it would encourage the spontaneous, direct expression of those demands. As I. F. Stone famously remarked, "the rich march on Washington all the time," often without doing more than picking up a telephone or a menu. The rest of us can trample all over the Mall in our hundreds of thousands and, most of the time, no one listens. In the good society, a march on Washington, civil disobedience in San Francisco, a neighborhood uprising in New York, a factory occupation in Hull, a march of women in London, would be an occasion not for response by national guardsmen or national prosecutors, but for listening; and the greater the number who marched or disobeyed, the more certainly would representatives know that they should listen and perhaps act. That sort of political culture, always submerged yet always ready to emerge, is the hidden but most important face of democratic participation.

IV

And yet: to the very extent that a good society encourages spontaneous activism and local self-protection against the appropriation of communal powers by an alien center, so too it must guard the powers and opportunities of individuals against the great and little tyrannies that are ceaselessly exercised by those very same communities. "Not in my backyard" is a perfectly reasonable slogan to oppose those who want to dump toxic wastes or build nuclear power plants; but it is an oppressive slogan to those who want only to be allowed to live with a backyard of their own. Direct action to prevent trailer trucks from being routed down residential streets is the essence of democracy; direct action to prevent the siting of homes for the mentally ill on those same streets is the essence of oppression. A good society must prominently feature institutions that constantly educate us about the nature of that difference.

The most negative aspect of the contemporary turn to communitarianism in democratic theory is precisely its obfuscation about the real nature of "community," and the attack on liberal rights and liberal individualism that is sometimes undertaken in its name. Thinking about the good society has to begin from an understanding that, outside the premodern tribe (perhaps), there is no such thing as an integral or homogeneous community. Here Mill is surely correct and Rousseau (as he himself implicitly recognizes in passages scattered throughout *Le contrat social*) is a hopeless visionary. All societies, large or small, are truly *pluralist*—not in the distribution of power, but in the distribution of values. "Homogeneity" is in fact nothing but the characteristic of a community in which repression is undergirded by conformist opinion rather than by force of arms; there, difference hides itself in the closet rather than freely asserting itself in the streets.

A good society, seen in this light, defines "the good" not as a particular set of values but as those processes which enable the bearers of different conceptions of the good to live in peace. Necessarily, then, the institutions of a good society must always to this extent be in tension with its popular will; for although a good society values alternative worldviews and life plans, people, even good people, do not. A good society is therefore not only tolerant of dissent and difference but actively enables the development of channels for their expression and dissemination. Whatever the existing modes of representation, civic freedom cannot survive their denial to minorities within the body politic, as history endlessly attests.

The denial of effective representation instantiates a hierarchy—of power rather than of moral value—among views of the good and the ability to communicate them to others: precisely the kind of hierarchy that destroys the fundamental processes of pluralism which are integral to the good society.[12] Similarly, whatever the existing technologies

12. The best contemporary exposition of the need to institutionalize effective representation of marginalized minorities is Young 1991.

of communication and representation, civic freedom cannot survive either monopoly or oligopoly in their ownership or control; nor exclusion or serious inequality in access to their use. This form of misrepresentation generates the deadliest form of alienation in modern societies, as the mass of people give up their power to see the world and describe it to others: the mass-produced image abstracts from, negates, and distorts the actual images that particular human beings have of their world, then returns the alienated image to them as though it were their own.

Of course the good society requires more than merely equal access to the means of communication, which can be abolished in an instant by a legislature, a bureaucracy, or an angry mob (see Green 1985, 219–24). Its crowning institutions are institutions for the positive protection of individual and minority rights—not just against the alienated powers of the center, but against the more authentic-seeming powers of the town, village, or neighborhood. Offensive personal behavior that does material injury to no one is, properly conceived, just as "private" as the organizing economic behavior of giant corporations is "public." An enforceable, written charter of rights; independent organs of judicial and administrative review to enforce those rights; civilian control of the police power; ombudsoffices in proliferation; special forums for the representation of isolated minorities; and, beyond such formal protections, an inculcated respect for the informal but equally crucial democratic processes of conscientious objection and civil disobedience: all of these are as much the lifeblood of the good society as political participation, neighborhood action, and communal self-help.[13]

This proposal to institutionalize the protection of rights is, to be sure, hardly uncontroversial. Judge Learned Hand, in a famous defense of judicial deference to majority rule, remarked that a court need not save any people in whom the spirit of liberty is alive and cannot save any people in whom it is dead. The sentiment is indeed beautiful and, in one sense, even true—but, in another, it is quite false. It is false

---

13. Since Americans have recently corrupted the terms "civil disobedience" and "conscientious objection," some explanation is necessary. Rights of conscience apply to the demand to be exempted from doing harm to others, and only to that; civil disobedience inheres in the refusal to submit to legalized injustice. Thus a doctor who wishes not to perform abortions ought not to be penalized for following his conscience, but has no right to harass women who are seeking abortions from other doctors. Thus also, the civil rights movement and Martin Luther King should have been supported rather than hindered by the federal government, but no one has a right to forcibly prevent others from *peaceful* mobilization, no matter how obnoxious their cause (e.g., racism or anti-Semitism). To do so is to commit *uncivil* disobedience, and no government need permit it, for it cannot be unjust for others to try to do only what we would insist on being allowed to do ourselves.

in that there is never, not even in a good society, *a* people, but only peoples, sometimes together but sometimes torn apart, in whose various collective consciousnesses the spirit of liberty sometimes waxes, sometimes wanes. It is a true sentiment, however, in that a good society, built on mutual respect for the plurality of communal values and individual life plans, cannot long survive the presence within itself of sectarian communities that insist on dogmatic adherence to their own values as the price of moral or legislative tolerance. The insistence that others ought to behave as we want them to behave, and that it is an infringement on our own rights if they fail to do so, is, as Mill put it, "so monstrous a principle" as can be conceived; and no communal demonstration, however spontaneous and however united, can justify it (Mill 1991, 99). In this single respect a universalistic *secular* liberalism is indeed, as both Left and Right have argued, an unyieldingly prescriptive philosophy: its spirit can tolerate any eccentricity but organized intolerance itself. In this respect, though, it is also the philosophy of a good society. To return to where this essay began, the wall of separation between church and state—that is, between any institutionalized moral belief and any institutionalized political power—is not merely incidental to our imagination of the good society. It is the very essence of the thing itself: without which not.

REFERENCES

Ackelsberg, Martha. 1993. *Free Women of Spain.* Bloomington: Indiana University Press.

Benewick, Robert, and Trevor Smith, eds. 1972. *Direct Action and Democratic Politics.* London: George Allen & Unwin.

Block, Fred. 1977. "The Ruling Class Does Not Rule: Notes on the Marxist Theory of the State." *Socialist Revolution* 7(3):6–28.

Carter, April. 1973. *Direct Action and Liberal Democracy.* New York: Harper & Row.

Cockburn, Cynthia. 1977. *The Local State.* London: Pluto Press.

Dahl, Robert A. 1962. *Who Governs?* New Haven, Conn.: Yale University Press.

———. 1989. *Democracy and Its Critics.* New Haven, Conn.: Yale University Press.

Dewey, John. 1927. *The Public and Its Problems.* New York: Henry Holt.

———. 1966. *Democracy and Education.* New York: Macmillan.

Gerth, H. H., and C. Wright Mills, eds. 1946. *From Max Weber: Essays in Sociology.* Glencoe, Ill.: Free Press.

Green, Philip. 1985. *Retrieving Democracy: In Search of Civic Equality*. Totowa, N.J.: Rowman & Allenheld.

———. 1990. "Robert A. Dahl's *Democracy and Its Critics*." *Social Theory and Practice* 16(2):217–44.

Hampshire, Stuart. 1993. "Liberalism: The New Twist." *New York Review of Books* 40 (August 12).

Hegel, G.W.F. 1952. *Hegel's Philosophy of Right*. Translated by T. M. Lenox. New York: Oxford University Press.

Jessop, Bob. 1980. "The Political Indeterminacy of Democracy." In Alan Hunt, ed., *Marxism and Democracy*. London: Lawrence & Wishart.

MacKinnon, Catherine. 1989. *Toward a Feminist Theory of the State*. New York: Cambridge University Press.

Mill, John Stuart. 1946. *On Liberty and Considerations on Representative Government*. London: Basil Blackwell.

———. 1991. *On Liberty and Other Essays*. New York: Oxford University Press.

Miller, Richard W. 1992. *Moral Differences*. Princeton, N.J.: Princeton University Press.

Mills, C. Wright. 1957. *The Power Elite*. New York: Oxford University Press.

Pateman, Carole. 1989. "Women and Consent." In *The Disorder of Women*. Cambridge: Polity Press.

Young, Iris Marion. 1991. *Justice and the Politics of Difference*. Princeton, N.J.: Princeton University Press.

Conclusion: Judging the Good Society

STEPHEN L. ELKIN

THE PAPERS PRESENTED in this volume are divided by whether their principal concern is with how human capabilities affect institutional design or with how we define the good society. The presumption underlying this division is that any competent account of good society thinking must have room for discussion of the systematic features of good society analysis and for a variety of accounts of the content of their constitution.

The first body of work is directed at building a set of general propositions that must be taken into account in any effort to foster a good society. These propositions will focus largely on the question of what is humanly possible in political life as this bears on institutional design. Through such work we can learn which modes of association demand too much of us in that they require regular displays of behavior—for example, the ability to sort out and weigh very large numbers of alternatives—that are beyond our competence. We can also learn how to compensate for human weaknesses and to strengthen human capabilities.

The second body of work concentrates on developing and criticizing a variety of sketches of good societies. Such sketches can run from accounts of the basic organizing principles of good societies and their underlying values to institutionally specific analyses of how good societies should work. The overall concern of such work is to build up a set of alternative conceptions, the critique of which will lead to more refined accounts and to a set of plausible analyses of the political constitution of a variety of good societies.

In this conclusion, I want to redefine these two themes, add to what has already been said about them, and introduce a new theme:

the character of the judgment that underlies an assessment that some societies are good and others are not. In doing so, not only do I mean to consider the connections among the papers and their contribution to comprehensive good society analysis. I will also be setting out an overview of the essential steps in any comprehensive good society analysis, whether as a matter of general reflection on the meaning and possibilities of such societies or as a preface to actual efforts to reform existing societies.

The three themes—institutional components, the character of political-economic wholes, and evaluation of those wholes—are, I believe, the essential components of good society analysis. As such, they are the substance of the political judgment that is exercised in good society thinking.

By considering the papers in light of these three themes, we should be able to conceive of their arguments in a new way. At this early stage in the development of good society thinking, such an additional perspective can only be to the good. In any case, the following overview, however sketchy, is an appropriate way to conclude a volume whose principal aim is to stimulate work on good society questions.

Policies and Institutions

It is common to think that the problem of political-economic reform is fundamentally a matter of good "policy." If we are in trouble, what we need are better public policies. The papers in this volume have a different premise: reform thinking, and reform itself, must focus on the design of political and economic institutions.

It is easy to see why this must be the focus for those who think that Western societies—the principal concern of this volume—are living off a vision of the good society that is no longer workable or capable of inspiring hope. It is the very essence of their task to think about the design of innovative institutionanl forms. If advocates of a new social vision are to be convincing, they cannot present a vague outline of their preferred good society but must spell out its institutional details. Thus, for example, Gar Alperovitz, argues that both democratic capitalism and any form of statist socialism are unattractive and ultimately unsustainable, and he begins the task of sketching in the fundamental political-economic institutional components of a new vision of the good society.

What is perhaps surprising, however, is that such a focus on institutional design is equally necessary for those who believe that the United States and other Western countries are by and large on the right track, committed, as they should be, to perfecting as their vision of the good society some form of democratic capitalism. Consider that those who think we are on the right track have a very serious problem to face. If we take the United States as an example, the difficulty is this: there is a constant stream of serious policy problems. Children are not learning as much as they might; the level of poverty and dependency shows no sign of declining and may well be increasing; the overall gap between rich and poor is growing wider; crime and violence are on the rise; and the rate of increase in economic productivity has slowed enough to raise questions about the future well-being of a growing population. Most generally, there is a widespread disillusionment with the public sphere and with the ability of government to reduce substantially the level and intensity of a wide range of social disorders.

Now a typical response to these problems is to say that what is needed is for Congress to enact a policy aimed at bringing about the desired results. There is nothing wrong with this response as far as it goes, for it is through policies passed by the national legislature, among other ways, that we attempt to implement our conceptions of what makes for a good society.

What is often missing in such policy thinking, however, is a sufficient appreciation of the sources of policy problems. Such problems are, in fact, largely a result of the failure of institutions. Or, what is even more unsettling, they are often the results of institutions that "work"—in the sense that their routines run smoothly and those who function in them feel they are doing a good job—but whose smooth operation itself presents the larger society with grave difficulties.[1]

Thus, as many observers argue, the problem with schooling lies as much as anything in the fact that public schools as they are now organized have little incentive to make a serious effort to educate students. Schools have a virtual monopoly in most places, these observers point out, and so they need not compete or respond to their clientele of students and parents. One might argue whether this is a case of schools smoothly pursuing their routines or, instead, showing significant signs of disarray. For the present discussion, this is not important. Nor is it important whether the diagnosis itself is correct. Rather, it is the focus

---

1. What is odd in such policy discussions is that there often is no realization that, in fact, institutional behavior is central to the policies that are proposed. Thus, it is typically assumed that these policies will be carried out by a government agency setting down regulations to which private actors must conform. This has come to be known—rather tendentiously to be sure—as relying on the device of "command and control." The real need may be to broaden the conception of, and bring to explicit consideration, thinking about institutional design.

on the institutions themselves—on the design of school systems—that is crucial.

The situation is, if anything, even more disturbing with regard to the distribution of income and the extent of poverty. It is increasingly obvious that something is wrong in the United States, and perhaps in other Western countries, with the way wages are set. It is now entirely possible in the United States to have a full-time job and to have an annual income below the poverty line. At the same time, very likely for the same reasons, the ratio of the salaries of top managers to those of workers has been growing worse, and with it the distribution of wealth and income.[2] Although the matter is very complicated, there is good reason to suppose that so long as workers have little or no ownership stake in business firms, the ordinary processes of wage setting can only contribute to substantial economic inequality and poverty.[3] In other words, the ordinary workings of business firms and labor markets—of institutions—are a major source of the difficulties.

Effective reform policy, then, must focus on institutional design. Those who are committed to a fuller realization of democratic capitalism need both institutional diagnosis of policy failures and, even more important, designs for new and more effective institutions. Instead of institutions that work badly or that work all too well but in the wrong ways, reformers need to look for institutions whose routine functioning, without regular "policy fixes," will bring the promise of democratic capitalism even closer.

And so, what is wanted, for example, are designs for firms where workers have ownership stakes or where other ownership forms will modify the present extent of inequality.[4] Similarly needed are designs for school systems that more closely tie teacher rewards and school resources to student learning.[5] The list could be expanded to include, for example, innovative institutions for land use control that make it easier for local governments to improve the quality of their physical environment and, through land ownership, to meet more easily their financial obligations.[6]

The paper by Elinor Ostrom is a powerful expression of this line

2. See the discussion in, among many others, Levy 1988; Philips 1990; and Kaus 1992.

3. See, e.g., Thurow 1977 and Dahl 1985, esp. chap. 3.

4. Again, see Dahl 1985, esp. chap. 5.

5. An early version of such proposals for market-oriented reforms can be found in Downs 1970. A sensible overview of the problem, with an eye to the implications of marketlike reforms for democratic citizenship—a question I will raise below—can be found in Barber 1984, chap. 10.

6. See Imbroscio 1993.

of argument. Ostrom does not confine her arguments to Western societies, nor does she explicitly say that her concern is with the reform of existing regimes, but that is clearly the implied context. More important, she contends that the development of voluntary associations among individuals through cooperatively enforced covenants is often a more efficient institution for the management of common property resources than "policy prescriptions formally made in a nation's capital." At the broadest level, her concern is with the design of robust institutional arrangements for efficient management of such resources, institutions that will be able to respond effectively to local problems.

The underlying point of view of Ostrom's paper is that well-run political-economic regimes are not built around a central governmental steering mechanism. They are instead composed of a wide variety of institutional forms for social problem-solving that, more or less autonomously, cope with their local dilemmas and, if necessary, work out cooperative arrangements with each other.[7] To be sure, she says, there are limits to such a decentralized self-governing political economy; but rather than looking toward Leviathan, we are better off looking toward the improvement of the less cumbersome and less remote problem-solving capabilities that are to be found in the array of modes of association through which we also conduct our collective lives.

A similar theme is present in the paper by Charles Anderson, although there the emphasis is on the point that all these problem-solving modes of association—Anderson elsewhere calls them "communities of practice"[8]—have a public dimension that makes regulation of them by political authority both necessary and desirable. Still, Anderson's good societies are distinguished by the simple fact that "things work"—which he attributes to an instinct for workmanship that has its basis in such well-run communities of practice. Anderson would then agree that the key to a good society is not its "policies," understood as laws made by central governmental authorities; rather, the key lies in an array of stable, problem-solving relationships that are fitted to their purposes. The principal task of government is to see that these relationships and the institutions that are built on them work well.

7. While the provenance of Ostrom's arguments is almost certainly the public choice literature, and from welfare economics and the economic theory of institutions from which public choice theory derives, a parallel set of arguments has developed independently from the same sources. This other line of argument makes no assumption that participants in institutions are economically rational, and it is open to a larger range of evaluative standards than the typical exercise in public choice. Two early and still very useful discussions are Dahl and Lindblom 1953 and Barry 1965, chap. 5. For an overview of such arguments and how they might be employed in a practice-oriented political science, see Elkin 1974.

8. See Anderson 1990.

Ostrom and Anderson illustrate the point that in good society thinking we must focus on institutions instead of policies. Both also make a second, more substantive point: that a good society is one characterized by a wide array of formal and informal institutions whose modes of association are well adapted to the problems they confront. Public authority is indeed to be wielded—but for the purpose of improving such modes, not replacing them. Indeed, the burden of providing social intelligence cannot principally be carried by government itself.

But what kinds of institutions? Granted that there must be a variety of such problem-solving institutions, is there anything more to say? The essays by Sołtan, Vanberg and Buchanan, and Dryzek all suggest at least one crucial point: namely, that institutions must be fitted to, among other things, an account of human capabilities for instrumental rationality. Dryzek is a good deal more suspicious certainly than Vanberg and Buchanan about how far such an inquiry can and should take us when we are designing institutions. To be more precise, he is less enamored of such an inquiry than devotees of the chastened kind of public choice theory that grows out of the work of Buchanan are likely to be, for Dryzek believes that rationality cannot be understood solely as means–ends thinking. But even Dryzek thinks that human beings do not have great capacities in this regard and that, insofar as such instrumental rationality is part of the "subjectivities" that citizens will invoke as they go about designing their own institutions, then it will (ought to?) lead to institutional designs that do not call for a level of rationality greater than can be exercised.

Among the additional features of human nature that the papers point to as being crucial in the design of institutions, at least one other receives more than passing attention: that human beings are self-interested but nonetheless capable of looking beyond their narrow interests. Sołtan's account of justice is premised on this conception of human nature, and I explicitly make the point in my account of lawmaking and citizenship in the commercial republic. There are, of course, other features of human capability that will need to be taken into account—for example, that human beings resent the arbitrary manipulation of their dependencies and that they have a deep need for both security and identification with others.

The creation of an attractive political constitution must be anchored, the papers imply, in just such reliable motives for action, taking human beings as they are or might plausibly become. This might mean that some motives should be deflected into harmless channels while others should be reinforced and their reach expanded. Thus, it may be better to have human beings tyrannize over their bank balances rather than over each other; and it may be crucial for a good society that the propensity to reach beyond one's own interests be given considerable scope and reinforcement. Moreover, at least in my paper and that by Sołtan, there is the suggestion that it will be particularly important that institutions that revolve around deliberation have an important place in a good society, since this is one way in which the limits of rationality can be stretched.

Taken together, the papers mentioned thus far suggest that any formulation of the content of political judgment in constituting good societies must rest on a determination of those features of human nature that are crucial in political life. If the list proves to be long, however, it is doubtful that good societies can be created by reason and choice, since the design task will simply be too great given human capabilities, even if the task is undertaken incrementally.

The other general consideration of great importance that emerges from these papers is whether institutional design should focus on compensating for human weakness, or whether it should attempt to compensate for that weakness but also to strengthen human capacity. Vanberg and Buchanan's paper suggests that they are more concerned with the former, Sołtan's that he is mostly concerned with the latter. I suspect that the choice turns as much as anything on the theorist's beliefs about whether the principal concern in good society thinking is to prevent the worst—a "good enough" society, as it were, anything else being too dangerous to contemplate—or whether humankind both should aim for and is capable of achieving more—a good society, if not the best society.

Putting the Institutions Together: Values and Regimes

Good society thinking cannot stop with a discussion of the great variety of problem-solving institutions, for in the end it is the *combination* of such institutions that is crucial. Institutions do not work on their own—with schools separate from workplaces, labor markets separate from local governments. They are connected up in a larger whole, a political economy. Moreover, I have until this point discussed only what might be called microconstitutional questions: the design of the problem-solving capacities of a good society. But who is to undertake and authorize such tasks? Even if it is supposed that such problem-solving institutions can come into being more or less spontaneously through the kind of cooperative efforts Ostrom describes, these institutions are not immortal and will need to be repaired, often in ways that those who run the institutions cannot do themselves. Even more obviously, many such problem-solving institutions will need to be set up and supported by authoritative institutions. In short, in thinking about the political-economic whole of the good society we must also consider the design of its major constitutive institutions, those which make its laws. Thus, the design of the constitution of a good society is in at least two senses a design for a political-economic whole.

In my paper, I set out some of the considerations that are central in designing the authority relations of one good society: the commercial republic. I will not go further here except to say that there is a substantial intellectual inheritance concerning the problems of constitutional design that, for the modern world, starts with Hobbes, is developed by Locke and Madison, and continues to the present day in the reflections of those who are attempting to set out workable and attractive authority relations for the new regimes of Eastern Europe and for the successor countries to the Soviet Union.[9]

Instead, what I wish to do here is consider the consequences for the constitution of good societies that micro- and macroconstitutional questions are significantly interconnected. The best way to make the point is by example. It is not improbable that organizing schooling along market principles (with a market, for example, driven by a system of vouchers handed out to each parent) will prove to be more efficient than the present system of public monopoly partly modified by the presence of private schools. But even if it turns out that students learn more than they do now, that the investment of resources is lower or identical, and that parents/consumers are more satisfied with the results, the discussion of the organization of schools cannot stop there.

Consider that any good society is likely to require some measure of public-spiritedness—understood as caring for public purposes and public destinations—from its citizenry.[10] As I have argued elsewhere in the present volume, such a disposition can be strengthened and given the right direction only through participation in a certain kind of local politics. In particular, that local politics must be participative and structured so that citizens have some experience with struggling to give concrete meaning to the public interest of the community. Now, it may not be the case that it is only through struggling over the proper content of schooling and its relation to the wider society that public-spiritedness can be reinforced in the necessary ways. But schooling will certainly be one of the central concerns of the citizenry of the various local governments that are a part of a good society—and if the rein-

---

9. See the overview in Elkin, "Constitutionalism: Old and New" (Elkin and Soltan 1993).

10. The phrase is Edwin Haefele's: see "What Constitutes the American Republic?" (Elkin and Soltan 1993).

forcement of public-spiritedness is to work, the concerns of local politics must be concerns that citizens care about deeply. A market in schooling will make such a local politics difficult to sustain since it will remove from local political life one of the things citizens care most about.

How, then, are the competing concerns of efficiency and citizenship to be brought together in the constitution of a good society? This particular example is one of many. Similar conflicts can be found across a broad range of domains between efficient institutions for problem solving, and institutions (for example) that are broadly representative and protect liberty. I will return to this question in a moment.

In considering how the various institutions that compose a good society are to be put together to form its way of life, however, there is a second important question: Can we pick and choose among the various institutional possibilities in a kind of rationalism of the machine shop, slotting in institutions simply in terms of the capabilities of each, taken one at a time?

At various points in their paper, Vanberg and Buchanan suggest that they think this is indeed the case. One interpretation of their arguments is that constitutional experts will inform citizens of the likely kinds of outcomes from the decision rules that might make up the constitution, and that the citizenry will then choose the combination they prefer. Vanberg and Buchanan may have something quite different in mind—a process in which the empirical constraints on certain kinds of institutions coexisting are given a more prominent place in constitutional choice—but the burden of their argument is closer to the first interpretation. Alperovitz also does not directly say what his views are concerning whether we can pick and choose. He argues that the institutional formation of the good society he sketches in his paper must be held together by some form of democratic planning. Insofar as this is not some sort of deus ex machina, then the good society he envisages is a set of mutually reinforcing institutions in which planning can work because other institutions work in certain ways, and these other institutions work as they do because of planning. This implies that only certain combinations of institutions can work.

The general point is simply that when we design constitutions, we are not just picking rules but creating institutions—which is to say, bodies of behavior that will variously support and undercut each other. It thus seems entirely likely that good societies cannot be composed of just any combination of institutions: there are "packages" of institutions, and constitutional choice is more nearly a choice between such packages than it is a choice of particular institutions.[11]

11. The deeper set of questions here is what kind of "totality" or "whole" are good

But for what purposes or ends are these packages of institutions to be put together? We want to know not only how the pieces may be fitted together, but why we engage in the exercise in the first place. What is the meaning of the "good" in the label "good society"?

In many ways, the simplest manner of answering these questions is to look to the design of the most efficient political economy, where efficiency is broadly understood, not tied to measures of costs and benefits that make what we lose and what we gain commensurable in some higher-order stuff such as money or utility. The microconstitutional tail will wag the macroconstitutional dog, as the principal task of the major constitutional institutions will be to foster intelligent problem solving among microconstitutional institutions. Ostrom and Anderson, I have said, are concerned with whether institutions work—with whether they do a good job in seeing that water resources are well used, medical care gets delivered to the right people at the right time, and so on. While nothing in their papers suggests that either of them is interested only in efficiency, it is not clear what will wag what. Their papers do, however, make it clear that we can understand a great deal about what makes for good societies by confining our attention simply to how to get a society to carry out, consistently and well, its major social tasks.

As a way of talking about intelligent problem solving, the concept of efficiency emphasizes that our resources are not boundless. In the inimitable words of Milton Friedman, "There is no free lunch." That it costs something need not be so constraining as he makes out, but it is still the case that lunch does not drop unbidden from the heavens.

If discussions within the domain of political science and political theory are any indication, it is all too easy to forget such points as we search for the real meaning of justice or freedom, or as we seek to learn who wins and loses in various political struggles. It is important not to move quickly past the question of whether any given version of a good society will competently carry out basic social chores as if this were a special concern of economists and largely a technical matter of no great moment. Efficiency is about intelligent problem solving, the effective use of resources to gain as much as we can of what we count as valuable. It really does matter whether the mail gets delivered reliably and at modest cost, as those who live in societies without such a service can attest.

We will, however, plausibly want to evaluate combinations of institutions by other criteria as well. It is unlikely that many people will

---

societies—or, for that matter, any sort of political economies. Here are the old and difficult questions concerning the relation of parts to wholes that has found modern expression in various kinds of system theory. A contemporary installment in this long-running debate can be found in Unger 1987.

sacrifice their lives in the battle for efficiency. But many of course have done just that in the struggle for freedom and equality. If nothing else suggests it, this fact alone ought to encourage good society theorists to think hard about how such other values might be realized. One suspects that they will in fact need little encouragement in this regard, since most good society theorizing has grown out of a dissatisfaction, not to mention disgust, with the all-consuming concern for economic efficiency.

Both Green and Alperovitz make clear what some of these additional value concerns might be. Thus Green considers at length the centrality of civic equality for the democratic organization of authority which, he says, must be at the center of any good society. Alperovitz also believes that any good society must have substantial equality, along with a sense of community and a deep commitment to liberty. It is no criticism of Green and Alperovitz to note that the values they point to are the standard ones of Western political discourse. For both, especially Alperovitz, this is an advantage because it points to the extent of our present failure: we are failing by our own lights, no less by some standard brought in from outside.

Green and Alperovitz, then, are engaging in what might be called "internal critique."[12] I take much the same path in my own paper, as does Anderson in less explicit ways. Instead of offering justifications and generalized specifications of various political goals, we simply take as given the more widely shared goals and standards, then consider the barriers to achieving them and the institutional arrangements that are necessary to serve them. Of these four papers, Green's is probably the most heavily oriented to making these political goals more precise by looking at what does not work. Green is suspicious of blueprints for what we should do instead. Anderson, presumably because his conception of the good society is a good deal more modest than Green's, does not think blueprints are, in fact, necessary—the prototypes of good societies can be found scattered across the political landscape. Alperovitz and I fall in between, thinking that good societies require more than Anderson allows (Alperovitz being more demanding than I am) and feeling confident that even if blueprints cannot be provided,[13] some institutionally specific things can be said. All four of us, though, might be understood as saying that there is a moral inheritance, which includes some conception of efficiency or effectiveness in the carrying on of political business, and that this inheritance is sufficiently well

12. Cf. Walzer 1987.
13. Can (and should) they be provided? Plainly that depends on what is meant by "blueprints." Do the *Federalist* papers constitute a blueprint?

established so that we can engage in an empirically oriented inquiry about what is necessary to give it concrete meaning. The assumption is that out of such analysis a more precise and coherent sense of the value and requirements of serving these ends will emerge. In short, we are all engaged in what Sołtan calls "rational reconstruction."

It is worth drawing a contrast here to Dryzek's arguments. Now that postmodernism is a prominent feature of our cultural landscape, he implies, it is no longer possible to accept that there is such a moral inheritance, or at least that we are in any way bound to it. Moreover, it seems likely that Dryzek would argue that any attempt to shore up this inheritance (with an inquiry into its foundation in conceptions of the right and the good) is doomed to failure. Western rationalism has suffered a stinging defeat in the cultural wars.[14] Thus, he joins hands with the four authors just considered in the thought that there is little profit to be gained from a sustained abstract inquiry into the precise meaning of specific political values. Dryzek, however, moves from such considerations to an argument about the "subjectivities" of individuals and their capacity to choose which values to invoke in different situations. Autonomy seems to be an unreserved good for Dryzek. The implication is that out of an inquiry into such matters will grow a citizen-generated art of institutional design. In this sense, Dryzek is much more suspicious of the kind of constitutional expertise that in one way or another is the subject of all the other authors in the present volume. For Dryzek, such expertise makes citizens hostage to narrow subjectivities.

The various essays that I have just considered—especially those by Anderson, Green, Alperovitz, and myself—demonstrate the wide range of constitutional designs that can emerge from efforts at rational reconstruction. This is, in fact, all to the good since it is useful to have a range of possibilities to compare. Still, at the end of the day we do want to be able to say just why one alternative is superior to the others, if only as a way of criticizing the choices that our own political economies are in the process of making. Good society analysis is important even for those who want to, or who are in a position to, do no more than consider the diagnosis of their own political despair.

I now want to consider one way of proceeding once we have before us an array of proto-constitutions of good societies that have emerged

14. I am unclear about how far Dryzek would want to carry the argument. There is no doubt that if he wished to go as far as the implications I have just drawn from his paper, he would have plenty of company. It is worth raising the question here of whether the cultural wars are the same as the philosophical wars, and whether the status of "discourse," "culture," and "values," and the like are not themselves a matter for philosophical inquiry.

through a process of rational reconstruction. To start, it is important to emphasize two features of any plausible account of our political values, even one rooted in some kind of philosophical inquiry. First, at the level of practical action, it is entirely likely that there will be multiple and incommensurable values. That is to say, there is unlikely to be "common value stuff" into which values may be converted so that we can more or less precisely judge the total worth of our actions. Of course, we do make rough weightings of values in our daily lives, but just how this is done is far from clear, and in any case there is no reason to suppose that such a process can be generalized and made acceptable to all those engaged in any collective weighting exercise.[15] This leads to, and indeed is a part of, the second point. Any account of political value that is widely accepted is unlikely to be comprehensive enough and precise enough to substantially guide action. In other words, rational reconstruction can take us down the right road, but not far enough to decide what precisely to do. We need something else. What might that be?

The best way to convey what I think might help is to use the common analogy—also invoked by Sołtan in his introduction to this volume—between constructing a political constitution and building a ship on the open sea. To elaborate, those who want to constitute good societies are like shipbuilders on the open sea who have some view of the directions they wish to sail, because the kinds of ports they prefer lie in those directions, and who know something about the conditions they will face as they move in their preferred directions. That is, they know some things; otherwise, they could not hope to build a seaworthy vessel. But they must build one that is adapted to a wide range of conditions since they cannot be sure what precisely they will face. As they sail and build, they learn—what works well under what conditions, how common certain conditions are likely to be, and whether it is sensible to keep sailing in the direction they are headed given their boatbuilding capabilities.

Described in this way, it is clear that the relations among the boatbuilders are fundamental, because it is they who must rebuild and modify the vessel as they learn, and they who must change course depending on what they ascertain about how their ship will do under various conditions. It matters whether their modes of association are such as to facilitate this learning and the attendant decisions they must make.

Even more striking, these modes of association are more impor-

15. For a very helpful overview of this whole problem of value pluralism, see Larmore 1994.

tant than the ports toward which they sail. That is because they can never reach them. As they learn what it will take to reach the ports toward which they sail, it may become clear that to go even farther is too costly and that they should head toward less costly ones. This process of reassessment will constantly occur since their resources are limited.

Moreover, if they do get close enough to glimpse a desired port it may well look less attractive. Certainly, if the analogy is dropped for a moment, it makes sense to stop when the people constructing a good society achieve "enough" equality, in a way that it does not make sense for the boatbuilders to say that they have enough Madagascar. In any event, the crew of boatbuilders will always be changing as some die and others are born, and what seemed attractive to one generation of boatbuilders may not seem so to the next.

So it is with constitutionmakers. They, too, are constantly learning and deciding but never arriving. Yet they do learn with greater precision what their aspirations entail through their concrete undertakings, and in the process they will undoubtedly modify them. And since they too must constantly adjust aspirations to realities, their political constitution must facilitate learning and adaptation of institutions and purposes if they are to survive.

Here, then, is how to begin to sort out the constitutional designs that issue from an exercise of rational reconstruction. We should favor those that promise to foster the ability to adapt to changing circumstances. A political constitution at its best defines how the people of a regime are to associate together in the face of the difficult-to-predict possibilities and problems that arise and the conflicts that come with their common fate.[16] A constitution is a design for political learning and, as such, those designs that take this task as central to political life are to be preferred.

Political Judgment

Political problems, at least as most human beings face them, are not then essentially moral or logical. They are *practical* problems, which are best approached through the exercise of practical reason— that is to say, through political judgment. Until now I have concentrated on the substantive questions that must be addressed by political judgment. What may be said about its general character, the manner of reasoning rather than its substance?

It is far easier to say what the manner of reasoning involved in

16. See Elkin, "Constitutionalism's Successor" (Elkin and Soltan 1993).

political judgment is *not* than to characterize what it is. I will therefore start with the negative.

I have implied that the design of the constitution of a good society is not akin to designing a factory for the efficient production of a set of outputs. To think of the exercise in this manner makes it seem as if we do not much care, as it were, about the relationships among the workers. But in political life there is a sense in which this concern, though it may not be *all* we care about, is a great part of what we value. That is so, I have argued, since there can be no clear sense of where "we" are going: no agreement precise enough to guide us is possible, and the problems of navigation are too complex to solve once and for all. The central political problem might be phrased as the creation and maintenance of desirable forms of relation we might have with one another wherever we are going. That is why we worry about such values as freedom, pluralism, and so on.

Put another way, and with an exaggeration designed to emphasize the point, procedures are all we have. They *are* us, and if we do not much like the way we are, it is these procedures which must be changed. If this seems an odd thing to say, consider that even if we set out to make the United States, for example, a more equal society, would we really think we had succeeded if we had simply altered the distribution of income. That, indeed, would be no mean feat and not without value—but I would argue that equality properly understood characterizes relationships, whether in the marketplace or in the polity. It is not some end state to be achieved, but an ongoing set of interactions of an egalitarian sort.

One response to observations like these is simply to say that we can add such values to our list of other, output-oriented values. This misses the point, however, and it amounts to continuing to insist that political systems are like factories and that the problem stems from a misstatement of the desirable outputs. But values such as freedom or tolerance are not *outputs* of the system: they *are* the system. They are the free or tolerant relations that serve to make it up, that give it its particular identity.

The basic point is simple enough. It is, in fact, the fundamental insight of constitutionalism: namely, that a constitution is a framework of institutions for indefinite future possibilities. It is not a program or a policy, and *because* the future is indefinite we cannot design institutions to maximize something substantive—that is, treat institutions as means to ends and design accordingly. Political-economic institutions are means through which we establish our identity—what kind of people we are. And they are the means, I have said, through which we will attempt to cope with an unending and unknowable string of problems and conflicts that are attendant on our living together. To talk about all this as a set of procedural values, simply to assimilate them to other values that are used to judge outputs, is a case of "saving the appearances," a matter of stretching a theoretical language past the point where it is illuminating. It would be better just to concede that here we have something different and then devise ways to talk about it.

Even if all this were to be conceded, there is still plenty of room for error. Most important, there is a temptation to argue, in the fashion noted above, that the problem is essentially one of logical coherence. We might then say: Yes, we need to focus on procedures, on the forms of relation among citizens; therefore, we need a blueprint for such relations. Then we can proceed to analyze whether the blueprint is logically coherent. Having directed our attention away from outputs, we now inquire, in the style of certain kinds of moral philosophers, into whether it is rational to hold the values that the institutions embody and whether it is logically and morally coherent to pursue a particular combination of values.

I have argued, however, that political institutions cannot be treated simply as embodiments of political values. The problem of how best to combine them thus cannot be understood as a question of the logical coherence of the various values given life by each institution. As I have said, institutions are modes of association, and whether they can be combined is at bottom an empirical question. Can the behavioral requirements of each institution coexist with those of the others?

There just *are* multiple values in the world, and no amount of ratiocination will get them into some coherent whole; nor can we tell without empirical investigation which institutions are mutually compatible. This is a description of our condition as human beings, not some evidence of our failings as philosophers. In addition, the existence of logically contradictory things—A and B are both valued ends, but to pursue A makes it harder to serve B—simply *is* a feature of the world. Individuals face such contradictions all the time, and so do political institutions and political regimes. The essential political problem, given the fact that there just *are* many valuable things that we wish for but that are incompatible, is this: How do we combine the institutions that bring multiple values to life? For combine them we must if we are to live together (or even alone).

There cannot then be a purely normative discipline of political judgment, one that is somehow separate from an inquiry into how and why things work as they do. As the papers in this volume demonstrate, political judgment is deeply empirical. To put it differently, we typically judge in order to act. Human beings do not have the advantages of gods who may contemplate the social order to satisfy their aesthetic longings.

Nor, perhaps more obviously, can there be a wholly empirical discipline of political judgment—not even one that is built around serving the expressed or revealed preferences of the citizens who compose the society. We will be tempted, I think, to go further and inquire into what underlies preferences, for it is reasonable to suppose that preferences have some underlying structure and are not merely a random collection of impulses. It is persons with identities, we might say, who have these preferences. We might suppose also that their identities are, in part, composed of relatively enduring preferences about preferences, which is simply to say: There is, distinct from the preferences revealed in behavior, something that deserves examination.

But this might be denied, and arguments could be advanced that human beings are *not* the sort of beings that can have preferences about preferences. The logical corollary, then, is that all that is possible with regard to a better life for human beings is an increase in the satisfaction of preferences as revealed by behavior. Although this can be presented as a conclusion of empirical theory, surely it is simultaneously the deepest sort of judgment about what sort of good we may hope for in the world. To exercise practical reason in the form of political judgment thus seems inexorably to direct us to the most fundamental question of all: What is the good life for human beings? What starts out as a matter of good practice ends up as a moral question.

What else can be said about the characteristics of the kind of reasoning that goes into political judgment?

Far and away the most important characteristic of political judgment is that it is an attempt to cope with the irremediable uncertainty of political life. Purposes are not easily defined in a manner sufficient to guide practice, and thus the principal concern of political judgment must be to constitute the collective engagement that is a good society in such a way that it remains intact as it attempts to make more concrete the political goods it seeks to serve. This is not an exercise to be judged by intellectual virtues, such as economy and simplicity. Political rationality cannot be found there. It is more nearly an exercise of what "fits," with all the uncertainty that this entails.[17]

Nor can one person, unaided, intelligently make the kinds of political judgments I have been describing. Thus, for these judgments to be a useful guide to action, they must also be collective, a pooling of the multiple judgments of many people. They must also, as I have

17. For a longer statement see Elkin 1985 and "Some Considerations on Political Judgment" (Elkin 1987, chap. 10).

said, be empirically based, for only experience can finally tell us what institutions can coexist. Finally, the judgments must be historical, because the best evidence of what a given people can accomplish is the record of what those who are most like them (i.e., those who came before them) have done.

The creation of a good society is, of course, a long journey—and one that is never completed. The expertise appropriate to such a journey is not that of a social engineer. This is indeed an explicit theme of several of the papers in the present volume, and it is implicit in all of them. This, among other things, is what gives these papers a coherent outlook even with the differences among them that I have described. Good society theorists are "friends of the regime" they hope to bring about. They talk to those whom they hope to make fellow citizens in the journey; they invoke ideals where these can be shared, point to the lessons of failures, and generally comment on the adequacy of steps that have been or might be taken in light of the kinds of considerations I have set out here. Not being social engineers, or for that matter prophets, this is the best they can do. But it is no small matter. In any case, ours is a democratic age, and no one person nor even a small group will be permitted to claim much more than that they are part of the effort of the people to construct their own framework for political living. Good society theorists, then, must be colleagues and collaborators with their more workaday fellow citizens who have not been granted the modest pleasures of sustained reflection concerning how "good" and "good enough" political regimes may be nudged into being.

Conclusion

Good societies may come into being by accident or force, but it is more likely that they must be constituted, brought into being by conscious choice and effort. In any event, neither chance nor the exercise of power alone can confer legitimacy. The constitution of good societies is the constitution of "regimes"[18]—of whole political economies that have an inner coherence of their parts that is an expression of the empirical possibilities for coexistence of various kinds of valued institutions. These regimes—in the metaphor I have been using—are like ships that have crews with a certain internal organization and that are oriented to a certain part of the horizon.[19]

18. See my other contribution in this volume (Chapter 7) and the reference there to Aristotle's *Politics*.

19. Since none of the papers in this volume takes up the theme, I will not consider here whether particular kinds of regimes are held together by particular social strata. If

Those committed to some form of democratic capitalism and those committed to a new political-economic regime must take this step of considering how to constitute a good regime. It is plain that those committed to something new must do so. They will need to make their vision plausible to those who will, naturally enough, be skeptical or even hostile. But even those who are committed to substantial reform of the present political economy must undertake the task. Those committed to a fuller realization of democratic capitalism need more than a theory of institutions *within* the regime. They also need a theory of the regime itself as a whole, an explanation of how its institutional pieces are to work together.

The work that the present volume seeks to promote is thus crucial not only for those who seek to develop new, and what they believe are more compelling, visions of the good society. It is also fundamental for those committed to a fuller realization of the reigning vision of democratic capitalism. Central to the work of both are the study of existing institutional experiments, the design of new institutional forms, and their combination into effective and attractive wholes. If there were well-understood ways to get existing institutions to work in the service of a more fully realized democratic capitalism, this might not be so. But the reality of present-day democratic capitalism seems to be one of an inadequate institutional structure.

In such circumstances, the line between the study of new institutional ways of realizing an old vision of the good society, on the one hand, and institutionally detailed accounts of a new good society vision, on the other, is likely to be thinner than is often supposed. Thoughtful conservatives are thus likely to find to their surprise that they have much in common with sophisticated radicals in exploring new ways of carrying on our collective life. While it is perhaps too much to say that good society thinking can be a nonsectarian undertaking, much of the best work on these topics nonetheless will likely turn out to be of the greatest importance to those committed to a broad range of good society visions.

---

that is so, then the design of good societies must draw on a mix of political theory and political sociology of the kind Aristotle initiated when he argued that a certain kind of good regime rested on the foundation of a middling social stratum.

REFERENCES

Anderson, Charles. 1990. *Pragmatic Liberalism*. Chicago: University of Chicago Press.

Aristotle. 1932. *Politics*. Translated by H. Rackham. Cambridge: Harvard University Press.

Barber, Benjamin. 1984. *Strong Democracy: Participatory Politics for a New Age*. Berkeley and Los Angeles: University of California Press.

Barry, Brian. 1965. *Political Argument*. London: Routledge & Kegan Paul.

Dahl, Robert. 1985. *A Preface to Economic Democracy*. Berkeley and Los Angeles: University of California Press.

Dahl, Robert, and Charles E. Lindblom. 1953. *Politics, Economics, and Welfare*. New York: Harper.

Downs, Anthony. 1970. *Urban Problems and Prospects*. Chicago: Markham.

Elkin, Stephen L. 1974. "Political Science and the Analysis of Public Policy." *Public Policy* 22(3):399–422.

———. 1985. "Economic and Political Rationality." *Polity* 18(2):253–71.

———. 1987. *City and Regime in the American Republic*. Chicago: University of Chicago Press.

Elkin, Stephen L., and Karol Sołtan, eds. 1993. *A New Constitutionalism*. Chicago: University of Chicago Press.

Imbroscio, David. 1993. "Reconstructing City Politics: Alternative Local Economic Development Strategies and Urban Regimes." Ph.D. thesis, University of Maryland.

Kaus, Mickey. 1992. *The End of Equality*. New York: Basic Books.

Larmore, Charles. 1994. "Pluralism and Reasonable Disagreement." *Social Philosophy and Policy* 11(1):61–79.

Levy, Frank. 1988. *Dollars and Dreams: The Changing American Income Distribution*. New York: W. W. Norton.

Madison, James, Alexander Hamilton, and John Jay. 1961. *The Federalist*. Middletown, Conn.: Wesleyan University Press.

Philips, Kevin. 1990. *The Politics of Rich and Poor*. New York: Random House.

Thurow, Lester. 1975. *Generating Inequality*. New York: Basic Books.

Unger, Roberto. 1987. *False Necessity: Anti-Necessitarian Social Theory in the Service of Radical Democracy*. Cambridge: Cambridge University Press.

Walzer, Michael. 1987. *Interpretation and Social Criticism*. Cambridge: Harvard University Press.

INDEX

accountability, role of, in good society, 177–81
Ackerman, Bruce, 94, 96
Adams, John, 148
agape, defined, 15
aggregate interests: in commercial republic, 120–28; deliberation and, 134–41
ahimsa, defined, 15
Aivazian, V. A., 88n.5
Alaska Native Claims Settlement Act, 66
alienation, institutional design and, 90–91
Alperovitz, Gar, 101–2, 146–62, 194, 196
anarchy, power and dependence and, 88–89
Anderson, Charles, 14, 101, 103–17, 190–91, 195–96
Arendt, Hannah, 78
Aristotle, 1, 3; on political deliberation, 109–10, 116
atars, robust design principles for *zanjeras* and, 28–29
Augustine, Saint, 58
autonomy: institutional design and, 69–70, 197–99; power and dependence and, 88–92; rationality as, 58
Axelrod, Robert, 89

Banks, Jeffrey S., 26
Barber, Benjamin, 105
bargaining: in commercial republic, 120–21; institutional design and, 89–90
barriers, to constitutional choice, 53–54
behavioral decision theory: institutional design and, 63–65; substitute measures, 82–84
Bentham, Jeremy, 165n.2
Berejikian, Jeffrey, 62
Berger, Thomas R., 66

Bill of Rights, wealth maximization and, 6–7
Bobbitt, Philip, 8
Bookchin, Murray, 153
Buber, Martin, 153
Buchanan, James, 4, 20–21, 23, 39–55, 191–92, 194
budget constraints, instrumental competence and, 9
Burke, Edmund, 58

Calabresi, Guido, 8
Calculus of Consent, 23
Calvert, Randall L., 26
Calvinism, diagnostic subjectivity and, 68
capital. *See* physical capital; social capital
capitalism: community and, 153–54; democratic participation in, 176–81; flaws in, 79, 147–48; gender issues in, 168–71; improvements to democracy through, 79–80; political inequality and, 171–75
care, morality of, 15
Carnoy, Martin, 10
Causal Theory of Justice, 8n.4
central planning, constitutional choice and, 50
Chicken (game), power and dependence and, 88–89
children, in democratic society, 165n.3
Chomsky, Noam, 5–6, 67, 76–77
citizenship: in commercial republic, 120n.7, 193–99; conceptions of, 14; constitutional choice and, 44–45; deliberative lawmaking and, 129–34; promotion of deliberation and, 135–41; public interest and deliberation and, 120–28

CONTRIBUTORS

GAR ALPEROVITZ, president, National Center for Economic Alternatives, Washington, D.C.; member of the Executive Board, Committee for the Political Economy of the Good Society

CHARLES W. ANDERSON, Glen Hawkins Professor of Political Science, University of Wisconsin at Madison

JAMES M. BUCHANAN, Harris University Professor, George Mason University; Nobel Laureate in Economics, 1986

JOHN S. DRYZEK, professor of Political Science, University of Melbourne

STEPHEN L. ELKIN, professor of Government and Politics, University of Maryland at College Park; chair of the Executive Board, Committee for the Political Economy of the Good Society

PHILIP GREEN, Sophia Smith Professor of Government, Smith College

ELINOR OSTROM, professor of Political Science and director, Workshop in Political Theory and Policy Analysis, Indiana University; past president, American Political Science Association

KAROL EDWARD SOŁTAN, associate professor of Government and Politics, University of Maryland at College Park; member of the Executive Board, Committee for the Political Economy of the Good Society

VIKTOR J. VANBERG, professor, Albert Ludwigs Universitaet, Freiburg

www.ingramcontent.com/pod-product-compliance
Lightning Source LLC
Chambersburg PA
CBHW021902020426
42334CB00013B/441